T0369773

Tactics of the Human

DIGITALCULTUREBOOKS, an imprint of the University of Michigan Press, is dedicated to publishing work in new media studies and the emerging field of digital humanities.

Tactics of the Human

Experimental Technics *in* American Fiction

Laura Shackelford

University of Michigan Press
Ann Arbor

Copyright © by Laura Shackelford 2014
Some rights reserved

ⓒ creative
commons

This work is licensed under the Creative Commons Attribution-
Noncommercial-No Derivative Works 3.0 United States License. To view a
copy of this license, visit http://creativecommons.org/licenses/by-nc-nd/3.0/
or send a letter to Creative Commons, 171 Second Street, Suite 300, San
Francisco, California, 94105, USA.

Published in the United States of America by the
University of Michigan Press
Printed and bound by CPI Group (UK) Ltd, Croydon, CR0 4YY

2017   2016   2015   2014   4   3   2   1

A CIP catalog record for this book is available from the British Library.

DOI: http://dx.doi.org/10.3998/dcbooks.12672514.0001.001

Library of Congress Cataloging-in-Publication Data

Shackelford, Laura.
    Tactics of the human : experimental technics in American fiction /
Laura Shackelford.
        pages cm
    Includes bibliographical references and index.
    ISBN 978-0-472-07238-5 (hardback : alk. paper) — ISBN 978-0-472-05238-7
(paper : alk. paper) — ISBN 978- 0-472-12068- 0 (e-book)
    1. American fiction—History and criticism.   2. Literature and technology
—United States.   3. Human body and technology in
literature.   4. Hypertext fiction—History and criticism.   5. Literature and
the Internet—United States.   6. Experimental fiction, American—History
and criticism.   I. Title.
PS374.T434S53   2014
813.009'356—dc23

                                                    2014023464

Contents

Acknowledgments

This book bears the marks of its intellectual and scholarly emergence, traversing several academic institutions, scholarly fields, and lively, ongoing dialogues. A few of these catalyzing forces and influences deserve special mention and recognition. Thomas Foster and Eva Cherniavsky have had an irreplaceable influence on this project since its earliest threads emerged through my dissertation work, under their advising, at Indiana University, Bloomington. I could not have found a more insightful and enlightening dissertation director than Tom. They continue to motivate me with their practice and vision of what scholarly work might entail. Purnima Bose and Helen Gremillion were similarly generous and circumspect contributors to the earliest trajectories that led to this book. Since I first attended the Society for Literature, Science, and the Arts (SLSA) conference in Buffalo, New York, to participate on a systems theory and literature panel, this diverse community of scholars, Katherine Hayles, especially, has been an incredible source of critical exchange and a much-needed, recognizable context for an area of study that has been peripheral until quite recently. Many of the ideas developed here have grown out of those conversations, networks, and exchanges. During a postdoctoral fellowship at Penn State University, Michael Bérubé and the American literary studies working group offered me an attentive audience and feedback on an earlier version of chapter 5. More recently, my colleagues at the Rochester Institute of Technology's College of Liberal Arts and, particularly our informal junior faculty writing group, have provided a crucial transdisciplinary audience for the project. Doris Borelli, Katie Terezakis, Elena Sommers, Cecilia-Ovesdotter Alm, and Sharon Beckford-Foster have been meticulous, thoughtful readers and provided insightful comments on individual chapters, as well as invaluable support and humor through the process of writing and revising.

The intellectual prompting and friendship of Louise Economides and Cristina Iuli are a continual source of insight and inspiration for me to pursue trajectories that realign expected scholarly and intellectual affiliations. I owe my first realization of humanities research as a collaborative, interdisciplinary activity to my experiences organizing and hosting the "Thinking Materiality: Language, Epistemology, and Embodiment" lecture series with them, as well as other stellar Indiana University faculty. This also initiated my first genuine interactions with scholars such as Andy Clark who made a lasting influence on my lines of inquiry here. The final stages of the book have also been thoroughly invigorated by Loss Pequeño Glazier and others active in the International E-Poetry Organization's events that he has organized at University of Buffalo, Kingston University, and the University of Mayagüez over the past three years. His sustained efforts to build on the communities of practice catalyzing and sustaining the digital literary have fed their way into my own work in a number of significant ways. I also owe an incredible debt to my thoughtful editor, Thomas Dwyer, for his unflagging support and guidance of my book project. I would also like to thank the anonymous readers who reviewed the manuscript for the University of Michigan Press. Their feedback was very helpful to me in consolidating the book's framing for multiple audiences.

The process of writing and revising this book has also been punctuated by visits and conversations with my mother Lynn; my sisters Kathy and Amy; my brilliant, kind, and most special niece Amber; and countless walks with Clyde the unstoppable, yet accommodating beagle-mix. A continual source of insight and a welcome reorienting of my usual trains of thought, they have each found their way into my thinking and purpose here. To them I remain especially grateful.

An earlier version of chapter 1 was originally published as "Narrative Subjects Meet Their Limits: John Barth's 'Click' and the Remediation of Hypertext," *Contemporary Literature* 46.2 (2005): 275–310; © 2005 by the Board of Regents of the University of Wisconsin System. Reproduced courtesy of the University of Wisconsin Press. An earlier version of chapter 2 was originally published as "Subject to Change: The Monstrosity of Media in Shelley Jackson's *Patchwork Girl; or, A Modern Monster* and Other Post-humanist Critiques of the Instrumental," *Camera Obscura* 21.3 (2006): 63–101; copyright © 2006 by Duke University Press. Reprinted by permission. An earlier version of chapter 3 was originally published as "Counter-networks in a Network Society: Leslie Marmon Silko's *Almanac of the Dead*," *Postmodern Culture* 16.3 (2006). Copyright © 2006 Laura Shackelford and The Johns Hopkins University Press. Revised and reprinted with permission by The Johns Hopkins University Press.

Introduction

Retracing Digital Cultures through American Fiction

This book returns to a series of American fictions published between 1991 and 2002, in the midst of the "digital revolution,"[1] to retrospectively unfold their literary contributions to understanding contemporary digital cultures. This fiction actively registers and responds to post–World War II biological and information sciences and their offspring: the Internet, World Wide Web, and other computation-based media, technologies, and scientific practices. Creatively transposing the spatiotemporal logics of information networks, hypertext linking, embedded scenes of material writing, real-time transnational social spaces, and other emergent digital practices into their literary print or digital hypertext fiction, these texts reveal untenable limitations to the polarizing oppositional terms in which we tend to perceive and read literary print and digital cultures. Through fiction, they tangibly grapple with the digital technologies and infrastructures impacting, though not exactly replacing, existing print cultures, their scenes of writing, modes of subject formation, and materially realized social spaces. I revisit their early forays into how digital cultures impact crucial boundaries and discourses of the human to illustrate the importance of these comparative, at once, literary print and digital forays. These are important precursors to more recent creative engagements that explore the literary's relations to computational media and digital cultures in the United States by directly reworking computational media to literary ends. Illustrating the key contributions of this trajectory of print literature to the digital literary, the book intends to complement and elaborate on this growing body of research on electronic literatures and other expressive digital practices. At a minimum, it provides additional evidence that the digital literary is neither a unique, stand-alone area of literary studies circumscribed by the "digital," nor an area of research confined to questions of typology, narratology, and digital textuality alone.[2]

The literary texts at the center of the book's inquiries attend to dynamic modes of interchange between textual practices, material technologies, material spaces, intersubjective social relations, economic circulation, and political forms such as the nation-state. Their intensive exploration of how computation-based digital technologies differentially enter into and facilitate subjectivities and social relations focuses much-needed attention onto these pivotal relays between writing technologies, textual practices, subject formation, social systems, and lived space. They also encourage a reconsideration of the kinds of work these literary practices can do. Through this early lens, the book rethinks how literary texts and a broader literary system participate in contemporary digital cultures. This overarching question continues to unsettle the literary and will certainly keep modern-day Scheherazades, attempting to answer it, alive for quite some time. Yet as I'll illustrate, it bears directly on how one understands and navigates these increasingly pervasive, dynamic digital cultures in the present.

Drawing on these literary texts, the book develops a mode of thinking through what many cultural theorists now acknowledge as a fundamentally distinct set of posthumanist perspectives on the human's relations to technologies emerging out of post–World War II scientific and cultural practices.[3] I engage these literary texts to better understand the literary's complex interrelations to digital cultures. In turn, through this literary mode of inquiry, I underscore what this fiction contributes to new understandings of the human that have accompanied postwar cybernetics, information and systems sciences, and digital cultures. The boundaries of the human and the very category of life are impacted by information and biological sciences on a daily basis. Seeing these boundaries to be highly malleable and, therefore, contingent, we increasingly come to realize that "what it means to be human is always negotiable," as cyberpunk science fiction has tried to teach us since the late 1980s.[4] Scientific practices draw and redraw the discursive, material, and technical threads linking human to animal to technology to lifeworld and back again. For instance, the life of the cell has recently jumped into silicon via some of these threads and will likely reenter the human, in due course. Researchers have just inserted artificial DNA molecules, not previously existing, into an organism. Electrical devices implanted into the brain by roboticists stimulate synapses enabling one, through focused concentration, to move a paralyzed limb. Frog cells grown in petri dishes are soon to be marketed as an animal-friendly, tissue-cultured meat for human consumption. Although such practices are becoming commonplace, they continue to raise new questions about the boundaries of the human and the consequence of this fundamental malleability, plasticity, and interconnectivity with material, technical, and discursive domains. They generate competing efforts to make sense of the human and to assess the current and/or potential impact of such practices on multiple dimensions of social life.

Interweaving a set of literary and extraliterary efforts to think the human in a transformative relation to contemporary technological, discursive, and material systems, I underscore the contours and consequence of this fiction's print cultural vantage on the human and her technicity. These literary engagements with digital technologies comparatively retrace the impact of these technologies on a series of charged sites. The importance of their historically contextualizing, print cultural literary perspectives on how technologies enter into and reshape social relations and material spaces has only increased since the 1990s. These literary texts already conceived of technologies as material practices that enter into and unfold in complex relation to existing social relations and lived space. In contrast, the prevailing, liberal humanist understanding of technologies as self-contained objects initially led theorists to read digital technologies and the virtual spaces they opened onto as distinct objects, or as secondary spaces categorically distinct from the real world. It is now quite apparent that computational media and processes are increasingly pervasive components of daily practices and lived space. As I will illustrate, this is one example of several crucial limits to liberal humanism's defining conceptualization of (human) subjects and (technological) objects as distinct entities that interact according to a relation of human users and wholly detachable tools, its oppositional, instrumental understanding of subject-technology relations.

This persistent oppositional understanding of human users over and against their technological tools and built infrastructures is both problematic and informative. Postmodern technocultures, unwilling to relinquish the human's perceived autonomy and authority, often prefer to read the newly apparent negotiability of the human as either a confirmation of the human's exceptional status as self-possessed, individual tool-user, or as a fearful reversal of that instrumental, subject-object relation. In the latter, frightening alternative, increasingly complex computational and biological practices now enlist the human as a tool in their totalizing technological systems rather than being subjected to the human's tool-based control. Perhaps sensing the inadequacy of both views on the human, these discourses frequently oscillate between these two attitudes toward the apparent negotiability of the human. On the one hand, they celebrate the human's transformation in computational worlds. On the other hand, they reject such a shift in the boundaries of the human, insisting that these technological changes simply allow us to more fully achieve an understanding of the human that remains unchanged. "Welcome to the human network," chime Cisco Systems' ads, suggesting that their teleconferencing and communications technologies will finally allow us to fully achieve human status.[5] Of course, the ads simultaneously raise the question of why we need a "welcome" to (re)join the human, unless it has been significantly transformed by its conjoining with these network technologies.

These two views of the negotiability of the human might initially appear to be polar opposites, one an emancipatory and the other a disenchanted account of the human's relation to technologies, yet they both oppose subject to object, user to tool, and active to passive. They only disagree in their analysis of who (or what) now occupies the subject position. In both instances, these readings rely on and run up against an impoverished, oppositional understanding of our relations to technologies. They also flag a crucial stake in such challenges to liberal humanism's instrumental "tool-user"—the agency of the human (above and against its nonhuman animal, material, and technical counterparts). Liberal humanism's exceptionalist model of human agency is undoubtedly confounded, if not more significantly qualified by, the liveliness of computational processes and "smart" technologies, by material environments in the midst of climate change, and by growing awareness surrounding nonhuman animal cognition and perception.

Reconsidering how digital technologies, informed by emerging information and biological sciences, enter into American culture and impact its technicity, I will suggest several ways to move beyond this persistent, reductive, oppositional view without losing sight of the impact of such shifting technics on how we understand the human among other agencies. The technological systems impacting us today are the—at times curious—outgrowth of post–World War II cybernetics and information sciences. One of the defining characteristics of these emergent digital technologies is their reliance on computation, on the digital computer's ability to recursively process information. Janet Murray insightfully describes this as the "procedural power of computers," their defining ability to execute a series of rules.[6] Because computers function procedurally, they are especially good at simulating processes. Computational methods involving information processing (and the recursive processing of processing) at multiple levels are at work in genetic engineering, nanotechnology, communications, reproductive technologies, digital games, financial networks, environmental sciences, robotics, artificial intelligence, and mobile telecommunications, to name a few fields. To understand contemporary relations to technology, then, it is essential to reckon with computationally enabled systems processes as these generate precisely the kinds of interrelations that perplex previous instrumental understandings of the human's technicity due to their recursive circularity. Philosophers Arthur Bradley and Louis Armand stress that it is "precisely this concept of technicity—as tool, instrument, or prosthesis—that now most urgently needs to be re-thought" in their recent collection of essays exploring the human's fundamental and defining reliance on technologies of various sorts throughout the species' evolutionary history.[7] Not surprisingly, they acknowledge "the meaning of technicity is more contested now than ever before."[8]

It is the book's primary thesis that this trajectory of American fiction substantially and insightfully contributes to these questions about the human's technicity and the difference that digital cultures, in particular, introduce. Its literary queries reveal that these questions surrounding technics require careful consideration if one intends to critically enter into contemporary biotechnological practices, "late capitalist" economies, and the struggles over "life" they introduce.[9] This fiction realizes what I'll describe as a mode of *systems thinking* that draws on contemporary cybernetics, information, and systems theory, while, as importantly, it modulates those theories and their key concepts by transposing them into or resituating them in relation to literary print poetics, cultural, and political forms. Approaching shifting understandings and practices of the human in contemporary U.S. digital cultures through the vantage of these literary texts, the book examines the co-imbricated critical space they open up through their comparative analyses of digital and literary print cultures.

Experimental Technics

Literary fiction may seem to be an odd, even irrelevant place from which to observe and reflect on digital cultures' impact on the human. If one takes into account the formerly privileged role literature played in reproducing and reflecting on human subjectivity and society, it should come as less of a surprise that these literary texts are especially invested in and adept at tracking these shifts. In fact, literature is an apt site to examine the impact of new technologies on the formerly absolute boundaries separating the human from nonhuman animals, machines, and their material lifeworlds. Dr. Frankenstein's creature, in Mary Shelley's classic, you'll remember, spent significant time reading literature in order to develop and demonstrate his humanity.[10] This particular literary text registers what was, in fact, the historical centrality of novel-reading in the development of modern subjectivities. Novel-reading and other literary practices played a tangible role in establishing and reinforcing modern readers' burgeoning sense of a private interiority and their participation in an emerging public sphere through this shared reading. Further, the literary continues to serve as a primary point of entry into legible humanity in that the demonstration of one's self-authorship in print narrative, so fundamental to abolition movements, women's rights, and civil rights struggles in the United States, remains a central means of social and cultural legitimization.

Literature has also reproduced the human in more literal ways to the extent that it has functioned as part of what Friedrich Kittler describes as a modern "discourse network," a historically, technologically, and socially distinct apparatus or material "framework within which something like 'meaning,' indeed, something like 'man' became possible at all."[11] Kittler and others in literary media studies underscore the fact that the material bases of literature—its text, reading, and circulation—establish specific, socially authorized bodily regimens, such as those that clearly guide skills like silent reading, cursive handwriting, or cognition's narrative tendencies. Although modern literature is more typically imagined to be the source of transcendent, immaterial meaning, it simultaneously plays a central part in physically coupling human bodies, subjectivities, and communications technologies, and in realizing social and political formations, like the nation-state, in distinct ways. This broader print literary and cultural apparatus is the unacknowledged precondition for the modern liberal humanist subject. The literary texts at the center of the book's inquiries, thus, reflect back on the role literary print practices play in the realization of subjectivities, social systems, nations, and lived space as a means of looking forward. They comparatively register the potential and consequence of emergent digital technologies as they alter and, at times, replace existing print-based subject-technology relations at multiple sites.

In the process, these literary texts creatively reconceive their literary occupation vis-à-vis digital technologies. They reconceive their own material, technical, social, and communicative practices in relation to emerging biological, information, and digital systems rather than simply depicting digital media's impact on U.S. social and cultural terrain. In particular, they incorporate digital rhetorics, poetics, logics, and modes of expression into the print medium (or reconsider print rhetorics, poetics, and literary cultures from within a digital hypertext fiction in the case of Shelley Jackson's *Patchwork Girl by Mary/Shelley and Herself*).[12] It is a practice that Jay Bolter presciently described as "remediation" in which the rhetorical forms of one medium are translated into another medium.[13]

The full significance of such practices, which continue to multiply, remains largely unrecognized. Reconceptualizing the literary moves between print and digital media in these and other literary texts as *experimental technics*, I argue that select comparative media practices such as "remediation" provide an essential, comparative means of registering the impact of digital media on the human and its current social, material, and technical corealization. Going well beyond Jay Bolter and Richard Grusin's theorization of "remediation" as a contest between *media* for primacy, these texts devise comparative media practices to explore the *social and cultural* as well as material and technological dimensions to transitions between print and digital technologies in contemporary American culture.

Earlier post–World War II American literary fiction that comparatively and self-reflexively incorporates other media and modes into its narratives is frequently aligned with (or confined to) an oversimplified account of postmodernism as self-conscious literary experimentation, as metafiction primarily concerned with the process of making fiction. The early work of postmodernists such as John Barth, Thomas Pynchon, William Gaddis, Joseph McElroy, Kathy Acker, or Don DeLillo, in this reading, is reduced to a kind of self-involved formal play with more or less esoteric language games. This initial reading of self-referential strategies in their fiction overlooked these postmodernist writers' exploration of their self-referential linguistic and literary signifying practices in direct relation to extra-literary material preconditions, contexts, and influences. It has since become clear that their experimentation with a wide range of media and signifying practices in post–World War II American culture initiates a distinct phase of literary media studies. They think through the literary's material and medial preconditions in relation to the larger social, cultural, and media systems significantly recalibrated by postwar cybernetic and information technologies. Their self-reflexive experiments with literary print technics, such as those

John Johnston theorizes in *Information Multiplicity: American Fiction in the Age of Media Saturation*, function as comparative methods to assess emergent media systems and their influence. As Johnston describes the novels of "information multiplicity" published between 1973 and 1991: "By both 'writing with' and in relation to new information technologies, these novelists inaugurate a writing practice fully cognizant of their own machinic relationship to the technologies and the fiction they produce within a larger information field."[14]

The fiction at the center of the book's inquiries draws upon, yet also extends, postmodern fiction's prior efforts to explore the dynamic shifts digital information technologies introduce into social systems. The literary texts under consideration here are similarly invested in exploring the literary's refiguration in relation to digital information technologies and computational processes and using the literary to diagnose the material, technical, and social shifts accompanying these digital media systems. Yet they more actively reckon with the shifting relations and *dynamic interchanges* between the discursive and material dimensions of social systems as they enter into processes of signification, subject formation, and the materially realized praxis and social space of late capitalist political economy. In this respect, they respond to the increasingly dynamic and disconcerting processes of re- and dematerialization accompanying these economic networks, and their catalyzing bioinformatic sciences, since the 1980s. As the book intends to illustrate, this trajectory of U.S. fiction further elaborates on and departs from prior strains of postmodernism by closing in on the points of interchange between literary texts, subjectivities, material and biological processes, economic and political networks, and the environments that sustain them. These texts are preoccupied with the dynamic, mutually transformative processes and epistemologically distinct system relations linking digital information technologies, intersubjectivities, and their material environments rather than with information systems and their seeming translation of the world into a field of information per se. Their fictional elaborations register, and even redeploy, new understandings and practices of materiality introduced through emerging physical, biological, and systems sciences and critically reengage prior material knowledges and practices in order to enter into (and exceed) emergent technicities. They presciently register tendencies now quite apparent in the social field, anticipating what has since developed into a widespread "new materialist"[15] concern with how material processes enter into signifying practices, subject formation, and are enlisted by late capitalist economies and nation-states. The diverse field of "new materialisms" designates a set of cross-disciplinary inquiries into how the new scientific practices, technologies, and knowledges defining digital cultures require us to revisit prior understandings of materiality and to query its relations to cultural processes in light of this altered context. Crucially, while they join efforts in their desire to open a "new" line of inquiry into conceptualizations of materiality and diverse material practices as they in-form intersubjectivities and variously circumscribe the politics of "life" today, their understandings of materiality most frequently draw upon prior historical, cultural, and philosophical knowledges and debates surrounding materialities and materialisms as they reapproach these fundamental questions from the vantage of present-day sciences, digital technologies, and their privileged modes of economic and cultural transmission.

The book engages these literary texts to cast into relief key changes in subject-technology and system relations accompanying digital technics. It examines the comparative literary strategies and other "speculative operations" they use to retrace established or emergent relations between readers, literary texts, print and digital media and technologies, subjectivities, social systems, and their lifeworlds, strategies serving to reveal how shifting subject-technology relations bring forth distinct subjectivities and social relations or solidify particular cultural values.[16] Their experimental technics undertake a "minor science," as other experimental media do, one that, in this case, comparatively explores the technicity of the human, past, present, and potential.[17] These texts actively elaborate, reiterate, and experiment with the relations to technologies enabled by digital media by translating those into the print medium and detailing their potential impact on existing print-based understandings of subjectivity, the nation, social relations, texts, and readers. John Barth's short story "Click"[18] incorporates hypertextual links and navigational strategies into its print text to register their impact on narrative, as well as the "self" authored and authorized through that narrativization; Shelley Jackson's *Patchwork Girl* rewrites Mary Shelley's classic print novel *Frankenstein* using blocks of digital hypertext, associative linking paths, and visual mappings of its narrative structure to explore the potentially liberating, multiplicit and decidedly queer feminine intersubjectivities such hypertextual narrative practices might enable; Leslie Marmon Silko's *Almanac of the Dead*[19] reconsiders contemporary information-based economic networks in light of the equally transnational circulations of indigenous American cultures and Maya almanacs that, it suggests, enact alternative, materially realized social networks through their spatiotemporal movements; Ruth L. Ozeki's *My Year of Meats*[20] compares the daily micropractices of food production, family, reproduction, and nation that global capitalist economic networks facilitate to those of previous eras, attempting to rethink their ongoing role in categorizing life along familiar gendered, ethnic, racialized, and species lines; and Jeffrey Eugenides's *Middlesex*[21] explores how contemporary genetics' evolutionary perspective of a gene moving from body to body and continent to continent through time informs U.S. nationalism's biopolitical embrace of a flexible, neoliberal logic of *becoming* American, yet might also open onto an alternate materialist perspective on, and posthumanist politics of, evolutionary becoming.

Drawing on the experimental technics at work in these texts, I pursue the question of how technics enter into the boundary formation of the human and her social systems and address the potential social, cultural, and political dimensions to such processes. At the core of their fictional, print cultural vantages on technics is an awareness of technics in their capacity as *socially embedded and embedding practices*, as interrelations between emergent technologies and existing social and cultural relations that are mutually transformative rather than a one-way street from technological to social change, or the inverse. I redescribe technics, following their lead and other recent thinking about subject-technology relations in philosophy, feminist science studies, systems theory, and critical geographies as *interrelations* between subjects, technologies, and systems to shift emphasis onto the productive, at once social, cultural, material, and technical relations that generate what later come to be seen as self-apparent subjects, technical objects, and distinct modes of material and symbolic circulation.

Recent efforts to think through the human's technicity and understand distinct subject-technology relations as system relations, emerging in a number of fields, open up an alternate understanding of these interrelations. More in keeping with the Greek root of technical, *technics*, systems theory allows one to understand subject-technology relations as *a process*, rather than as preexisting subjects and neutral instruments or tools. These emerging theories of technics shift emphasis onto the processes or productive relations that generate legible, delineated subjects and objects. They also foreground multiple dimensions to our relations to technologies, what Donna Haraway, and then Karen Barad, describe as the "entanglements"[22] through which recent technological developments intertwine nature and human culture in distinct, formative ways. These entanglements require and open onto more complex understandings of the dynamic, ongoing interrelations between the human and her technologies than an instrumental understanding of our relation to technologies allows.

This perspective on technics as ongoing, multidimensional relations that recursively realize, reiterate, and transform subjectivities and social relations sheds oblique light on the less straightforward, less unidirectional or linear social, cultural, and material dimensions to technological shifts well under way in digital cultures. It provides an important contrast to work in media studies focused on competition between media alone or media-centric theories that imagine wholesale, linear, progressive media change, that is, a digital revolution (always, of course, paradoxically, only partially realized). The book reckons with what are, otherwise, perplexing, uneven interrelations between existing print and emergent digital cultures in contemporary American social systems such as those that led theorists to initially presume a wholesale end to nation-states was imminent in the wake of late capitalism's transnational economic networks. It proceeds to think through the ongoing, mutually transformative impact of digitally based, transnational economic and cultural networks on the nation-state and, by extension, on contemporary U.S. cultural and political life. This allows the book to reckon with practices, such as those Lisa Nakamura describes as "cybertyping," through which existing ideologies of race, gender, and sexuality are persistently rerealized in human/computer interfaces and interactions online and off.[23]

These literary texts' efforts to think through *technics* as system relations take on a new significance when situated within this larger theoretical and cultural context. The book explores the emerging perspectives on the human these texts open onto, unpacking several distinct ways in which systems-theoretical understandings of the human and her relation to technics unfold in recent cultural, political, and biological life. Examining competing, contested posthumanist reunderstandings and practices of the human and her technics, as informed by recent research in feminism, gender studies, science studies, philosophy, and comparative media studies, the book aims to (1) underscore the particular relevance of these literary texts' vantage on shifting technics of the human; (2) identify their valuable contributions to larger, ongoing, charged conversations about digital cultures and their current and potential politics in the United States; and (3) convey the ongoing importance of these literary modes of comparative media practices for engaging with system relations in digital cultures of the present.

Reorienting Systems Thinking

Importantly, the systems thinking these literary texts and recent cultural and literary theory draw on is hardly unified and continues to evolve. It develops out of, and against, the first-order cybernetic theory that emerged from the interdisciplinary post–World War II Macy Conferences and Norbert Wiener's influential work in catalyzing this field.[24] Developing their theories of systems in order to link humans, animals, and machines into a shared informational circuit, first-order cybernetic theory was primarily interested in how such recursive feedback loops between phenomenally distinct entities enabled one to secure more stable, homeostatic (i.e., self-regulating), self-enclosed system boundaries. Although cybernetic systems made apparent the interconnections possible between humans, animals, and machines, their primary goal in doing so was to render the system more amenable to totalizing human guidance (*Cybernetics* is derived from the Greek word *kubernētēs*, or "steersman") and control. This understanding and practice of systems, what Donna Haraway describes as "C3I command-control-communication-intelligence," is the apotheosis of instrumentalization and control that has defined modern bureaucracies, totalitarian states, and Fordist economic organization.[25] C3I also remains an obscure object of desire driving post-Fordist economic formations and much technoscience.

First-order cybernetics imagined its systems as closed, totalizing systems securing the human's control over a wider, more complex environment. Thomas Pynchon's narrator in the novel *Gravity's Rainbow* famously captures this view of the postwar terrain, proclaiming, "Living inside the System is like riding across the country in a bus driven by a maniac bent on suicide," that is, like succumbing to a literal death drive.[26] These systems are perceived to be plodding toward an inescapable, entropic heat-death, the antithesis to life. They are premised on systemic *closure* from a larger environment. This cybernetic pursuit of stabilizing closure was intended to secure the human's instrumental control, though as Pynchon's narrator suggests, such totalizing systems, once under the sway of a military-industrial project, are distinctly inhuman from the vantage of a former GI.

Both understandings of systems, as human or inhuman, rely on and fail to recognize the conflict between first-order cyberneticists's penchant for "self-enclosed meaning" and its foil, "the dream of pure and unimpeded becoming," a conflict that, philosopher Claire Colebrook argues, "mark[s] the problem of the living being as such."[27] Colebrook underscores the conundrum posed by this apparent contest between a desire for human subjectivities' and social systems' closure and, simultaneously, a desire for openness to nonhuman species and a natural environment. Noting how it plays out at the level of the human subject, she states: "The living body cannot be a self-enclosed world unto itself but must be open to the needs of life. In terms of the species, living beings cannot simply act for self-maintenance and continuity but must in some way become other than themselves in order to have a future."[28] While "Living inside the System" generates heightened desire for systemic openness and access to some kind of material or spiritual outside through which to transcend the system, Colebrook insightfully underscores the fact that this conflict is, when approached in this way, unresolvable, paradoxical, as Pynchon's novel seems to concur. On the one hand, systemic closure is believed to secure the human and his instrumental control over a more complex environment. Alternately, systemic openness is perceived to provide access to some sort of environmental, existential, or even supernatural real. Yet as long as these questions are posed in this way and framed by an instrumental opposition (and its requisite choice between closure or openness, system insides and outsides), *system relations* will continue to elude us, as will a genuine alternative to the unanswerable question of whether human social systems are either open or closed to their material environments.

Second-order cyberneticians came face-to-face with this paradox of a first-order cybernetic understanding of systems' closure. They realized that the "total loops" of instrumental closure, so desired by first-order cybernetics, in fact, turn into "strange loops of the sort imaged by M. C. Escher's Möbius strips," as Cary Wolfe describes this pivotal shift in systems theory and its philosophical consequences in *Critical Environments: Postmodern Theory and the Pragmatics of the "Outside."*[29] Analyzing a variety of *autopoietic* (self-making) or self-referential systems that recursively use their own output as input, that is, as a feedback loop that guides future operations like the famous ouroboros symbol of a snake eating its own tail, second-order cyberneticists and information theorists came face to face with the contingency of observation and its transformative consequence to systems and systems thinking. With recursive, self-regulating systems, whether mechanical or biological, this feedback loop entails a relation of circular causality. The float in a modern flush toilet sinks as the water level in the tank decreases and its lower level then prompts the inflow of new water until it reaches its allotted height; it uses its output of water to guide its input of water. Or, in the case of a person reaching out to catch a softball, each movement of the hand is guided by its near-simultaneous receipt of proprioceptive information about the remaining distance, speed, and trajectory of the softball. "A and B are mutually cause and effect of each other," as Steve Heims describes this theoretical insight in his history of the Macy Conferences.[30] This reveals the importance of the observer in identifying and differentiating cause and effect in what are, in fact, more complex systems. It is the observer who identifies the toilet's loss of water when flushed as the causal force leading the tank to refill with water or, in the second example, who decides whether one is moving one's hand to catch the softball or the softball position in flight provides you with information on how far and fast to reach. These are recursive operations entailing both/and rather than the either/or an oppositional understanding of subject-object relations typically requires.

Second-order cybernetics acknowledges how recursive processes in such systems confound their predecessors' assumptions about causality, agency, and instrumentality. Facing up to the indistinguishability of cause and effect in recursive systems, second-order cybernetics points to the deciding role observation plays in understanding these complex interrelations. They argue that it is the observer who attributes agency in such system relations, reductively turning a more complex system into a straightforward, unidirectional, causal relation leading from A to B. The observer selectively constructs a highly contingent description of the world from a more complex, multipotent reality. As Heinz von Foerster claimed in his foundational second-order cybernetics text *Observing Systems*, "a description (of the universe) implies one who describes (observes it)."[31] As a result of the multipotentiality revealed by the contingency of observation, second-order cybernetics and subsequent systems theorists turned to pursue questions of *system formation* to try to understand how a wide range of systems (social, subjective, biological, etc.), through their distinct modes of operating, participate in an "an ongoing bringing forth of a world through the process of living, itself."[32] This approach foregrounds the constitutive role a particular system's operations play in establishing a distinct modality of relating to the world, a specific, co-productive, dynamic enframing that guides future observations. If the existence of other observing systems of various sorts (and not necessarily human) is taken into account, then it becomes clear that the material effects and knowledge produced by any system's distinct engagement with an environment at a particular time could always be realized otherwise.

Quite paradoxically, the resulting attention to ongoing processes of system formation in second-order cybernetics actively dismantles this defining term, *system*. Systems are no longer understood, as they were in first-order cybernetics, in terms of systemic control, instead, "system" comes to be understood as a kind of "nonlinear recursion, and that is equal to unpredictability," as is apparent in the work of German sociologist and social systems theorist Niklas Luhmann.[33] More recent systems thinking continues to elucidate challenges cybernetic and information systems pose to an instrumental understanding of our relations to technologies and technological systems and to propose alternate methods of approaching these relations. Extending second-order cybernetics to more thoroughly think through *social* systems, Luhmann identified systems thinking as a crucial resource in better understanding how historically and culturally distinct societies and human intersubjectivities emerge from a more complex environment and, through processes of communication and material operations, recursively reproduce themselves.[34]

A systems-theoretical perspective, when combined with more recent work in feminist science studies, philosophy, and critical geographies, I suggest, provides important insight into how technics unfold through recurring, material processes of boundary formation that regularly rerealize subjectivities, national social spaces, other material spaces, and their affective, intersubjective, as well as political economies. From this point of entry, I examine the processes through which the human is negotiated, even co-produced, in relation to technological, economic, and social interrelations in contemporary U.S. cultures. I engage this systems thinking to ask how the human and her social systems co-emerge out of a series of ongoing, dynamic interrelations with a material environment. If the human is negotiable (at discursive, material, and technical levels), how, in fact, do specific subject-technology relations, social formations, and economic systems co-produce distinct understandings and experiences of the human (and not others) in American culture? How are modes of gendered, racialized, and ethnic intersubjectivity consistently produced and what also allows them to change over time? How does the human negotiate technical, social, and material shifts, such as those accompanying computation-based technologies and media? In turn, how do emerging digital cultures have to negotiate existing, embedded social forms and understandings of the human?

These questions are far from simply theoretical ones these days. There are crucial reunderstandings of the human, social systems, and their environments at stake in competing understandings of the human's technicity. These shifting practices, experiences, and understandings of the human have an immediate, tangible impact on subjectivities, their differentiation along intersecting lines of sex, gender, race, ethnicity, subalternity, and sexuality, and the intersubjective experiences they open onto. They enter into national identities still resolutely defined against an inhuman "outside." Further, they impact how we understand the place, privilege, and politics of the human in relation to nonhuman life and material environments. Considering that structural inequities in the world system have become *more*, not less, precise since the 1990s and that they tend to reinforce previous patterns of privilege and exploitation, the stakes in these reunderstandings of the human remain

quite high for those subjects, like women and subalterns, who have historically been assigned to positions deemed liminally human, as well as for nonhuman animal counterparts and material environments.

Putting this systems thinking into conversation with these literary texts,
the book marks the significant changes it makes to the way we think through
the technicity of the human. Observing the co-productive interrelations between distinct material technologies, processes of subject formation, modes
of intersubjectivity, and material lifeworlds, systems thinking focuses attention onto the mutually transformative relays through which what we later
perceive as distinct subjects and objects are materially realized. It looks into
the unacknowledged preconditions for, and the processes through which,
something as apparently intransigent and self-contained as subjectivity, or
a social system improbably comes to be probable and can then be taken for
granted.

In particular, this perspective on technics helps to clarify how systems
relations in contemporary U.S. social systems at the interrelated levels of
subject formation, literary systems, national and transnational social spaces
and their geographies are, at once, highly contingent, ongoing dynamic processes that must be continually reiterated and, equally, are coercive, forceful,
seemingly intransigent structures in daily life. The literary texts at the center
of the book's inquiries illustrate both dimensions to technics. As philosopher of technology Don Ihde argues in his analyses of subject-technology-
embodiment relations, this room for maneuver or "multi-stability" allows
for "unintended use[s] and consequence[s]" of technologies as they are taken
up and transformed in different cultures, at different moments, in different
hands.[35]

Creatively redescribing technics through a comparative juxtaposition
with their own print technics, these literary texts examine how digital technics enter into, transform, and recapitulate print cultures and values, yet
might also be deployed otherwise. They reveal how this multistability of
technics leaves room for interpretive, tactical play in such relations. In this
way, they explore how their own and, by comparison, other mediums and
material technics enter into our subjective experience, social networks, reading practices, and lived space with a productive difference. In light of the
ongoing, dynamic character of such systems relations, these novels and short
fiction search out opportunities to tactically register and to reorient the existing and emergent technics that enter into system formation at multiple
levels within contemporary U.S. digital cultures.

In order to fully think through the material, technological, social, and cultural dimensions to technics, as these relations are taken up by these literary texts and also as they continually, recursively reenter subjectivities, social systems, and material spaces, the book engages systems thinking by researchers working in feminist science studies, gender studies, phenomenological philosophy, and critical geographies, along with earlier biological and social systems theory.[36] The work of Katherine Hayles, Karen Barad, Sara Ahmed, Doreen Massey, Nigel Thrift, Judith Butler, and Elizabeth Grosz,[37] among others, redirects a systems theoretical concern with the dynamic, reciprocal, mutually constitutive relations between subjectivities, social systems, technologies, and their material environments. Their work elaborates in significant ways upon the interrelations described as "structural couplings," "a history of recurrent interactions leading to the structural congruence between two (or more) systems," by second-order systems theorists Humberto Maturana and Francisco Varela.[38] These theorists are particularly determined, as are new materialisms more broadly, to rethink the relations between material and cultural processes as impacted by contemporary technoscientific and economic practices. In this way, they contravene and complexify liberal humanisms' affiliated instrumental oppositions between technologies and subjects, nature and culture, feminine and masculine, passive and active, nonhuman and human, nonwhite and white, space and time. To this end, they introduce additional intellectual perspectives drawn from cognitive science, quantum physics, phenomenological theory, queer theory, postcolonial theory, feminist philosophy of science, critical geographies, among other disciplinary knowledges, which helps to shift their emphasis away from the meaning-centered, constructivist preoccupations that key strains of postmodernism share with Luhmann's social systems theory. Luhmann, for instance, absolutely differentiates between matter and meaning, between systems at the level of their operations and at the level of their observation in meaning, considering all matter wholly outside meaning-based social systems.

These reengagements with processes of materialization and with materialisms of various stripes rethink technics so as to unsettle, not reinforce, the Cartesian subject-object dualisms opposing matter and meaning, physical body and immaterial mind, nonhuman and human, oppositions through which subject-technology relations are most often understood. Their rethinking of systems relations is cognizant of the alignment of women, subalterns, and nonhuman life with a generic, impassive, static material world and interested in troubling the hegemonic gender roles, sexualities, and environmental philosophies these oppositions lend reality. They explore how these co-productive system relations coordinate distinct phenomenal domains without simply translating across, or otherwise overcoming, the differences between these domains. Subjectivity, for example, is reconceived as a "structural coupling" that links the biological body and cognitive self in a reciprocal relation, both of which are, in turn, informed by a larger social apparatus and its privileged technics. Acknowledging how one's individual embodiment is enlisted in socially and cognitively distinct modes of subjectivity, this approach underscores how the body's material facticity as a biological system remains both indispensable and significantly unknown. Though the latter may sound counterintuitive at first, it is quite apparent in everyday situations such as when one suffers from an illness doctors are unable to diagnose.

Bringing these critical, new materialist reengagements with material knowledges and practices into this discussion of system relations, the book inquires into the unknowable yet transformative material dimensions to social systems, subjectivities, and their environments. Such inquiries neither assume material forces into, nor foreclose them from, the domain of human meaning. Registering the transformative, co-productive force of structural couplings at the level of *observation* (in meaning) and *operation* (in matter), interrelations that Luhmann's social systems theory severs, I reveal how such processes might, instead, be seen as processes of *reorientation*, expanding on Sara Ahmed's concept in this systems-theoretical context. Capitalizing on the phenomenological sense of *orientation* as a means of approaching and relating to objects and to a larger world, Ahmed explores the ways in which bodies are "oriented towards things"[39] and she addresses the dynamic material impact spaces and spatial orientations have on bodies and their respective agency and knowledges. Arguing that subjects or social systems and their lifeworlds are reoriented through specific kinds of technics, the book's approach to thinking about how technics enter into and help realize distinct systems relations recognizes the mutually transformative material and epistemological force and import of such interrelations at multiple scales and sites.

Gathering and juxtaposing these systems theories, the book expands the scope of questions that can be addressed. It opens up a consideration of how sex, for instance, the material facticity of which remains largely unknown and unrealized, nonetheless, remains a crucial presupposition for the emergence of the human. How sex enters into processes of human boundary formation is well worth exploring, not bracketing, as long as the limits to our knowledge of sex, always observed and experienced from the vantage of particular social and subjective systems, remain, equally, in view. Thinking through systems relations in this way, the book actively identifies and pursues these feminist and subaltern stakes and, in turn, anatomizes the conceptual tools this broader discourse of systems thinking can contribute to understanding technics and, in particular, literary engagements with them.

Important work on systems thinking in American literature has been undertaken by Joseph Tabbi in his *Cognitive Fictions*,[40] which develops a systems-theoretical approach to literary systems to explore how a series of American novels published since the late 1980s deploy self-reference as a model and means for reflecting on the self-referential processes that also define human cognitive systems, consciousness, and their blind spots. More recently, Bruce Clarke's groundbreaking *Posthuman Metamorphosis: Narrative and Systems*[41] illustrates the fecundity of Luhmann's social systems theory, recombined with science studies work on systems by Bruno Latour and others, for understanding narrative. His impressive book reveals how "neo-cybernetic systems theory" (his gloss on second-order systems theory) allows us to see "narrativity as a significant allegory of systemic operations," as an enfolding or enframing of broader systems relations between psychic systems, social systems, and material lifeworlds within literary narratives, an allegorizing at the level of meaning that, nonetheless "resonate[s] with the operational evolutions—the mutations and occasional catastrophes—of natural and social systems."[42]

This book contributes new dimensions to such systems thinking in and about the literary, while it shares their preoccupation with the lively, principled reciprocity between social, medial, and subjective environments and the literary, a concern with the "interlocking observations of sociohistorical systematics *and* textual formalisms," as Clarke describes his systems-theoretical approach.[43] In particular, the book pursues the material dimensions to technics as they impact and are entangled by bodies and lifeworlds, rethinking their transformative relations to the narrative and cognitive dimensions of social systems privileged within former constructivist frames. As an end result, the book's rethinking of technics as materially realized and reiterated systems relations proceeds to identify technics as a necessary and unavoidable means for reapproaching, registering, navigating, even subtly reorienting emerging digital cultures.

Tactically Yours

Redescribing the simultaneously sedimenting, intransigent and the dynamic, transformative dimensions to technics, as anatomized in these texts and recent systems thinking, the book illustrates how and why technics are key *tactics of the human*. Using the register of the tactical, I underscore how the technics explored in these texts confound notions of proprietary ownership and the subject-object dualisms that undergird concepts of ownership and use. As Michel de Certeau argued, "tactics," as opposed to "strategies," are deployed by those who have only temporary and imperfect access to the resources they borrow and hope to lead astray.[44] Redescribed as a tactical relation between the human, technologies, and broader technological infrastructures, technics are understood as practices involving the insinuation of each into the other's place, an ongoing dance of mutual appropriation that confounds any clear sense of a stable dividing line. The models for such tactical practices "may go as far back as the age-old ruses of fishes and insects that disguise or transform themselves" by borrowing from their immediate environment "in order to survive," which are less sophisticated, yet similarly adaptive and transformative 'ways of operating.'[45] There is no genuine ownership or fidelity that precedes these encounters between the human and her technics. Instead, as tactics of the human, technics come to be understood as co-productive, transformative relationships between subjects and technologies and systems. At the same time, when approached in the register of the tactical, it becomes clear that there is room for maneuver in these interrelations. In their active experimentation with the destabilized and destabilizing technics digital media introduce, these works of fiction encourage us to explore select technics as tactics of the human that reorient us toward the world and might do so with a noticeable difference. Aware that technics enter into and materially shape subject relations and thereby structure intersubjectivity in their terms, these texts recommend how we might take creatively playing on the negotiability of the human as a necessary and serious pursuit.

This is not to suggest, in any way, that technics or their end-games are to be embraced. The book's perspective on technics as socially embedded practices and its envisioning of tactical, not determining engagements with shifting technics contributes its literary perspective to broader efforts to address both the vital, productive and the deadly, nullifying force of technics at once, as these feminist and subaltern texts certainly do. In *Improper Life: Technology and Biopolitics from Heidegger to Agamben*[46] Timothy C. Campbell surveys the contemporary terrain of philosophy of technology and stresses that modern technicity, since Heidegger, is most often approached in terms of its role in delineating or clarifying what is improper or proper to man and, therefore, becomes closely aligned with death and opposed to "proper" human Being and life. Such theories of technicity also, in his view, remain unduly preoccupied with questions of mastery due to Heideggerian lines of thinking on which they continue to draw. This emphasis on technicity's thanatopolitical tendencies is front and center in Kittler's reading of discourse networks 2000 as a totalizing, inhuman, intensified form of closure within media systems whose vitality outstrips our own. In this context, it seems incredibly naive to acknowledge the plastic, productive potential of technics to reorient systems relations, rather than claiming they likely ensure more and more totalizing forms of system closure. To do so, even with serious qualifications, appears to fall back onto understandings of the human as the penultimate, masterful "tool user," the flip side of thinking about technics as relations of mastery. Hayles characterizes this theoretical conflict as a choice between either embracing a human-centric embodiment or privileging the disciplinary enframing by a totalizing media regime, neither of which adequately explains technological change as it joins in human evolution and social systems.[47] At both extremes, such readings of technicity are unable to reconcile the play, reiteration, and degrees and kinds of change that enter into these relations, which are as immanent to such system relations as are their sedimenting force. For this reason, the book shares Campbell's interest in exploring technicity to open onto a different way of thinking *techne* not linked primarily to a defense of the self and its borders but rather as an opening toward the relational.[48] The book contributes to such efforts to think the deadly and affirmative force of technics at once with a careful attention to how subject-technology relations are incorporated into and play themselves out politically and socially in contemporary U.S. social systems and might be encouraged, at select sites, to unfold somewhat differently.

In the chapters that follow, I pursue a series of literary queries and differing engagements with emerging digital cultures and computational media, from Silko's *Almanac of the Dead* in 1991 to Eugenides's *Middlesex* in 2002. Each of the chapters, in turn, identifies a different site at which technics enter into and rerealize twentieth- and twenty-first-century social systems. They move from shifting technics at the scene of writing, to those impacting gendered and racialized subject formation, to technics entering into materially realized social spaces such as transnational economic networks and the U.S. nation-state, to the technics informing micropractices of eating, food production, sex, reproduction, family, and the closely affiliated affective economies subtending the nation-state, and end with an inquiry into the novel's relationship to bioinformatic circulatory systems of "late capitalism" and the modes of becoming American U.S. biopower encourages and overlooks.

Chapter 1 returns to one of the literary system's most influential first encounters with digital narrative—early hypertext theory—to rethink these "Literary Turns at the Scene of Digital Writing." Reading John Barth's short story "Click" in this context, it illustrates how the story's literary print remediation of digital textuality—translating digital hypertext rhetorics and spatial organization into a story in print—actively interrogates shifting relations between literary narrative, its medium, and its writers and readers as these are impacted by emerging digital media and their hypertextuality. In addition to the clear comparison and contest between media taking place in such texts, I identify a cultural questioning and concern with the impact of technological materiality on the human's agency and embodiment in this print remediation of digital hypertext. Understanding subject-technology relations as socially embedded and embedding practices clarifies the social and cultural stakes in the transition of writing scenes from print to digital media, especially as they impact a conception of (masculine) subjectivity as a form of self-authorship. While Barth's story addresses the shifting material conditions of its literary narrative and their potential impact on subjectivity's realization through narrative, its aim in doing so is to transcend those preconditions in the name of the human and preserve the gendered, instrumental oppositions the print textual apparatus and technics of author, literary text, and reader secure. Contrary to its aims, the story unwittingly reveals how digital media are transforming narrative, scenes of writing, and the legibly human subjects they engender in ways that comparative media practices such as remediation might, instead, bring more productively and critically to the fore.

Chapter 2, "Tracing the Human through Media Difference," explores literary and theoretical practices of remediation that pursue this alternative and more actively reckon with the technicity of the human. Literary texts such as Shelley Jackson's digital hypertext, *Patchwork Girl* engage media difference as a resource to reconsider, even reconceive processes of human subject formation. Reading this digital hypertext fiction in the context of posthumanist theory, I examine its reconsideration of the human's co-emergence in transformative relation, not opposition to, material worlds and technologies. *Patchwork Girl* joins posthumanist theories that extend cybernetics, information, and systems theory to develop an understanding of technicity as a recursive system relation characterized by dynamic, reciprocal feedback loops, rethinking the familiar, oppositional relation of subjects and objects, users and tools. Drawing on several strains of second-order systems theory, its adaptation into social systems theory by Niklas Luhmann, and recent new materialist systems thinking from physicist and philosopher Karen Barad, I consider the significance of their alternate views on technics as ongoing, reciprocal, structured, yet shifting interrelations between subjects, technologies, and social systems to thinking about gendered and racialized processes of human subject formation. What are seen from the vantage of an instrumental print narrative framework as monstrous couplings between media, bodies, and enactive selves are reimagined in light of social and biological systems theory and *Patchwork Girl* as a remarkably transformative relation between the human and her technics. Jackson's creative rewriting of Mary Shelley's print classic *Frankenstein* raises the question of whether reconceptualizing the instrumental understanding of technics familiar to print cultures, and revaluing the material objects they disregard might shift the gendered, heterosexist instrumental subject relations the former subject-object dualisms help secure. Noting how scars, stitches, and hypertext links serve in this fiction as models for mutually transformative, reciprocal, dynamic, non-instrumental, hybrid relations between subjects and technologies, meaning and medium, and among variously feminine subjects, this chapter considers what happens when material complexity and the subjects aligned with it are given a gloriously monstrous role in the co-production of the human. In turn, it considers the limits to this and other creative cyberfeminist and material feminist engagements with digital technics and their poetics in light of the less than liberatory functioning of digital networks' material practices for women and for subalterns positioned quite differently within neoliberal late capitalist economies.

To address these limits, chapter 3 shifts its attention from the scale of subjectivity to that of social space to address the simultaneous material reorganization of social space accompanying digital media networks, what sociologist Manuel Castells describes as the emerging spatial logics supporting informational capitalism's "network society." These, and accompanying shifts in spatial organization, such as the dismantling of the "three worlds system," draw attention to social space as the product of dynamic, socially embedded, yet ongoing material practices; a revelation that opens the way for resistant spatial practices and social formations that reflect both a feminist, new materialist rethinking of technics and a postcolonial concern with the operations of global capitalist networks. Arguing that such space-making processes are best understood as processes of reorientation and drawing on Sara Ahmed's critical materialist and phenomenological theorization of the forces that enter into our experience of lived space and gendered, racialized, and sexualized spatial relations, I explore Leslie Marmon Silko's novel

Almanac of the Dead. The novel's spatiotemporal mapping of the Americas, which reimagines networks as a means of channeling energy both materially and symbolically, redescribes late capitalist information networks and resituates them within a five-hundred-year system of imperialist and colonialist expansion in the Americas. Attending to the material and discursive dimensions to technics of space-making, past and present, the novel recommends a series of tactical engagements with hegemonic material spaces as a crucial means to override and unsettle the unequal social relations and spatiotemporal epistemologies social spaces such as late capitalist networks and their digital technics otherwise resolidify. This chapter reveals how the novel's counternarrative of networking as materially realizing possibilities in the world, or "Realizing the Vitality of 'Dead' Spaces," as the chapter's title expresses it, anticipates more recent tactical media practices circulating via new media, and recommends one role for place-based, locative narratives and an increasingly distributed literary system that unfolds through distinct interrelations between literary narratives, material places, and embodied intersubjective relations.

Chapter 4 changes scale once again, registering the U.S. nation-state's recalibration in response to late capitalist networks at the level of national micropractices of eating, food production, sex, reproduction, and family. I explore how transnational practices of production, consumption, and exchange alter preexisting industrial modes of categorizing and differentiating forms of "life" and pose problems to American nationalisms and their affective economies. The chapter centers on Ruth L. Ozeki's novel *My Year of Meats*, which examines transnational feminist networks such as the affiliations between a Japanese American and a Japanese woman, brought together through global capitalist networks designed to produce and market American beef to a Japanese audience. The novel's feminist critique of nationalist discourses' reliance on women as the unchanging, static "meat" or "medium" for national reproduction insightfully anatomizes the materially realized technics on which nationalist discourses and nation-states rely. Developing an Asian American, feminist counterhistory of U.S. nationalism, the novel illustrates how transnational networks require nationalisms to confront the existing cultural, ethnic, racial, and religious complexity already within their geographic (if not symbolic) space, a by-product of cultural and economic imperialisms. I complicate readings of the novel's transnational feminism and the role of affect in solidifying these relations by paying close attention to the novel's concern with shifts global capitalist networks introduce into communication technologies, literary texts, technoscientific practices, industrial food production, and reproductive technologies, all of which quite viscerally impact micropractices of eating, sex, racialization, gendering, family, and desire. These shifting technics unsettle and realign the nation's racialized, gendered, and classed affective economies, its privileged and highly differentiated modes of creating relations of belonging and of disgusting and, thus, instantiating variegated degrees and kinds of intimacy and distance. *My Year of Meats* is interested in how shifting technics, at this micropolitical scale, might noticeably impinge upon American nationalism's dominant affective economy and, in this way, help generate new modes of living and new ways of linking and inhabiting bodies, texts, human and nonhuman animals, and transnational communities. It aims to attune American nationalism's affective economies of desire and disgust to a slightly different, multicultural and transnational key. Registering the visceral impact of technics on individual, social, and national bodies and their modes of relation, the novel raises the question of how feminisms can inhabit, register, and engender national and transnational affective economies to open onto more ethical and enjoyable modes of life. It also forces a consideration of what limits there may be to playing on nationalist logics of desire and disgust and, in this way, "Counting on Affect" to enable new modes and kinds of belonging.

Chapter 5, "Novel Diagnosis of Bioinformatic Circulations," continues the previous two chapters' inquiries into how literary print novels enter into and respond to American nationalism's re-articulation in relation to late capitalism's transnational economic and cultural networks and their dynamic de- and reterritorializing logics. It focuses attention onto the contemporary novel's shifting role in relation to genetics, late capitalism's increasingly bioinformatic flows, and the dynamic, evolutionary perspective on the human species that emerges from them. Engaging Jeffrey Eugenides's novel *Middlesex*, I suggest that it provides a diagnosis of emerging geo- and biopolitical circulation that intervenes in hegemonic modes of bioinformatic networking and late capitalism's neoliberal becoming by exploring unexpected outgrowths of these emerging perspectives on material and cultural transmissions in evolutionary time. The novel identifies a rearticulation of American national belonging as a more dynamic process of becoming American over the course of the twentieth century, which heightens awareness of the ongoing evolution of American nationalism as a political form. Its retrospective, comparative analysis of twentieth- and early twenty-first-century modes of *becoming American* foregrounds the hinging of geopolitics and biopolitics in modern and emergent American nationalisms and considers the consequence of genetic sciences' bioinformatic modes of circulation, and the flexible logics of accumulation they encourage, for contemporary U.S. bio-power. *Middlesex* traces the Greek American Stephanides family through their twentieth-century transnational immigrant tale of becoming American and through the twenty-first-century tale of grandchild Cal's realization of his transgender subjectivity and intersex. The novel embraces these deter-ritorializing, nonbinary migrations across national lines and across the lines of the sex/gender system, and then proceeds to resituate these and its own novelistic becomings in a materially unfolding evolutionary time. Its critical reengagement with genetics, sociobiology, and genetic sciences of material transmission reveals how Darwinian evolutionary theory might provide an important counter to neoliberalism's own lust for becomings, its relentless pursuit of processes of productive differentiation. Reading the novel in rela-tion to philosopher Elizabeth Grosz's account of Darwinian evolutionary theory's feminist potential, I illustrate the need to differentiate between mul-tiple strains of becoming. The novel's rethinking of intertwining material and cultural processes as "smuggling operations" suggests a crucial way to re-cast the instrumental, presumably limitless, flexible logics of neoliberalism, and to engage complex processes of sexual differentiation and other kinds of becoming to other ends. This chapter concludes the book's inquiries into the different ways in which materially realized technics co-produce distinct and shifting modalities of the human, illuminating how these fictions creatively diagnose, register, and reorient such tactics of the human. In a concluding coda, I return to the overarching question of how the literary participates in U.S. digital cultures, drawing from these literary texts' experimental technics to clarify literary poetics' abilities to comparatively engage and enter into digital cultures with a tangible, though perhaps underestimated, difference.

The book's inquiries both begin and end with this question of the liter-ary's current and potential relations to digital cultures and its political rel-evance to how we understand and then reengage emergent modalities of the human in U.S. culture. In reviewing this select prehistory to the literary's increasingly cross-platform, distributed sites and modes of elaboration, I in-tend to illustrate how literary poetics can take up, modulate, and cast com-parative light on the actualized and unactualized potential of emerging tech-nics to forestall, engender, and reorient shifting modes of the human and her social life. I identify these and more recent literary texts' comparative media practices as an important resource, among others, for creatively re-tracing complex systems and, thus, diagnosing the processes through which they emerge, transform, and are reoriented. These literary print texts, as they experiment with digital technics in another medium, have much to teach us about "the function of literature in the technical age" without "succumbing to the uncritical lure of the technical and the new," as Friedrich Block has argued in relation to electronic poetry.[49] In this way, the book speculates on how literary poetics, through these and other experimental technics, can contribute to, and continue to incite, timely modes of engagement in contemporary social systems and their ongoing, multileveled, multiagential system formation. It hopes to elucidate and facilitate the remarkable ways of reunderstanding and reengaging the technicity of the human in digital cultures that these literary fictions open onto.

1 / Literary Turns at the Scene of Digital Writing

> Today . . . we are experiencing the deep opacity of contemporary technics; we do not immediately understand what is being played out in technics, nor what is being profoundly transformed therein, even though we unceasingly have to make *decisions* regarding technics, the consequences of which are felt to escape us more and more . . .
>
> More profoundly, the question is to know if we can predict and, if possible, orient the evolution of technics, that is, of power (*puissance*).
>
> —Bernard Stiegler, *Technics & Time, 1: The Fault of Epimetheus*[1]

> Objectively material means (*technology*) and the tropology of subjective desire (*poiësis*) are bound in an irreducible intentional relation as a revelatory bringing forth (*technë*) that, in its diverse historical and personal practices, makes matter meaningful and meaning matter.
>
> —Vivian Sobchack, "'Susie Scribbles':
> On Technology, *Technë*, and Writing Incarnate"[2]

As the computer entered our homes, and the Internet followed with the unprecedented draw and reach of its World Wide Web in the 1990s, these and other digital media have prompted close analysis, raising anew questions about the relationship between the human, its technologies, and their shared materiality and co-realization through social and cultural systems.

What philosopher Bernard Stiegler, one of the most apt theorists of these contemporary technics, describes as their "deep opacity" signals the complexity and urgency of such questions, while underscoring our desire to render these interrelations more transparent. If we aspire to simply lessen their opacity, the question remains: how to understand and think through the co-productive relays joining print and now digital media to processes of subject and social formation? What kinds of historical, material, social, and cultural processes enter into and transform the human-technology relations now described under the sign of technicity?[3] What kinds of access do we have to such transformations and to the broad-scale, increasingly abstract, and painfully concrete power relations that are their trade and traffic? How do we nonetheless register these emergent relations at multiple levels in the most quotidian experience of sitting at the computer to write?

This reference to the scene of writing is far from incidental to these lines of inquiry. In fact, early encounters between print literary texts and emerging digital writing practices and their theorization in early hypertext theory, if scrutinized, reveal the complex, multidimensional relays comprising what are more often thought as unidirectional and one-dimensional text-based transitions between print and digital media. The scene of writing continues to serve as a foundational site for existing and emergent understandings of the human and her appropriate and inappropriate relations to technology. It is the site of, and a continued source of anxieties about, the relation of writing practices to human intentionality, embodiment, and technological materiality. It is, therefore, a useful starting point for reconsidering how technics work within and through existing social and cultural processes to inform and reform the differential boundaries and modalities of the human. Returning to the scene of writing—that apparently straightforward coordination of writer, textual instrument, desk, medium, reader, and environs—will illustrate the consequence of this extended apparatus to a series of technological relations that unfold, in multiple directions and at various scales, from it.

Reconsidering early hypertext theory and literary print remediations of digital writing as an influential first encounter between literary print and digital textuality, I will identify a missed encounter with technics, with the co-productive interrelations between these distinct material technologies, processes of human subject formation, and modes of intersubjectivity. I return to early hypertext theory's inquiries into the relation between print literary and digital textual practices in order to complicate their understanding of subject-technology relations. These transfers between print and digital media (and more recent ones) shed important light on technics as a shifting set of subject-technology relations with historical, material, social, and cultural, in addition to technological, dimensions. This perspective opens up inquiries into how technics function, at multiple levels, as *tactics of the human*, as dynamic, enactive processes through which subjectivities, technological configurations, and social systems together and alternately variegate the grounds for experience, movement, interaction, expression, and imagination. But first, a bit of backpedalling and extrapolation is necessary. Understanding these interrelations and their tactical relevance to the human requires thinking through the secret life of technics as socially embedded and embedding processes, as technological relations that simultaneously enframe, alter, and are, in turn, transformed through social praxis.[4] Relentless and fruitless discussions of whether the effects of digital media are new or the mere repetition of previous technological relations in slightly altered guise continue apace, unwilling to address the complex negotiations between existing and emergent subject-technology relations and subject forms or larger social formations. These discussions continue to underestimate how digital technologies unfold against, as well as in complex relation to, earlier, liberal humanist oppositions and print-based modes of subjectivity.

To illustrate the complexity of technics as they work in and through social and cultural systems to co-produce intersubjectivities and to elaborate social relations, and to underscore the consequences of leaving these crucial levels to technicity unexplored, I want to reexamine a few influential first encounters with digital textuality. Early hypertext theory by George Landow, Jay David Bolter, and Richard Lanham is instructive, not simply because it was one of the first attempts to grapple with digital textuality and its impact on subjectivities, but, as importantly, because it adopted a comparative approach to examining technics, alternating between print and digital rhetorics in the same transmedia viewfinder.[5] Juxtaposing a literary print textual apparatus and its institutionalized interrelations to those perverse, associative links and trajectories digital texts and the World Wide Web were introducing, hypertext theory cast into relief the interactions between authors, texts, readers, modes of subjectivity, and their medial, institutional, and social apparati. Returning to ask why this initial attempt at a comparative approach to technics fell short of its aims, I will suggest how rethinking technics comparatively, done differently, opens up a line of inquiry into technics as tactics of the human. This approach keeps in view both a specific "history of techniques" and technicity as a recurring relation of the human.[6] A comparative approach to technics, if fully developed, clarifies the social and cultural dimensions to media practices and enables a consideration of their potential recalibration. It allows one to recognize more thoroughgoing modes of *experimental technics* that actively explore discursive and material, cultural, and technical dimensions to such practices. I want to reconsider why early hypertext theory and literary print remediations, such as John Barth's short story "Click,"[7] did not opt to pursue this potential, multi-leveled querying of technicity, which, I'll argue, other American literary fiction identifies and engages as an important occupation for the literary in emerging digital cultures.

The Secret Life of Technics

Hypertext theory represented one of the first attempts to grapple with digital media and their impact on liberal humanism's print cultures, their textual apparati, and their privileged modes of subjectivity. Hypertext, a term coined by computer scientist Ted Nelson in his Xanadu Project[8] well before its distinct (albeit less ambitious) materialization on the World Wide Web, describes primarily text-based digital media with "multiple reading paths, chunked text, and some kind of linking mechanism."[9] George Landow, Jay Bolter, and Richard Lanham, clearly influenced by poststructuralists' engagements with the material apparatus to which distinct discursive formations are indebted, extended the more philosophical queries of Jacques Derrida in *Of Grammatology* and *Archive Fever*[10] by attending to the impact of digital hypertext, specifically, on reading, writing, and "selves."

The promise and lure of early hypertext theory was its apparent attention to the transformative relation between subjectivities and digital media at levels material, discursive, social, and cultural. Stressing the revolutionary difference of digital media, Landow, Bolter, and Lanham suggest that hypertext "leads us to the many twentieth-century attempts to release language from the traditional rules print has dictated."[11] All three saw digital hypertext as actualizing a deconstructive critique of linguistic transparency. In his influential *Hypertext 2.0: The Convergence of Critical Theory and Technology*, Landow claims "hypertext embodies many of the ideas and attitudes proposed by Barthes, Derrida, Foucault, and others," more succinctly, "contemporary theory proposes and hypertext disposes."[12] Digital hypertext was perceived to render subjects' construction in and through language, the constitutive role of discursive practices in subject formation, visible as deconstructive theory attempts to do.

Characterizing digital hypertext as an empirical realization or literalization of deconstructive theory, Landow, Bolter, and Lanham appear poised to grapple with the transformative interrelations between these emergent digital technologies and processes of subject and social formation. They appear poised to address the constitutive, material, and discursive dimensions to our emerging relations to digital hypertext, dimensions that are front and center in their critiques of literary print media. Instead, they present digital hypertext as a means to overcome or remedy the conflict between language as an expressive instrument and language as a constitutive, opaque force in subject and social formations. In their view, digital hypertext provides individual, stand-alone subjects with a means to manage and manipulate this conflict between subjects' expressive relation to language and their constitutive formation through it. It provides subjects with a means of alternating between and manipulating the transparency and opacity of any language and, thus, overcoming specific limitations that it might impose on subjectivity or subjects' self-expression.

Presenting digital hypertext as a remedy to print limitations on subjectivities, optimistically suggesting that this writing technology provides subjects with more various and flexible means of self-construction, early hypertext theory reverses the defining premise of poststructuralism and constructivist theory. The latter theories insist that discursive technologies are constitutive, not secondary to, processes of subject formation and, thus, cannot be separated from these processes, let alone manipulated as distinct, merely additive prostheses or tools. In hypertext theory, the constructive, constitutive force of print media and cultures is replaced by its apparent opposite: an instrumental relation to digital hypertext. In their readings, digital hypertext provides subjects with the means to more actively participate in their own construction, as a tool for self-construction. In relocating subjects in a position of mastery over their writing technologies and, by extension, their discursive "construction," Landow's, Bolter's, and Lanham's accounts of digital hypertext sidestep a genuine encounter with the reciprocal, mutually transformative coupling of digital hypertext media to processes of subject formation.[13] They envision a literally *retooled* liberal humanist subject, relying on an instrumental understanding of technics as a relation of user to tool, subject to object, self to writing technology. Underlying their revolutionary rhetoric, then, is an understanding of technics that is anything but radical. Their constructivist account of print writing technologies positions digital hypertext as a liberating remedy to the restrictive, constitutive enframing of print media, proposing digital hypertext will return us to (or perhaps finally make good on) liberal humanism's understanding of writing technologies as transparent expressive tools.

An underlying, unacknowledged reliance on an instrumental under-standing of subject-technology relations leads early hypertext theory to over-estimate the ability of digital media, alone, to transform subjectivities and to misconstrue the character of that transformation, using it to reinstall and resolidify the very print narrative assumptions these theories, on another level, claim to escape. Theorizing the revolutionary transformation of au-thors, readers, and texts (and the print scene of writing it secures), Landow and Bolter paradoxically maintain authors, readers, and texts—the defining terms of an instrumental, print framework—as distinct, self-contained, self-apparent entities. While clearly searching for a language to describe emer-gent subject-technology relations developing out of digital hypertext writing technologies, their theories of hypertext extend a series of print narrative assumptions about authors, texts, and readers to explain digital hypertext.

Subsequent theorists, Espen Aarseth, Lev Manovich, Katherine Hayles, Sue-Ellen Case, and Jenny Sundén, among others, question the literary print terms in which Landow, Bolter, Lanham, and others theorize this new terrain of digital hypertext. They propose alternate approaches more responsive to what Hayles describes as the "media-specific" character of digital hypertext *multimedia*, as well as writing.[14] Subsequent analyses of new media writing, Matthew Kirschenbaum's *Mechanisms: New Media and the Forensic Imagina-tion* prominent among them, explicitly counter hypertext theory, arguing that it begins and ends with oversimplified, unexamined assumptions that, for instance, electronic texts are always "ephemeral, for example (in fact, data written to magnetic storage media is routinely recovered through mul-tiple generations of overwrites), or that electronic texts are somehow inher-ently unstable and always open to modification."[15] Kirschenbaum, invested in exploring the elided "physical" level to new media writing technologies, in tracing "the bits all the way down to the metal," usefully complicates the theoretical enthusiasm of early hypertext theory.[16] He extends Hayles's and Manovich's nuanced work on the distinct levels to digital textuality and its complex relation to media-specific, materially realized computation (includ-ing software and code, machine language and inscription). Kirschenbaum in-troduces what he terms the "forensic" level of computational inscription and storage, where the bits hit the metal, and differentiates it from the "formal materiality or "formal environment for symbol manipulation."[17] Drawing attention to the elided forensic level to digital technologies, Kirschenbaum, nonetheless, resists identifying the forensic level as an originary ontology for digital media. Instead, he attends to the perplexing independence of the formal material level's numerous softwares and platforms from their "underlying computational environment," an independence that has led theorists to focus on the computer screen and to disregard its processes of inscription, though the latter enables and, in some subtle ways, informs the materiality and textuality of the screen.[18]

Redirecting early hypertext theory's limited engagement with digital textuality, this chapter shares Kirschenbaum's interest in thinking through these multiple levels to digital scenes of writing (levels that include computational inscription that goes well beyond the computer screen). I am particularly interested in the ongoing, reciprocal relays between digital inscription, materially realized symbolic practice, and the cultural imaginaries they unsettle and resolidify. Pursuing a comparative media approach to writing technologies, I will focus on how these interrelated dimensions to digital textuality are and are *not* registered by distinct conceptualizations of digital scenes of writing and in practices as commonplace as sitting at the computer to read, play, or write. If there is no way to banish medial ideologies *tout court*, as the history of recent media studies surely illustrates, they might, instead, be comparatively engaged as a resource. For instance, it is worth asking why an instrumental framework for understanding these relations and their textual apparatus reappears at the very moment digital hypertext comes along and unsettles so many of its defining assumptions—the unchanging print text, clear distinctions between authors, readers, and texts, the unidirectional relationship between authors, texts, and readers. Thinking through the mutually informing and opaque relays between the computer's physical operations, its software and interfaces, and the digital textualities that emerge through these interactions, it is worth considering both how and why print narrative assumptions are so surreptitiously, at times even sub- or nonconsciously transferred and applied to a new medium and technology that unsettles those very terms. How and why are early hypertext theory's revolutionary claims about digital hypertext accompanied by a reassertion of oppositions so out of step with emergent relations to this digital medium? As importantly, what is the alternative to this medial view? How and why does an alternate view matter and, in turn, what new blind spots might it introduce?

Hypertext theory's transposition of the key components of a literary print scene of writing, and its binary, gendered, spatiotemporal logics onto digital writing unwittingly illustrates the socially embedded and embedding character of technics. Its analyses of digital writing remain bound by the conceptual contours of a literary print scene of writing and its investments. If one, instead, takes into account the socially embedded and embedding character of technics, that is, the recursive, co-productive relations between an emerging digital scene of writing, intersubjectivities, and existing social formations, then the overlapping of emerging and recuperative media practices begins to make perfect sense. What at one level are physical circuits also involve conceptual, cultural processes. The conceptual, cultural level emerges from an ongoing process of reading and renegotiating emergent and existing media relations, as well as from interdependent physical and formal levels of digital media. It is through such ongoing acts of reckoning with the kinds of intersubjective relations digital media such as hypertext writing make available and take away that understandings and practices of textuality emerge.

Acknowledging this secret life of technics allows one to comparatively trace some of the recursive and transformative loops through which human subjects are engaged by and engage with specific media. This perspective points the way toward a comparative technics that wrestles with the similarities and differences between print and digital writing practices and, importantly, grapples with their impact on modes of intersubjectivity, on temporal and spatial enframing, and the social and cultural relations they engender. Aware of complex exchanges and cross-media translations between existing print and digital media, Jay Bolter coined the concept of "remediation," and later developed it with Richard Grusin to describe print texts' efforts to mimic and appropriate the rhetorical and medial practices digital hypertext introduces and, conversely, to explain digital hypertexts' transcription of print conventions such as virtual earmarks or tropes of page-turning to this new medium.[19] Bolter and Grusin suggest that "remediation," or "the representation of one medium in another,"[20] is a process that allows media to "critique and refashion" one another. This process of inscribing in its own language the effects produced by other media is necessitated by the fact that other technologies remain "reference points by which the immediacy" of new technologies is measured.[21] The paradox that Bolter and Grusin identify via their "double logic of remediation" is that new media aspire "to get past the limits of representation and to achieve the real," yet they can only appear to do so by either citing the limitations and opacity of other media or by foregrounding their own forms of mediation and openly acknowledging their own opacity, the reality of the text, as a substitute.[22] In either case, the aim is to feign transparency, to disavow the transformative effects of mediation. Explaining these transmedial dynamics as an ongoing contest between *media* for technological primacy in a broader media ecology, Bolter and Grusin's concept of remediation forestalls full consideration of the social and cultural negotiations under way in such transpositions across media.

Reconceived as a comparative mode of experimental technics, remediation comes to be seen as a means of reflecting on the differential capacities of media to materially and conceptually encourage certain intersubjective modalities, relations, and the epistemological assumptions to support them, rather than mere attempts by media to establish their primacy. The multiplication and diversification of modes and methods of remediation over the past ten years illustrates this ongoing reckoning with media difference and the modalities of experience distinct media and their affordances make available and take away. It heightens the importance of rethinking the practices falling under the general sign of remediation. In the introduction to a recent collection of essays on narrative media studies, narratologist and comparative media theorist Marie-Laure Ryan cites nine varieties of remediation.[23] This proliferation attests to the ongoing social and cultural, as well as technological stakes in this traffic across media.

If understood to involve social and cultural, as well as technological, transfers between media, remediation comes to be seen as a practice of comparative technics actively investigating the socially embedded and embedding force of technics.[24] Such practices of media transposition and cross-fertilization cast the rhetorical, material, social, and institutional operations of different media into relief through juxtaposition. In doing so, these processes experiment with what Don Ihde usefully describes as the "multi-stability" of technologies, the room for maneuver in subject-technology-embodiment relations that allows for "unintended use[s] and consequence[s]" of technologies as they are taken up and transformed in different cultures, at different moments, in different hands.[25] The do-it-yourself TV program *This Old House* humorously invokes "multi-stability" in its weekly "What is it?" segment featuring the hosts' hypothetical uses for an unidentifiable tool before revealing its "proper" use for which the tool was supposedly designed.[26] An instrumental understanding of technics explicitly forbids such plasticity by presuming that, as a tool, by definition, its use is determined in advance. It refuses to allow, as postphenomenological theories of technics like Ihde's, or as new materialist and systems-theoretical approaches to technics like my own, do, that these relations are both "overdetermined" due to certain technological affordances *and* plastic.[27]

Redescribing select varieties of remediation as a form of comparative technics that plays on this multistability opens up a line of inquiry into the social and cultural exchanges occurring through these practices. It allows these frequently unnoticed dimensions of technics to be reconsidered. Not surprisingly, feminist and subaltern writers and theorists have been at the forefront of experimenting with and reflecting on digital technics in their capacity to enact and enable intersubjectivities not defined by binary, gendered, and racialized subject-object dualisms. They are astutely aware of how emergent, digitally enabled social formations, subjectivities, and material spaces are extending, as well as recalibrating, liberal humanism's and industrial capitalism's oppositional logics and political forms. The writers and theorists whose work I examine in subsequent chapters comparatively register *and* reimagine print and digital technics and the binary spatiotemporal logics they often renaturalize. Playing on the unacknowledged multistability of technics as they enter into subjectivities, social formations, and material spaces, their work develops an experimental technics. This experimental technics traces these dynamic, shifting interrelations and the modalities of the human they enable in order to creatively diagnose unseen potentialities in these relations.

Literary Print Returns to the Scene of Digital Writing

Although transfers between print and digital scenes of writing clearly generate inquiries into the cultural, material, and technological dimensions to such textual practices, a thoroughgoing engagement with technics was initiated, yet not fully pursued, by hypertext theory or by many early literary print remediations of digital hypertext, in spite of their expressed interest in precisely these transformations. In stopping short of this more rigorous line of inquiry into technics, hypertext theory and early literary print remediations of digital hypertext such as John Barth's short story "Click" are, nonetheless, instructive. They evidence the cultural strategies and stakes informing transitions between print and digital media and reveal strong investments in a literary print scene of writing, investments that remain in place and are well worth recognizing.

As critics of hypertext theory were quick to note, early accounts of digital media often attempted to reproduce the preexisting *cultural values* of liberal humanism's print cultures within an emergent screen culture. Concerned that print remediations of new media function "in the service of retaining the dominance of print culture by re-writing, or correcting its traditions," as "strategies to retain writing amid screens" by "writing about writing, in order to maintain its ground through self-referentiality, or writing in emulation of the screen's potential for hypertextuality," Sue-Ellen Case underscores what is at stake in these transmedia exchanges.[28] An overt investment in print apparati and their primacy provides little cover for the more substantial investment these works have in the epistemological assumptions, cultural values, modes of subjectivity, and modalities of the human these print cultural practices serve to reinforce and instantiate. In her feminist and queer performance studies approach to digital media, Case flags the pivotal relation between digital technologies and the practices through which gendered and sexed subjectivities are realized, whereas first-generation hypertext theorists' emphasis on the potential "uses" of digital media presumes that these technologies, as tools, remain at any (abstract) subject's disposal. Rather than simply providing "new opportunities for self-definition," as Bolter and Grusin suggest, existing and emergent technics help to establish a set of relations in which specific understandings of gender, sexuality, and race are already in circulation well before a subject accesses the Web.[29] These preestablished, though dynamic, interrelations with different media and media systems reinforce a limited and differentiated set of subjectivities and intersubjectivities and delimit those to whom such an opportunity for self-definition is extended (i.e., those who are recognizable as autonomous human subjects able to "use" a technology) in the first place. From this vantage, early hypertext theory's extension of an instrumental, print-based understanding of textual apparati from print to digital hypertext maintains the privilege of print's instrumental framework and its clear, gendered distinctions between authors and readers, while it may overtly acknowledge possibilities for flexible movement among these (two) positions.

To clarify what is at stake in how literary print remediations and other comparative media practices redescribe the digital scene of writing and its impact on textuality, I turn to John Barth's literary print remediation of digital hypertext in "Click." Barth's fiction plays a pivotal role in reexamining the writing scene as it encounters digital technologies and in reflecting on the literary system's shifting role in relation to digital cultures. Rereading the story will help illustrate how reapproaching remediation in light of the socially embedding and embedded character of technics opens up an alternate perspective on these intertwined processes of social, cultural, and technological change. If print remediations of digital media (and vice versa) are a means of exploring and experimenting with the social and cultural possibilities and consequence of shifting technics, of resisting or enhancing multistable relations to distinct writing technologies, then both their conservative and expansive movements may be read and valued in significantly different terms.

What Print Narratives Remember and Forget

Translating the rhetorical strategies and effects of digital hypertext into the form of a literary narrative in print, or remediating hypertext, John Barth's short story "Click" is clearly interested in the impact of digital textuality on the scene of writing and on its own scene of writing as a work of literary fiction, in particular. Published in the *Atlantic Monthly* in 1997, this short story continues Barth's long-standing interest in the self-reference of language and the limits of the literary. "Click" and his subsequent novel *Coming Soon!!! A Narrative* link their standard metafictional concern with language and the literary form to an exploration of digital hypertext and are particularly concerned with the challenges digital hypertext poses to subjectivity, which is understood, in relation to literary print narrative, as a form of self-authorship.[30] As Daniel Punday argues in his insightful analysis of "fictionality" in postmodernism, "Barth develops an understanding of what it means to write fiction precisely by working through the institutional occasions of his writing and searching for principles that occur within those occasions."[31] Punday underscores Barth's recurring concern with the nitty-gritty occupation of the literary as it responds to shifting institutions of writing, publishing, education, and social life. In spite of this prescient awareness of the literary's impending transformations, Barth's understanding of the fictional impels him to first confront and then attempt to "transcend the occasion of writing" by finding underlying continuities that lead beyond the shifting material and cultural grounds of fiction.[32] His fiction pursues the very logic Barth identifies in Jorge Luis Borges's work, revealing "how an artist may paradoxically turn the felt ultimacies of our time into material and means for his work—paradoxically because by doing so he transcends what had appeared to be his refutation."[33]

Barth's print remediations of digital hypertext, read in this light, clearly attempt to engage the digital scene of writing as a means of disabling or surpassing its challenges. Examining how and why Barth's short story "Click" sidesteps the occasions of its writing clarifies the significance of the specific "occasions" it attempts to, but cannot, transcend. It also underscores the impact of a shifting digital scene of writing on the literary and on the modalities of the properly individualized, human subject of writing the literary here attempts to secure. "Click" asks what happens to the print scene of writing as it encounters digital writing technologies such as digital hypertext on the World Wide Web, and what impact the encounter has on the liberal humanist subject, imagined and legibly materialized through this print scene of writing as self-author. Its answers to this question acknowledge the transformative material, technological, and cultural dimensions to shifting writing practices. They do so to then move to higher ground, maintaining an understanding of fiction and of a narratively realized subjectivity that supersedes these upheavals. In staging this encounter between a print and digital scene of writing, "Click" nonetheless casts into relief precisely those "occasions" of writing it would prefer to elide and illustrates what is conspicuously absent from its thinking about technics. Its remediation, in other words, evidences what is lost in its translation between these material writing practices. In this way, the story helps elucidate the material and conceptual processes through which existing subject-technology relations are transposed onto new media and how the multistability of emerging technics, if registered, can thoroughly unsettle such gestures.

"Click" describes and enacts a couple's navigation of a website on the World Wide Web so that the narrative mimics, as best it can, the movements afforded by early web-based digital writing, indicating, and apparently following, underlined keywords as if they are hypertextual hot links. In spite of the story's interest in digital hypertext as an emergent writing technology—evident in its enactment of the rhetorical strategies of a digital hypertext and simulation of the latter's material specificities—"Click" emphasizes the fundamental similarities between print and digital textual practices. It presents both hypertext on the World Wide Web and print fiction as *narrative* technologies: narrative means of managing the complexity of the world. The story chronicles a couple's troubling encounter with "The Hypertextuality of Everyday Life" as they explore a website on the World Wide Web and make their way to the National Aquarium.[34] The narrator describes this "hypertextuality" of everyday life as the "all-but-infinite array of potential explanations, illustrations, associations, glosses and exempla, even stories, that may be said to lie not only behind any verbal formulation but also behind any real-world image, scene, action, interaction," as opposed to the "the literal menus-of-menus and texts-behind-texts that one finds on CD-ROMS and other computer applications."[35] Hypertextuality is, thus, presented as a figure for narrative complexity that is assumed to transcend its particular, material manifestation (or occasion) in print or online.

Using digital hypertext as an opportunity to reconsider the value and limits to narrative, "Click" undercuts the difference of digital hypertext, which is often characterized and heralded, in opposition to narrative, as a nonlinear or multilinear mode of writing that "challenges narrative and all literary form based on linearity" and "calls into question ideas of plot and story current since Aristotle," as George Landow states with characteristic hyperbole.[36] Illustrating through its metafictional narrative the equal potential of print narrative to be recursive, nonlinear, multivalent, and multilayered, the story lays bare the illusion of literary narrative conventions such as the well-made plot and chronological sequence and the always imperfect production of that illusion. "Click" critiques this conventional understanding of narrative by demonstrating nonlinearity, recursivity, and the multivalences of textual meaning as an unacknowledged, but essential, basis of, and backdrop for, any momentarily achieved, but ultimately illusory, linearity, closure, or univocality in narrative. Redefining narrative in metafictional terms, terms comparable to emerging digital hypertextual rhetorical forms, the story undercuts the latter's novelty and reasserts the primacy of narrative (albeit in a self-reflexive, metafictional guise) over what is often described and valued as an antinarrative writing technology.

Admittedly, "Click" is not alone in its conceptualization of narrative, in the abstract, as a means of managing complexity that is primarily *unchanged* by shifts in media. It continues the legacy of a structuralist-born narratology and a hermeneutic tradition that privileges narrative meaning and disregards its means of production, its differential realization in a specific medium that informs that meaning at more than one level. Recent work in narrative media studies continues to grapple with the question of what happens to narrative in its encounters with digital writing technologies and computational practices. This work asks whether narrative remains fundamentally unchanged or is increasingly recast in relation to the textual, organizational, and cultural forms privileged by digital media, such as the database. Researchers in a range of fields—social semiotics, game studies, digital narratology, literary studies, new media, and software studies—have recently joined forces to detail the differences digital writing technologies and computational media introduce into narrative practices and literary poetics.

While "Click" has plenty of company in its conception of narrative as above and beyond media, the impact this has on the story's reading of digital hypertext merits pause. This exclusive emphasis on the narrative dimensions of digital hypertext leads to a wholesale elision of significant material differences between these textualities and downplays their transformative impact on intersubjectivities. Digital hypertext's capacity, as a material technology, to challenge the primacy of narrative or challenge the translatability of a certain conception of narrative, unchanged from medium to medium, goes unremarked. While the different modes of access to complexity provided by print and digital writing technologies prompt the story's inquiries, by conflating digital hypertext with an abstract concept of hyper*textuality* "Click" renders all complexity in narrative terms and firmly situates all textuality within the domain of narrative. This recuperative move overlooks the fact that verbal language is not subjects' exclusive mode of access to the world or means of expression. Barth's subsequent novel, *Coming Soon!!! A Narrative*, provides a telling counterexample to this presumption. In one of a series of exchanges between an aging author of "p-fiction" and a young upstart writing "e-fiction," the youth translates the acronym "WWW" as "A Way With Words" or "Away With Words!"[37] "Click" evades this concern that digital hypertext and other hypermedia, in their capacity as multimodal visual, aural, and tactile, not solely verbal, media, might *challenge*, if not thoroughly unsettle, a print narrative framework. In only considering the continuities between digital hypertext and print narrative, the story reductively incorporates digital hypertext within its print narrative framework.

Further, "Click" conceives hypertext as a figure for narrative meaning, which means it does not engage digital hypertext at the physical level as a technology at all. This oversight is a familiar by-product of the hermeneutic tradition's privileging of abstract meaning and its disregard for the material textual apparatus or processes of production.[38] This prioritization of thought stands in the way of a genuine grappling with the reciprocal, transformative, co-productive, inscriptive, formal, and conceptual relays established with writing technologies such as digital hypertext. As Mark Hansen characterizes twentieth-century humanism's refusal to register the material force and impetus of technology, which he terms "*technesis*": a "progressive assimilation of technology to thought" subordinates and "sacrifices technological materiality in order to maintain the integrity of thought."[39] Hansen argues that the

> extensive invocation of technology by twentieth-century philosophers and theorists from Freud and Heidegger to contemporary cultural critics remains faithful to the logocentric foundation of philosophical humanism—the privilege of thought and/or the thinking agent. . . . An initial move to embrace technology is in each case compromised by a defensive gesture: at some point or other, the radical alterity of

technology is sacrificed to preserve thought as the ultimate tribunal of experience.[40]

In a similar way, "Click" gestures toward the technological materiality that escapes linguistic capture, yet then proceeds to recontain the material difference between print narrative and digital hypertext, reducing both to the role of a "mere material support for the all important—and all engulfing—process of subject constitution."[41]

In spite of Barth's extensive concern with the matter of writing as it transformatively enters into fiction writing and reading, he maintains the secondary status of this apparatus as a stand-alone tool ultimately in the hands of its autonomous human user, that is, the author, and, by extension, human subjects conceived as self-authors. It should be stressed that this very concern is both prompted and betrayed by the fact that writing technologies indirectly structure the very emergence of legible subjects and continue to inform subjectivities at perceptual and experiential levels that may not be registered at the level of consciousness at all. In her phenomenological mediation on a contemporary toy writing automaton, "'Susie Scribbles': On Technology, *Technë*, and Writing Incarnate," Vivian Sobchack addresses the multiple levels at work in "relations between technology and embodiment in the matter—and meaning—of writing."[42] She describes her experience acclimating to writing technologies (pencil, ball-point pen, typewriter, and computer), stressing that "activity, object, and subject are enabled and mediated through a particular writing technology that spatially and temporally qualifies the embodied manner and objective style in which we write."[43] In addition to the material co-emergence of written self-expression with writing implement, "the meaning of writing and its material technologies are historically and culturally enworlded—in particular embodied techniques and the meanings that in-form them."[44]

Sobchack's attention to the matter of writing technologies reveals their multilayered influence and ability to amplify and transform specific modes of experiencing, interacting, communicating, and being in the world at levels physical, social, and cultural. Writing technologies are materially incorporated and embodied, and, as importantly, these embodied techniques are socially embedded; they are learned and convey "learning" to others. Sobchack reminds us that there are appropriate and inappropriate ways to write, and these serve "as an indexical sign of subjectivity, a symbolic sign of class, and a pragmatic form of social empowerment."[45] It is no accident that a black "Susie Scribbles" is accompanied by two other writing automatons: a

white, blonde, blue-eyed "Susie Scribbles" and "Skippy Scribbles," a domes-
ticated brown bear, are her equally, if differently, mechanical, and, therefore,
ambiguously human, counterparts.

"Click" is equally though differently preoccupied with the relay between
writing bodies and writing technologies that Sobchack explores through Susie Scribbles: "what writing is and how it is accomplished" is once again
hinged to "what is—or is not—'human' about writing."[46] Disregarding the
material level of the medium or its impact on readers and writers in its
thinking through these relays, "Click" downplays the transformative character of technics. The story focuses exclusively on linguistic complexity, a
complexity over which subjects retain some conscious control, rather than
the "semiosis of the lived body," as Sobchack's analysis does.[47] In "Click,"
hypertext writing technologies serve as an occasion to reconsider the limits
of narrative and, as importantly, the limits of subjects' self-mastery in narrative without letting go of an instrumental understanding of technics and the
individualist, autonomous human subjectivities it intends to secure.

The story chronicles Mark's and Val's encounter with the "hypertextuality of everyday life," which is the source of a lovers' quarrel that the narrator
describes as a conflict between "fundamentally opposite views of and modes
of dealing with the infinitely complex nature of reality," two conflicting
modes of managing complexity.[48] Mark and Val are figures for two "contrary
narrative impulses of equal validity and importance" and, thus, their story
is employed in the service of the story's self-referential narrative about narrative.[49] Mark is described as an "Expediter" who wants to "get on with" it
by getting to the point or to the ultimate destination, and Val is described
as an "Enhancer" who is "fascinated by the contiguities, complexities, inter-
scalar resonances, and virtually endless multifariousness of the world."[50] The
couple's eventual truce signifies the necessity, in print fiction, of balancing
these two narrative tendencies. In the narrator's words:

> A satisfyingly told story requires enough "Valerie"—that is, enough
> detail, amplification, and analysis—to give it clarity, texture, solid-
> ity, verisimilitude, and empathetic effect. It requires equally enough
> "Mark"—that is, efficiently directed forward motion, "profluence,"
> on-with-the-storyness—for coherence, anti-tedium, and dramatic ef-
> fect.[51]

As an aspiring writer, Mark, with his predilection for the temporal progression of the plot and for narrative meaning represents a privileged ten-

dency within nineteenth- and twentieth-century realist literary print narrative, which has traditionally focused on meaning and considered narrative as a means to this end, as a means to Truth and narrative closure. Val, on the other hand, is aligned with the spatial dimensions of narrative and its textuality, the poetic occasions of writing that realist literary print narrative attempts to transcend in the service of meaning. Importantly, this is a poetic spatiality and textuality that hypertext enables and revalues, allowing for the apparently limitless amplification and enhancement that Val so desires.

The story's gendering of these narrative tendencies is far from incidental to its concern with narrative. "Click" indexes the inextricability of a specific textual economy and a specific, heterosexual sexual economy, revealing that the story's concern with the transformation of narrative tendencies is equally a concern with the transformation of a sexual economy that this understanding of narrative has secured. "Click" is self-reflexive, if not self-reflective about the fact that, in Judith Roof's words: "Gender ideology and narrative coalesce into an insistent form that reiterates a tension between male and female as occupiers of particular narrative (and [re]productive) functions—the male as 'creator of differences' and the female as 'matter' or undifferentiated space."[52] Even without specific evocations of gender, as Roof rightly insists, "we are halfway to heterosexuality; defining oppositions in terms of complementary differences [which] creates a heterology, a play of differences that seems to be minimally necessary for any narrative activity to occur."[53]

"Click" completes its "heterology" by situating a heterosexual union as the desired end of its narrative about narrative and its ends. It depicts the "complementary differences" between these narrative tendencies and these gender roles in quite familiar terms. It is quite easy to read Mark, the masculine writing subject who is aligned with narrative progress as the "active principle of culture, the establisher of distinction, the creator of differences."[54] Val, the feminine reader, is just as easily read in terms of the "feminine" position: she is aligned with that which "is not susceptible to transformation, to life or death."[55] Situated in proximity to the scene of writing, an inscription surface, "she (it) is an element of plot-space, a topos, a resistance, matrix and matter."[56] Far from questioning its stereotypical gendering of these narrative tendencies, "Click" actively participates in reinforcing the equation between what are presumed to be masculine and feminine narrative tendencies and masculine and feminine sexual tendencies by suggesting that Mark's and Val's relations to narrative reiterate this sexual difference and vice versa. According to Mark, Val was "a Gemini who preferred hors d'oeuvres to entrées both at table and . . . in bed" and, according to Val, Mark was "a bullheaded whambamthankyouma'amer of a Taurus whose idea of foreplay was three minutes of heavyweight humping to ejaculation instead of two."[57]

Advocating a "truce" or balance between the "masculine" tendency toward expediting (i.e., temporal narrative progression) and the "feminine" tendency toward enhancing (i.e., poetic spatial immersion), the story attempts to remedy realist literary print narrative's subordination of the spatial dimensions of narrative and textuality. In this respect, it attempts to acknowledge or "Mark" the limits of narrative and, presumably, the limits to the (masculine) subject's instrumental mastery of narrative—limits that are, not coincidentally, figured as feminine textuality and immersive textual space. Val, the "Enhancer," is paying attention to language itself as a thing by clicking on words rather than subsuming these linguistic contingencies to the aim of representation, the "expedition" of the plot. Juxtaposing her "feminine" engagement with language as a sensuous aesthetic object and end in itself to Mark's "masculine" engagement with language as an instrument, "Click" acknowledges digital hypertext's capacity to stage the conflict between language as a transformative, opaque medium that structures and enhances that which it figures and language as a somewhat transparent instrument of representation or tool. Richard Lanham describes this conflict as the oscillation between "looking at," a focus on the poetic dimensions of language, and "looking through," a focus on its representational function, its ability to be a window on the world.[58] Lanham admits that this oscillation is nothing new, that writers have always used strategies to trigger some version of this oscillation in narrative. Yet he also assigns digital hypertext a special status by arguing that it literalizes this conflict by allowing readers to choose between and combine these two strategies. According to Lanham, new media such as digital hypertext are distinguished by subjects' *self-conscious* reflection on "looking at" and "looking through."

"Click" counters this view of hypertext's novelty with its own print-based oscillation between "enhancing" or "looking at" language and "expediting" or "looking through" language. As a work of metafiction, the story shifts its attention back and forth from the narrative ground of meaning-production to the figure or narrative meaning. Self-referentially attending to the process of meaning-production, to the process of its own narration, the story charts the production of narrative meaning out of its linguistic ground. It accomplishes this by shifting its attention from the necessary transparency of language in the service of narrative meaning to the opacity of language, which it aligns with the textual complexity that this transparency subtends. In one of many asides, the narrator notes that if one chooses to attend to "apparently insignificant elements" such as "<u>The,</u> for example or the <u>of</u>" in a phrase such as "the hypertextuality of everyday life," one finds that "[a] good desk dictionary will list at least eight several senses of the homely word 'the' in its adjectival function, plus a ninth in its adverbial ('the sooner the better,' etc.)—twenty lines of fine-print definition in all."[59] According to "Click," narrative—whether it takes the form of a digital hypertext on the World Wide Web or the form of a literary narrative in print—always entails a reduction in, and partial bracketing of, textual complexity. In this respect, digital hypertext remains as selective, as much—a "<u>virtual hypertextuality</u>"—as any literary narrative in print in that it requires one to click or select.[60] Digital hypertext may render that process explicit, yet as a work of metafiction that makes that very process of selection the subject of the narrative, so does "Click."

"Click" underscores the selectivity of its own print engagement with the "hypertextuality of everyday life" by drawing analogies between hot links to additional information in hypertext and parentheses or footnotes in fiction, between bullet points and other devices for ordering information in hypertext and chronology in fiction, and between online names in hypertext and characters' names in fiction. The story suggests that these all serve as modes of abbreviating and, thereby, managing the complexity that underlies, and escapes, any narrative. Its title and its repeated reference to the command "click" stresses the necessarily selective limits to narrative, which always requires some kind of "click," a selective remembering and forgetting or simultaneous enhancement and reduction of that complexity. This selectivity is what fuels narrative according to "Click," which both presents and enacts this understanding of narrative as a circular, ongoing process of remembering and forgetting, an always incomplete, interminable, circular process that begins and ends with another selection, with a "<u>Click</u>."[61]

This selectivity not only fuels and limits narrative, according to "Click" it also motivates and limits subjectivity, which the story conceptualizes as a form of self-authorship (in line with a "possessive individualist" understanding of subjectivity).[62] Insisting that the reconciliation of Mark and Val, and an entente between the narrative tendencies they figure is of relevance not only to those with a "professional interest in storytelling," the narrator describes "<u>the self itself</u>" as a

> "posited center of narrative gravity" that, in order to function in and not be overwhelmed by the chaotically instreaming flood of sense data, continuously notices, ignores, associates, distinguishes, categorizes, prioritizes, hypothesizes, and selectively remembers and forgets;

that continuously spins trial scenarios, telling itself stories about who it is and what it's up to, who others are and what they're up to; that finally *is*, if it is anything, those continuously revised, continuously edited stories? . . . finding, maintaining, and forever adjusting from occasion to occasion an appropriate balance between the "Mark" in each of us and the "Valerie" ditto is of the very essence of our self-hood, our being in the world.[63]

Acknowledging the limits of narrative and the *narrative* limits to the (masculine) subject's narrative mastery or self-authorship serves, in "Click," as a means of repurposing this conception of subjectivity as a form of narrative self-authorship *in spite of its limits.*

The story's engagement with textuality and its acknowledgment of the limits to the subject's mastery of narrative is motivated by its sense that digital hypertext might upset this opposition between "expediting" and "enhancing" altogether. Digital hypertext might contribute to a disequilibrium between the presumably masculine and feminine narrative tendencies by privileging or enabling the reader's engagement with textuality to such an extent that it might eclipse or elude the masculine writing subject—embodied in the figure of the author—and his instrumental mastery through narrative altogether. If literary print narrative overlooks the *process* of meaning-production in favor of its end—narrative meaning—digital hypertext allows one to become so immersed in the instruments and scene of meaning production that one forgets the point of narrative altogether. In "Click" Val provides a cautionary example of this latter possibility, spending much of the story exploring a website depicting the webmaster/narrator's writing desk, then proceeding to examine the view out his window. Due to her tendency to elaborate, enhance, and, in this way, to digress, she is utterly incapable of telling a story, according to Mark. Val here represents the inhuman, process-based iterability unleashed by the digital scene of writing. She is, not co-incidentally, aligned with the very material and technological occasions of writing that the story wants to mitigate, if not transcend.

How Media Make a Difference

"Click" evokes precisely the dis-ease it attempts to vanquish by confining digital hypertext to the abstract realm of narrative complexity. In flagging the selective limits to print and digital narrative, the story unwittingly reveals the nonequivalence of these media-specific and technologically distinct means and modes of selectivity. It raises the question of what exactly a particular medium and medial interface affords, what exactly it encourages us to remember or forget through its selective enhancement and reduction of the complexity of the world. The title of the story identifies the media-specific sound and movement one makes when using a mouse to navigate a website and to select one link over others, suggesting that the mode and means of selection afforded by any medium matters. Whereas print and digital writing both entail a selection from the complexity of the world, which the story associates with the click of a mouse in digital writing, the introduction of the mouse, invented in the 1960s by digital interface pioneer Douglas Engelbart, "initiates the move from tool as prosthetic extension to technology as environment, a space to be lived in and explored."[64] The "click" of a mouse marks a significant turning point in the digital scene of writing and initiates its reconceptualization as a material space one enters into, rather than as a writing accomplished with a stand-alone tool. In fact, recent research in human-computer interactions is intent on developing human-computer interfaces able to engage a broader spectrum of our perceptual, expressive, and embodied experience in these computational relays, an aim Golan Levin's digital installation art creatively and insightfully achieves.[65] He underscores how the mouse-click places especially severe restrictions on human expressivity, illustrating why the specificity of the technology and medium of writing matter quite a bit.

Insisting that medium is "a category that truly makes a difference about what stories can be evoked or told, how they are presented, why they are communicated, and how they are experienced," Marie-Laure Ryan proposes a middle ground to avoid the "media-blindness" on display in texts such as "Click," a blind spot that leads to the "indiscriminating transfer of concepts designed for the study of the narratives of a particular medium (usually those of literary fiction) to narratives of another medium."[66] She develops a comparative media studies approach to reveal how different media "support a distinct type of narrativity" as a result of their "unique combination of features," such as the "senses being addressed"; "priorities among sensory tracks"; "spatio-temporal extension"; "technological support and materiality of signs"; and "cultural role and methods of production/distribution."[67] Asking, "Will New Media Produce New Narratives?" Ryan underscores the transformative force of a medium and the distinct technics it realizes, describing how

The interactive character of digital texts manifests itself as a feedback loop that sends information from the user's body and its extensions (mouse, keyboard, joystick, magic wand, data glove, or headset) to the processor, often through the mediation of a virtual user-body; from the processor to the display, which is modified by the execution of the command issued by the user; from the modified display to the mind of the user; and back to the acting body. Digital media do not simply place us in front of a static text; they situate us inside a system that continuously produces a dynamic object.[68]

As her detailed sketch of this scene of digital writing suggests, digital textuality is transformed and, I would stress, transformative, at multiple levels. In situating readers and writers amid this system, these different modes of writing enter into the boundary formation of intersubjectivities and their experience, expression, and interactions in unexpected ways.

Quite interestingly, as "Click" turns to the scene of writing, its recontainment of digital hypertext within a print narrative framework falters, and the force of a significantly distinct digital writing system intrudes upon its instrumental, print technics. Focusing on the textuality that escapes any narrative and compromises subjects' self-mastery through narrative, the story imagines the difference between literary print narrative and digital hypertext (with its seemingly limitless capacity for textual elaboration), in quantitative terms, hiding its actual concern with the genuine, qualitative, material differences between these mediums. "Click" avoids qualitative differences between these media by engaging digital writing only at the level of meaning-production, by presenting the scene of writing in narrative terms as the story behind the story. This emphasis on an abstract process of narrative meaning-production causes "Click" to underestimate the significance of its own media-specific writing practices. It fails to engage or acknowledge its own material instantiation in a print periodical as more than incidental to its meaning. Identifying parenthesized material, "stuff that might be left out of or cut from" the story, as a print precursor to the information now being "'hypertexted' behind the bare-bones description, to be accessed on demand," "Click" turns a blind eye to the fact that the way that "textual complexity" is "managed" or evoked matters quite a bit.[69] Placing textual amplification in parentheses may serve a comparable need in writing, but the impact and effects of parentheses and hot links in print fiction and digital hypertext, respectively, differ substantially. Attempting to foreground the circularity of textual production, regardless of the medium, by approximating the "virtually endless reticulations of the World Wide Web," the circular structure of the story, which begins with and returns to the word "Click?," forgets that the sequential arrangement of the *Atlantic Monthly*'s pages or its twinned columns place distinct constraints on the endless, cyclical recurrence of its story.[70]

The narrator of "Click" is also the webmaster of a website that the couple explores, yet when the story self-referentially turns to this scene of writing, the story's elision of the material differences between these writing technologies results in the absurd depiction of this narrator/webmaster at his desk with a *fountain pen*. This scene reveals the story's underlying concern with the nontextual threat digital hypertext poses as a technology that might not retain such a strict delineation between user and tool, between author and instrument or writer and reader.[71] Figuring Val, the "feminine" reader, looking at a website depicting a picture of the author/webmaster at his desk with phallic fountain pen in hand, this scene encapsulates the story's various attempts to transpose or superimpose these instrumental, gendered, binary user/tool relations between readers and writer onto digital hypertext.

Contrary to its intentions, "Click" draws attention to the technological differences that it elides in order to do so and reveals its investment in narrative to be equally, or more importantly, an investment in the instrumental understanding of technics that print narrative has secured. The narrator characterizes the World Wide Web as an "electronic labyrinth, the black hole of leisure and very antidote to spare time," and Mark insists that it is "time-expensive, too, and—like dictionaries, encyclopedias, and hardware stores [this last in Mark's case; substitute department stores and supermarkets in Val's]—easier to get into than out of."[72] Aligning digital hypertext with these and other *immersive* spaces, "Click" is wary of digital hypertext, as a technology that blurs the boundaries between user and tool, and the threat it seems to pose to the (masculine) liberal humanist writing subject's autonomy. Literally and figuratively, Mark and the narrator and, thus, the narrative, depart from Val, who is left navigating the hypertext website, "'progressing' unhurriedly toward . . . two intriguing points of land" in the distance, leaving her "to circulate indefinitely with the spawning eels," in order to get to the point of the story and move the story forward in time, toward narrative closure, rather than simply dwelling within what the narrator perceives as the regressive, aquatic, feminine textuality of hypertext.[73]

Aligning digital hypertext with immersive, feminine spaces of natural reproduction and mass consumption, "Click," nevertheless, releases the specter of a technics that does not conform to a rigid, instrumental delineation of user and tool. This alternate understanding and engagement with technics, instead, resituates user and tool inside multiple, intersecting systems of dynamic, transformative interrelation. Within humanism's instrumental view of technics, such "immersive" relationships to technologies render subjects passive and, thus, the subject-technology relation is transformative in a wholly negative way. To be acted on or by, or subsumed within, a technological system generates a familiar liberal humanist anxiety with mass cultural forms, susceptible feminine readers, and technology, all of which disturb the masculine author/subject's symbolic, immaterial autonomy and unique, human individuality.

Since Heidegger, modern technology has been perceived to sever writing from its more originary, essential, and proper realm of the hand.[74] As Timothy Campbell suggests in his analysis of Heidegger's influence on contemporary philosophies of technology, Heidegger was concerned with the typewriter's "capacity to occlude handwriting, and with it, the character of the individual who writes by hand, [which] alters the relation of being to Being."[75] Heidegger's work on technology establishes a distinction between proper and improper relations to writing depending on "the relation of man to his writing mechanisms."[76] As Campbell stresses, this "distinction between proper and improper" relations to writing is at the core of Heidegger's "division in life . . . between one *Art*, or species of man, associated with proper writing and another with improper writing."[77] We can see a remarkable continuation of this line of thinking about technicity in "Click," as it reoperationalizes a gendered distinction between human subjects based on whether they maintain their individualized mastery of a writing technology or are, by contrast, perceived to be deindividualized, passive masses subjected by that writing technology.

Shifts introduced through digital scenes of writing introduce crucial alternatives to these habits of thinking technicity. They reveal contradictions in the former, liberal humanist illusion of an instrumental relation to technologies and its absolute delineation between user and tool. In the former case, technologies are embraced when they are conceived as prosthetic (i.e., additive) extensions of the human that "enhance" perceptual abilities, aptitudes, and means of communication. This subject form is, simultaneously, unwilling to acknowledge the reductions and qualitative, transformative changes that necessarily accompany any "enhancement" of the autonomous human individual. Understanding technologies as merely additive instruments, tools, or prostheses effectively reinforces a "doubled desire" to profit from technological enhancements (as additions or prostheses) and, paradoxically, to deny the very transformational effects that one desires.[78] The extensions, additions, and enhancements technics introduce necessarily involve transformative gains and unacknowledged diminishments. Such efforts to manage the impact of modern technology on the human's individuality and assumed self-mastery are predicated on a productive differentiation of properly human writing subjects from those subjects supposedly mastered by their relation to writing and other technologies. As we are today well aware, the latter, undesirable, transformative aspects of subject-technology relations are frequently attributed to feminine, racialized, and subaltern subjects and, thus, symbolically and materially redistributed. This distinction between proper and improper relations to writing technologies continues to enable the former, privileged instrumental relation to technologies to appear uncompromised when simply unproblematized.

As "Click," through its print remediation, makes apparent, digital scenes of writing and textuality unsettle this understanding of technics and the gendered and racialized distinctions between desirable and undesirable relations to technology subtending it. Under the pretense of acknowledging and equalizing a "masculine," instrumental relation and a "feminine," transformative relation to writing technologies, establishing a "truce" between the "masculine" tendency toward expediting and the "feminine" tendency toward enhancing, "Click" reinstalls an instrumental understanding of technics and its gendered oppositions. Figuring the limits to the masculine subject's narrative mastery as an immersive, feminine textuality, this distinction reasserts and renaturalizes the opposition between an instrumental and an instrumentalized relation to writing technologies. In this regard "Click" offers a familiar, thoroughly unconvincing collaboration that leaves no room to register transformative relations to writing technologies otherwise.

As digital hypertext and other new media writing practices continue to trouble this understanding of technics, the translation of this gendered distinction to new media helps reproduce these familiar relations to writing technologies. By literalizing the relation between these sexual and narrative tendencies, "Click" underscores the inextricability of these textual and sexual economies, what Judith Roof describes as the "heteronarrative, the ideological/structural link between the structure of narrative and the conjoinder of opposites understood as heterosexual that explains and produces binary gender."[79] Even when these relations to narrative are conceived as interchangeable, as relations open to either gender as opposed to grounded in one's biological sex, such moves "unsettle the valence or characteristics of each side of the binary, but not the binary itself, even if they seem to multiply or displace it."[80] As in the story, this underlying framework reproduces the same (formerly) gendered binary and offers the same two relations to writing technologies: a (masculine) position of active mastery through an instrumental use of language and its other, a (feminine) subjectification to, immersion in, or equation with the interface, which is the former's foil. While "Click" responds to and engages with the transformative potential of relations to digital hypertext writing, it reads these relations back into its literary print framework. In doing so, and trying to mitigate the perceived threat of transformation, the story's remediation of digital hypertext reproduces a binary concept of gender, which "work[s] as a synechdochal lynchpin that not only grounds older systems, but that also enables a safe swing into the new."[81] This "safe swing into the new" qualifies the revolutionary claims that are often made in the name of digital textualities. It also underscores the ongoing relays between writing technologies, subjects of writing, and the differential human boundaries they materially and symbolically realize. "Click" remains unwilling and unable to pursue the subtle and not so subtle differences the material affordances of writing technologies introduce. It cannot register the transformative, reciprocal, material force and co-productive influence of writing practices on human subjectivity beyond the hierarchical, gendered oppositional positions of user and tool, active and immersive. It reinforces binary gender through this understanding of technics rather than exploring the different, dynamic ways in which technics enter into embodied experience. Most strikingly, it is unwilling to maintain its initial insights into how human subjects may come into relation with their writing technologies and how such material occasions matter (for better and for worse).

In an interesting parallel to "Click's" narrator/author with fountain pen in hand, the mechanical doll "Susie Scribbles" is "fashioned to write with a pen rather than at a computer."[82] In Sobchack's reading, she "hyperbolizes the mystery not of writing as technical enterprise but as an expression of the human hand," encouraging us "to reframe 'the question concerning technology' to accommodate the intentional and lived body-subject in the act of writing not only the word, but the world and herself."[83] "Susie Scribbles" and the narrator in "Click" intersect in conveying a pervasive cultural questioning of, and anxiety over, human agency, intention, embodiment, and technological materiality amidst digital writing practices. Pen in hand is a synecdoche for a liberal humanist subject whose relations to writing technologies appear well clarified. Notably, both cultural texts simultaneously unsettle the distinction they long for. "Click" both registers and recontains the transformative, qualitative matter of media and its impact on intersubjectivities and, as Susie scribbles with a pen in hand, "inscribing its singular intentionality in acts and marks of *expressive improvisation*," she is, quite ironically, a mechanical doll, not the human girl or mode of being she doubles, which renders the human more than uncanny.[84] Sobchack eloquently describes the relays that compromise any notion of the human hand uncoupled from her technics:

> In sum, objectively material means (*technology*) and the tropology of subjective desire (*poiësis*) are bound in an irreducible intentional relation as a revelatory bringing forth (*technë*) that, in its diverse historical and personal practices, makes matter meaningful and meaning matter.[85]

If technics paradoxically, should I say, intentionally, remain in the hand of the human in these print-inflected scenes of digital writing, human intentionality is simultaneously in the hand of its appropriately digital (i.e., originally meaning "discrete" like the segments of one's fingers) technics. That intentionality, and the gendered and racialized "human" subject of writing it is believed to secure, is always already redescribed by the recurring material practices that subtend its writing as both these texts, in their own ways, illustrate. It is, therefore, worth recognizing the impact of this human/computational admixture on the intentionality of lived bodies. Rather than a new and improved tool, digital writing technologies involve us in recursive, dynamic relations with an extended, multilayered, multiagential system that informs our writing, the differential human selves it enables, and their potential experience, interactions, and relations to larger lifeworlds.

This alternate perspective on technicity is worth pursuing and, I'd stress, is hardly unique to digital writing and the emergent technics these practices are unleashing. Introducing their collection of essays on handheld computer technologies, *Small Tech: The Culture of Digital Tools*, Byron Hawk, David M. Rieder, and Ollie Oviedo situate these handheld mobile devices along an ongoing, dynamic, evolutionary trajectory of mutually transformative relations between humans, language, and technologies. They cite French anthropologist André Leroi-Gourhan's account of how Paleolithic human's technics, cave painting and phonetics in particular, led to a separation of gesture from the human body.[86] As insightfully documented by Bernard Stiegler, Leroi-Gourhan's work retraces a history of human technics in which the parts of the human body itself and their uses—including limbs and physical capacities that technologies are often assumed to model or double—are far from self-apparent or originary. Sharing Leroi-Gourhan's view that "the twentieth-century is producing a return to the techniques of the hand," Hawk and coauthors suggest that

> having been separated from the body through the development of writing, the hand is being (re)integrated into a new context. Rather than being an extension of the human body, the hand becomes a small technology in its own right, with the ability to enter into material combinations with other digital devices and material events to create new possibilities for communication and action.[87]

From this vantage, a return to the hand in digital scenes of writing and the textualities they are unleashing is transformative, once again, in co-relation with these distinct technologies.

Co-productive, multistable, shifting relays between human subjectivities and their technics as they are materially engaged with social and cultural meaning, as I've suggested, open up the human to a variety of distinct modes of communication and interaction, and not others. It is through these relations to distinct writing and communication technologies and the technics they enable that human subjectivities gain differential degrees of legibility and expression and, thus, through a reengagement that these technics serve as tactics to regain aspects of the embodied human currently under erasure or rendered illegible. Such an experimental technics, as explored in the next chapters, might alternately engage the multistability of technics and the modalities of the human they help realize in order to acknowledge and exploit the transformative material potentiality recontained by "Click's" liberal humanist self-author and "Susie Scribbles."

2 / Tracing the Human through Media Difference

The scene of early digital writing also catalyzed comparative media practices that opted to pursue these distinct affordances of new media. Such fiction actively gauges, even celebrates the transformative influence of these writing technologies on boundaries of the human, contrary to liberal humanist print cultures' tendency to wishfully posit such boundaries as stable and secure. These early literary encounters with digital media exploit media difference and sites of interchange between print and digital cultures as a resource for reflecting on how emergent writing technologies, and the technological apparati they draw on, influence subjectivities and social relations in more or less tangible ways. *Patchwork Girl*,[1] Shelley Jackson's digital hypertext remediation of Mary Shelley's literary print classic, *Frankenstein*,[2] devises comparative methods to register the impact of media difference on the realization of gendered and racialized intersubjectivities. These comparative methods, in turn, generate new vantages on the past and present technicity of the human. If read with particular attention to its observation and engagement with formative, ongoing subject-technology relations or technics, this first-generation hypertext fiction contributes in significant ways to broader, ongoing conversations about the technicity of the human and her social systems. It, in turn, suggests how we might engage digital hypertext and digital media through an experimental technics, developing this as a means to comparatively register, perhaps even elaborate on the boundary formation of the human through distinct technics. *Patchwork Girl* exploits digital hypertext to inquire into the processes through which distinctly gendered, sexed, and racialized human boundaries, and the intersubjective relations they co-authorize, are repeatedly rematerialized. It explores the transformative impact of technics on existing modes of human subject formation. *Patchwork Girl*'s continued critical prominence, while references to other hypertext fiction written using the Storyspace authoring program tend to focus on their limitations vis-à-vis more recent digital literatures (with a few notable exceptions), is likely due to continued cultural concerns with the apparent negotiability of the human, which have only intensified since Its first publication.

As I'll illustrate below, *Patchwork Girl* joins an expanding set of efforts to think through the technicity of the human. These efforts are numerous and quite diverse, though they tend to draw upon several of the same influential sources: philosopher Gilbert Simondon's accounts of the emergence of the human through an ongoing process of technically induced "technogenesis;"[3] André Leroi-Gourhan's evolutionary history of the human's coproductive relations to language and technology;[4] Bernard Stiegler's thoroughgoing consolidation of the former theories in his two-volume work on technics and time;[5] Katherine Hayles's history of cybernetics and ongoing analyses of electronic literature and literary cultures of computation;[6] phenomenological philosophy of technology; second-order cybernetics and systems theory; and feminist science studies, including cyberfeminist and more recent "new materialist" engagements with contemporary physical and bioinformatic sciences and technologies by Donna Haraway,[7] Sadie Plant,[8] and Karen Barad,[9] among numerous others.

Work on the technicity of the human often identifies itself as posthumanist due to its defining tendency to call into question the rational mastery of the human (as opposed to the nonhuman animal), his unique status as tool-user, and his supposed autonomy from material embodiment and technological and material lifeworlds. Posthumanist theories question the rational superiority and autonomy that are defining trademarks of the human within liberal humanist discourses. Importantly, posthumanist accounts of the technicity of the human do not theorize the end of, or a wholesale break with, humanism, as the "post" might initially suggest. Instead, they work to develop perspectives on the emergence and transformation of the human and the divergent discourses that have supported and sustained that species understanding across cultures and over time. For this reason, most posthumanist theorists differentiate the *posthuman*—which includes a wider variety of efforts and attempts to literally and theoretically go beyond the human, including those that perpetuate humanist discourses of transcendence, self-invention, or the new—from *posthumanisms*.[10] The latter problematize humanist modes of understanding the human, attempting to provide more responsive accounts of the species-being of the human as it is implicated within complexly material, nonhuman, and technical environments. As Cary Wolfe stresses in *What Is Posthumanism?*, "The decentering of the human by its imbrication in technical, medical, informatic, and economic networks is increasingly impossible to ignore," and, thus, these attempts to think the human-in-relation respond to the necessity of finding "a new mode of thought" to grapple with the status and situation of the human. [11]

Drawing on research in cognitive science, molecular and evolutionary biology, computer science, philosophy, philosophy of technology, sociology, physics, and feminism and gender studies, posthumanist theories of technicity attempt to think the human in dynamic, constitutive interrelation to material, nonhuman, and technical environments and to query the conceptual, practical, and ethical consequences of this departure from humanist discourses of species-being. In spite of key differences I will address below, posthumanist theories typically share an enactive understanding of the processes through which human and nonhuman subjects and environments contingently *co-emerge* and *co-evolve* through the very processes of living and acting in the world.[12] They proceed to explore the material, technical, discursive, and phenomenological processes through which distinct modalities and delimitations of the human come to be, and continually come to be transfigured in time rather than beginning, as humanisms do, with a foundational concept or claim about the identity, being, or substance of the human. As Karen Barad describes this theoretical turn in her work, instead of fixing

> the boundary between "human" and "nonhuman" before the analysis ever gets off the ground, [such theories encourage and require] a genealogical analysis of the discursive emergence of the "human." "Human bodies" and "human subjects" do not preexist as such; nor are they mere end products. "Humans" are neither pure cause nor pure effect, but part of the world in its open-ended becoming.[13]

Posthumanist theories assume that the human animal is embedded in a biological and natural world, participating in an evolutionary process of technogenesis, which involves the human in an originary, ongoing technicity. In this, they extend Jacques Derrida's insistence on the supplementarity of the human. They attempt to register biological, material, technical, psychic, and discursive dimensions to his co-evolution, directly countering liberal humanism's Cartesian belief that consciousness guarantees the autonomy and integrity of the human. Instead, they pursue questions raised by recent cognitive science that suggest consciousness is only quite mistakenly understood as the whole show.

Situating *Patchwork Girl*'s comparative, digital hypertextual exploration of technics alongside other prominent posthumanist efforts to think through the technicity of the human accentuates the important new lines of inquiry they open into the processes through which highly contingent modes of subjectivity develop out of ongoing interactions with worlds material, technical, and discursive. It foregrounds, in particular, their relevance to thinking through the emergence of those defining features of human subjectivities: sexual difference, gender, and sexuality. Gender, its relation to sexual difference, and the relation of both to sexuality are "a precondition for the production and maintenance of legible humanity," Judith Butler reminds us, making these dimensions of the human a core concern in assessing contemporary renegotiations of the human.[14] For this reason, considering the impact of technics on such primary parameters of human boundary formation provides one good register of what can be gained and lost as a result of how we conceive human/nonhuman subject formation in conversation with contemporary technics. These questions surrounding sexual difference, gender, and sexualities, which were central to early cyberfeminists and continue to preoccupy more recent inquiries into the differential emergence of human subjectivities, are one specific, though also special, case of this broader theoretical line of inquiry into the boundaries and boundary formation of the human.

Crucially, reflecting on how technics enter into gendered, sexed, and racialized human subject formation and intersubjectivities brings to the fore several striking differences between prominent posthumanist theories and suggests what we might learn from these discrepancies. At their core, theories of human technicity pivot upon the vexing problem of "determining where the biological, the psychic, the discursive, the social begin and end" and describing their interrelations.[15] This is a dilemma Butler describes, suggesting that "sexual difference is the site where a question concerning the relation of the biological to the cultural is posed and reposed, where it must and can be posed, but where it cannot, strictly speaking, be answered."[16] While posthumanist theories join in rethinking the human's material embodiment and transformative relation to complex social, material, and technical environments, they differ quite dramatically in how they understand materialities (biological, technological, and physical) to enter into social systems and human cognition and in how they conceive of multiple agencies within such relations.

The status, role, and interrelations between subjectivities, technics, embodiment, and material lifeworld is of particular concern in understanding these processes. Arguing that it matters not just if, but how materialities reenter accounts of the human, this chapter juxtaposes influential strains of posthumanist theory, such as the social systems theory Niklas Luhmann[17] develops out of second-order cybernetics, to *Patchwork Girl*'s inquiries into the technics of gendered, sexed, and racialized human subject formation, and both to more recent, new materialist theories similarly engaged in rethinking the status and character of materialities in light of the new physical, biological, and informatic sciences impacting human subject and social formation.[18]

The increasing prominence and diversity of such posthumanist efforts to think through the contributions material and technical processes make to the human is literally instructive. It reveals the need to juxtapose and recombine these approaches to develop the hybrid theoretical and conceptual methods necessary to work through the kinds of dynamic, technically realized material processes that resolutely confound us today. In the introduction to their recent collection, *Emergence and Embodiment: New Essays on Second-Order Systems Theory*, Bruce Clarke and Mark B. N. Hansen stress the urgency of these questions about the boundary formation of the human in light of "the technoscientific processes that are everywhere transforming the material world in which we live today."[19] They claim the only approach that "can rescue agency—albeit agency of a far more complex variety than that of traditional humanism—from being overrun" is their account of the "operational closure" of social systems and psychic systems from their material environments, which follows from influential strains of second-order cybernetics and Niklas Luhmann's social systems theory.[20] They maintain that social systems are wholly self-referential and realize themselves in meaning, unable to perceive the ontological world that sustains their operations as they blindly attribute meaning to their self-described environments. Interestingly and tellingly, the essays included in the collection diverge in significant ways as they elaborate upon second-order cybernetics and Luhmann's social systems theory's presumption of "operational closure," suggesting some recognition of the need to complicate this and other key concepts from these theories in light of what we now understand about digital technics. Sharing their sense of urgency in thinking through these questions about human boundary-formation, this chapter recommends that working through the complex questions about system formation currently being raised on several fronts and also critically comparing and combining those queries with other posthumanist theories of the human's technicity is a more pressing and productive task than maintaining the purity or purchase of a single theoretical concept or framework, especially in light of what Hansen acknowledges in his contribution to the collection as the *multiple sites and scales* at which human boundary formation is currently under way.[21]

Second-order cybernetics and social systems theory, which emerge in close conversation with the informatic sciences at the core of contemporary technics, provide a valuable set of approaches to questions now also being broached from quite different directions by new materialist and other strains of posthumanist theory. Focusing in on questions of gendered, racialized, and sexed human subject formation and intersubjectivities, I will draw on *Patchwork Girl* to juxtapose and selectively recombine these efforts to think through the boundary formation of the human to reconsider how we might register the materialities that enter into such processes. While social systems theory does not adequately think through sexual difference, gender, or sexualities, its efforts to think through the question of where and how material, biological, cultural, and technical practices join together bear directly upon how we might understand sexual difference and its linkages to the emergence and consolidation of gender and sexuality. *Patchwork Girl* helps to combine this systems thinking with the investments and insight of feminism and subaltern studies into these processes of human boundary formation, among others. Together, they draw upon a thick history of inquiries into the technicity of the human and her gendered and racialized instrumentalization and raise key questions about the negotiability of the human. In light of women's historical alignment with the material, with the natural, the organic, the embodied, and the impact of these discourses on nonhuman animals and material environments, it is especially necessary to query how materialities are reconceived and how they reenter discourses of the human.

New materialist theory considers how shifting technics prompt and trouble our very ability to distinguish between matter and meaning, between ontology and epistemology, modes of being and knowing. It intends to register interrelations among the material, biological, psychic, and discursive, however contingent these interrelations, and our conceptions of them, may be. These theories think through the influence of different social, material, and medial environments on these relations and the lived experiences they enable or foreclose. They explore shifting technics as a means to register, reflect on, and enter into human boundary formation with a difference. Feminist philosopher Claire Colebrook has recently underscored the limitations to what she describes as vitalist theories emerging from the life sciences, cognitive sciences, new media theory, and philosophy.[22] Juxtaposing these competing posthumanist theories of the human's technicity, I will suggest the need to find alternatives to both vitalism's unproblematized organicity and to social system theory's constructivist bracketing of the agency and meaning of the material world as an operationally closed constitutive "outside" to the human and to social systems.

As I will illustrate, if attention is paid to its engagements with technicity, digital fiction such as *Patchwork Girl* suggests a compelling way to experimentally query the impact of new media technics on the boundary formation of the human. *Patchwork Girl*, in addition to its clear status as a groundbreaking work of digital hypertext storytelling, continues Mary Shelley's exploration of the "human debt to technical systems," its concern with how "life is calibrated according to the technical trajectories and capacities of particular machines," as Catherine Waldby describes Shelley's text's preoccupations in "The Instruments of Life: Frankenstein and Cyberculture."[23] In this regard, Jackson's influential digital hypertext rewriting of Mary Shelley's text is a defining text of modern technics, as is its predecessor. As *Patchwork Girl* pursues these feminist inquiries into modern technics, it enlists digital hypertext to explore shifting possibilities for enacting gendered, sexed, racialized, and species-specific bodily boundaries, and for understanding how they emerge through quite specific cultural, historical, technical, and material practices, or technics, that conjoin mind and body, human and nonhuman, discourse and matter, authors, texts, and readers in distinct ways. *Patchwork Girl* revisits Mary Shelley's literary-print inquiries into the production of gendered, sexed, and racialized human subjectivities, and their monstrous otherness and others, from the multimodal, multimedia vantage of digital hypertext and other "bodily" technologies such as sewing, quilting, surgery, and speech. Through this comparative analysis of human technics, *Patchwork Girl* reconceives the co-productive, monstrous subjectivities we enact in conversation, collusion, and conflict with a range of physical bodies. It also raises key questions about how to register what it views as the gloriously monstrous agency of the material world. It explores how processes of materialization enabled by digital technics, in particular, impact human subject formation, intersubjectivities, and material lifeworlds, concerns that increasingly vex theorists today.

Systems Theory's Strange Relations

These posthumanist engagements with technicity are, to a significant degree, the strange offspring of post–World War II cybernetics, information, and systems theory. The latter sciences, as mentioned in the book's introduction, were initially bent on extending the human's instrumental control over his environment. Yet from its very inception, cybernetics called into question the ontological distinctness of the human through this effective coupling of human, animal, and technological though communication networks and mechanical relays and, thus, unwittingly opened onto a serious, sustained crisis in species-understanding and prevailing humanist discourses. This is just the first in what might best be described as an ongoing series of bifurcations, digressions, and reencounters within cybernetics, information, and systems sciences as they develop into fields of informatics, bioinformatics, molecular genetics, and cognitive science (to name the most prominent) and circulate well beyond these fields into and through contemporary digital cultures. Thus, although cybernetics might seem remote today, its legacies are the very fields that undergird and inform contemporary digital cultures in the United States even if we most often confront their knowledges and practices as a kind of unseen, ubiquitous "technological unconscious"[24] that structures the coded spaces, objects, and infrastructures in our daily life (as opposed to encountering these knowledges and practices in a more explicit or conscious way). Because these fields and the knowledges and practices they generate continue to evolve in response to complex social, cultural, technological, and material relations, it is worthwhile to identify a broader *systems thinking* in order to account for a range of contemporary sciences, technological practices, social relations, and expressive forms that reconceive themselves as, or in terms of, dynamic systems. This is a systems thinking directly or indirectly influenced by these sciences, yet, as carried out in much new materialist theory, it is no longer confined to systems theory or second-order cybernetics per se in that it has spread from this specific scientific, cultural, social, and technological configuration to others and continues to be engaged and recombined in ways worth registering.

Systems thinking is, in many respects, indebted to second-order cybernetics' influential reorientation of postwar cybernetics and information theory in the 1970s, which opened a line of inquiry into the epistemological questions raised by circular causality in systems that function recursively through feedback loops. Second-order cybernetics is often described as the "cybernetics of cybernetics," because it turned to consider how it is we can understand or observe the kinds of circular processes and nonlinear feedback loops that cybernetics worked to extend and intensify through its networks of communication between humans, machines, animals, and their physical environments. In his foundational *Observing Systems*, Heinz von Foerster consolidated second-order cybernetics, arguing that it is only through a second-order observation of circular, recursive, self-referential systems that an external observer can selectively attribute linear, unidirectional causal relations and agency to what is, in fact, a more complex, circular system dynamic.[25] Cybernetic systems such as thermostats or missile guidance systems, which use their own outputs as inputs to guide and adjust their subsequent operations, make the paradoxes resulting from circular causality especially apparent. In such systems, "A and B are mutually cause and effect of each other," as Steve Heims describes the kinds of strange loops and complex relations that came to preoccupy scientists and philosophers at the post–World War II Macy Conferences and well after those discussions.[26] As he notes, an action as basic as reaching for a glass of water includes such relays: I extend my arm to pick up a glass and receive visual and proprioceptive signals that serve as feedback signaling how close my hand is to the glass, which then guides subsequent action, allowing me to gently pick up the glass as a result of these recursive feedback loops.[27] I stretch my arm to pick up the glass, and, in turn, the position of the glass guides my arm's movements. In such relations, "not only does A affect B but through B acts back on itself," which means that "A cannot do things to B without being itself affected."[28] Second-order cybernetics addressed the undecidability of causal relations in such system relations, arguing that the attribution of a causal relation is, in fact, a secondary attribution or description of the system that is always relative to the position of the observer describing that system. As von Foerster claimed, "A description (of the universe) implies one who describes (observes) it."[29]

German sociologist Niklas Luhmann draws upon second-order cybernetics and initiates another significant bifurcation in its systems thinking with his elaborate extension of their accounts of self-referential systems to reconceive *social systems, in particular*.[30] It is in this sense, as well as others I'll suggest below, that *social systems theory* is all about strange relations. Luhmann adapted key concepts from influential second order-cyberneticists—Chilean biologist Humberto Maturana and his philosopher collaborator Francisco Varela—to develop his extensive systems-theoretical approach to social systems. Continuing second-order cyberneticists' interest in epistemology, Luhmann's theory explores how social systems emerge and reproduce themselves self-referentially in meaning and connect their operations with psychic systems via communication. In his account, social systems are neither the outgrowth of human consciousness, nor the simple reflection of an existing ontological world. Instead, they emerge through a defining relation of *nonidentity* with their environment and with the other subsystems and the individual psychic systems that co-emerge with, but do not comprise, them. In Luhmann's dynamic, nonfoundational account, social systems produce themselves through an ongoing process of making distinctions, continual acts of selectively differentiating the system from a more complex environment. Social systems are, thus, understood as observing or meaning-processing systems and, crucially, ones that remain blind to their own operations and to the constitutive distinction that allows them to differentiate their own processes from a more complex environment.

Social systems' *autopoiesis*, or self-making through their processing of meaning, relies upon the circularity and self-reference of their operations, which Luhmann describes as their "operational closure" from their environments.[31] Social systems' self-referential closure might mistakenly be read as an extension of first-order cybernetic sciences' military-industrial dreams of control to social systems, that is, the latter's use of systems thinking to secure and direct efficient causal relations between components in a system, as in war efforts to develop guided antiaircraft missiles by calculating the trajectory between a shooter, his aircraft, and target; or, in organizational systems theory's post-Fordist strategies to maximize efficiency. Instead, the relations of nonidentity that define Luhmann's systems theory are indebted to second-order cybernetics' confrontation with the strange loops of circular causality in such systems, which cast causal relations, control, predictability, and aspirations of systematic totalization into questionable doubt.

Following on second-order cybernetics' inquiries into the undecidability of causal relations in such system relations and, thus, pursuing their view of the contingency of any description of such systems, Luhmann's work plays out this central concern with the contingency of knowledge, the fact that "everything said is said by someone," as second-order systems theorists Maturana and Varela put it.[32] Luhmann develops on this to propose that social systems emerge through a set of mutually constitutive, contingent relations with an environment, arguing that the system uses its own self-referential distinction from its environment to selectively reproduce itself over time. Luhmann's insistence on the self-referential, circular dynamics of social systems is the basis for his pointed rejection of humanism's instrumental subject-object dualisms and the representational, unicausal logics they impose. Conceiving the social in a linear, causal relation to its material environment, humanism has tended to render the social as a mirror or representation of that material reality, or the inverse, to see that material reality as largely a refraction of the social's discourse. Luhmann, instead, redescribes the social in a more complex, reciprocal, circular relation to its environments. Further, rather than suggesting this circularity to social systems secures human meaning and ensures some sort of systematic control, in Luhmann's work "'system' means nonlinear recursion, and that is equal to unpredictability," not systemic control, just one example of how his theory entails a deconstruction of its defining term, as Dirk Baecker insightfully stresses in his essay "Why Systems?"[33]

Reimagining the relations between the social system and its environment as relations of nonidentity, Luhmann rejects the representational view that social systems reflect, correspond to, or produce their environments. Instead, social systems and the psychic and other systems in their environment all emerge as a result of their self-enclosure as autopoietic, self-making systems. In this regard, Luhmann's theory of social systems is comparable to other constructivist theories. But it differs in crucial respects as a result of its distinction between systems at the level of their self-descriptions or observations and at the level of their operations. In Luhmann's social systems theory, the term *observation* designates a system's making of distinctions, its self-description, whereas *operation* designates the level of a system's actual processing, which remains inaccessible so long as it forms the basis of that particular system's observations. This differentiation of these systems' observations from their operations has the potential to account for both the incommensurability and interdependence of these systems and their environments, at once.

Describing social and psychic systems at both the level of their self-referential observation, and the level of their operations, Luhmann's systems theory provides a way of theorizing the interrelations and interactions between distinct kinds of biological, social, and psychic systems while simultaneously preserving their significantly different modes of operation (using biochemicals, meaning, or consciousness). It refuses a unidirectional, causal relation between social systems or psychic systems and their environments, estranging our usual assumptions about these relations, if not about relation per se. Systems are "perturbed" or "triggered" by their environment, but these relations are defined in terms of an "*indeterminate* causality," as "causes that do not effect effects," in Baecker's appropriately paradoxical phrasing.[34] In turn, systems' self-referential operations are defined as an effect that is "the cause of its own cause," primarily circular, in other words.[35]

These strange loops in Luhmann's systems theory complicate both essential-ist and constructivist theories of subject and social formation. The latter are polarized over the question of psychic systems' and social systems' openness or closure to their material environments, yet also paralyzed by a shared, representationalist assumption of a causal, unidirectional relation of corre-spondence between subjectivity or a social system and the material world it either expresses or constructs.

Claiming that "sociocultural evolution does not proceed from matter to mind, from energy to information; it leads, rather, to combinations of corporeality and functionally specific communication that are increasingly demanding and increasingly dependent on specific aspects,"[36] social systems theory's rethinking of the interrelations between a range of systems and en-vironments opens up crucial lines of inquiry into these combinations, the various ways in which social and cognitive systems enlist and engage the complexity of the "highly complex agglomeration of systems" known as "the body" and vice versa.[37] Unfortunately, these are lines of inquiry systems theory does not fully pursue.

In Luhmann's framework, the relations among psychic systems, nervous systems, and social systems—like the relations between social systems and their environments—are all cast as relations of difference, not identity. As operationally closed, autopoietic systems, they establish themselves via a founding distinction or differentiation of the system from an environment. This means, for instance, that psychic systems are not contained within so-cial systems but constitute part of the latter's environment, and nervous sys-tems are, similarly, part of psychic systems' environment. As nonsensical as this may sound, it is central to the theory's insistence on the incommensura-bility of each system's operations. As self-producing systems, social systems produce themselves by processing communication, psychic systems produce themselves by processing consciousness (or the perception of perception), and nervous systems produce themselves by processing biochemicals. Due to their distinct, system-specific modes of operation, none of these systems express or in any way reflect the reality of an external, material world, as foundationalist accounts of subjectivity and the social would insist.

Social systems and psychic systems can observe and attribute meaning to the systems in their environment or to their own operations, yet they remain unable to observe or in any way overcome the differences in their respective modes of operation, the enabling differences that allow them to produce themselves as distinct systems. According to Luhmann, "the external world is as it is" in spite of social and psychic systems' ongoing differentiation of the world in the form of meaningful distinctions.[38] In this theoretical move, he usefully counters constructivism's tendency to reduce everything to discourse or meaning and also resists a liberal humanist tendency to make meaning the exclusive province of human agents. Luhmann's systems theory differentiates social and psychic systems' meaningful observations from both their own and from other systems' operations, operations that escape the meaningful observations of these systems.

Through the concept of "structural coupling," taken from second-order cyberneticists Maturana and Varela, Luhmann attempts to explain how social systems, psychic systems, and nervous systems, despite their distinct modes of operation (processing communication, processing consciousness, and processing biochemicals), are able to both connect their distinct, systemic operations and use this closure to create openness, to at once separate and connect the system and environment. Maturana and Varela, working to describe what characterizes living organisms—from the level of a cell, to a multicellular organism, to a human member of a linguistic community, develop the concept of "structural coupling" to convey the simultaneous closure and openness of the relation of any organism to its environments. They use the concept to describe "a history of recurrent interactions leading to the structural congruence between two (or more) systems."[39] Luhmann extends this concept, characterizing the boundaries between structurally coupled systems as a "cut" or "break" that "binds" systems due to their dual capacity to differentiate and, thereby, to connect distinct systems. As structurally coupled systems, psychic and nervous systems are understood, on the one hand, to "collaborate"; yet on the other hand, the boundary between these systems mediates or conditions their contact so that "processes which cross boundaries (e.g., the exchange of energy or information) have different conditions for their continuance . . . after they cross boundaries."[40] This means that nervous systems may trigger or perturb psychic systems, but it is the psychic system that determines how the unbound material, energy, or possibilities are to be used. In Luhmann's words, "What the human body is for itself we do not know."[41]

Insisting that social and psychic systems blindly attribute meaning to their environments and the other systems within them from a closed, self-referential, systemic inside, Luhmann here convincingly describes such strange relations of nonidentity, but also appears to undercut his own argument that the self-referential closure of social systems enables their connectivity, a relation of productive difference or reciprocity, to the systems in their environments. Self-referential, autopoietic closure appears to trump environmental openness in such passages. Arguing that social systems are self-constituting and therefore realize themselves in meaning, rather than in living systems, as biologist Maturana would counter, Luhmann installs an absolute divide between meaning-processing systems such as social and psychic systems, which are composed of communication, and the physical and organic systems, the "'substructure' . . . of energy, material, or information" that the latter must presuppose but cannot access in any form other than in meaning.[42] The problem with this move is that not knowing what the nervous system is for itself does not override the necessity of a contingent, but nonarbitrary, relation between nervous and psychic systems.[43]

Quite problematically, this distinction between nervous and psychic systems reasserts the latter's autonomy as meaning-processing systems. The inaccessibility of organic and neurophysiological operations (except in the form of blind attributions from within the autopoietic closure of social and psychic systems) results in a disregard for the integral role systems that process energy or chemicals play as "triggers," "perturbation," and "disturbances" prompting meaning processing.[44] As the changing "infrastructure in reality"[45] that social systems presuppose, "physical, chemical, thermal, organic . . . conditions of possibility"[46] are persistently invoked and then elided because Luhmann tends to, in Hans Ulrich Gumbrecht's view, "implicitly or explicitly anathematize as 'ontological' whatever does not appear unambiguously constructivist."[47]

His claim that meaning is not "vibrating in tune"[48] with that substructure regularly slides into a more familiar, less convincing, constructivist view, which begins by asserting a lack of correspondence among social systems, psychic systems, nervous systems, and their environments and ends by bracketing the environments of meaning-processing systems altogether. In addition to rendering the distinction between meaning-processing systems and physical or organic systems absolute and absolutely unthinkable and maintaining the purity of their distinct systemic operations, this move reinforces a long-standing privileging of meaning and disregard for the agency of the material world. Although Luhmann does usefully uncouple meaning from (human) consciousness, material processes have no significant relation to social systems and psychic systems' meaning. As a result, systems theory's attempts to conceptually secure the openness and radical contingency and, perhaps even, the radical alterity of material complexity, are predicated on a simultaneous foreclosure of that complexity from any force (i.e., beyond a minor "trigger," "perturbation," or "vibration").

This conceptual blockage has led critics such as Gunther Teubner to argue that "relation, according to Luhmann, is a nonconcept."[49] In Teubner's view, "Luhmann tries to minimize, if not to eliminate, the interaction, the translation, the interrelation" between systems and their environments, and, as a result, "Luhmann's systems theory cannot deal with the environmental relation 'as such,' but only asymmetrically, either from the internal perspective . . . or the external perspective of an outside observer."[50] While his critique doesn't fully acknowledge Luhmann's rationale for insisting on the asymmetry of such "relations of nonrelation," it does put its finger on this shortcoming of social systems theory and prompts the crucial question of how to understand the strange relations of nonidentity that traverse perceived phenomenal domains without resorting to an assumption of either an equivalence and symmetry, or of an unbridgeable, unthinkable gap. In a conversation with Luhmann at the Institute for Advanced Study at Indiana University in Bloomington in September 1994, Katherine Hayles challenged him on this very issue, and described her interest "in what happens at the dividing line, where one side meets the other side," an interaction that "has two, not one, components," an interest that she has pursued in more recent work through her concept of "intermediation," which I'll address below.[51]

Where Luhmann's deployment of the concept of structural coupling falls short, it identifies the need to theorize the kinds of mutually transformative, enactive relations that traverse phenomenal domains and combine material and discursive components in complex ways. Social systems theory's nonrepresentational understanding of social and cognitive systems, its insistence on their fundamental nonidentity with their environment, provides a useful means of thinking the complexity and contingency of cognitive and social systems and the increasingly complex ways that emergent technics reelaborate or calibrate these systems' relations to their environments. Its deconstruction of the opposition between closed and open systems, by recommending that self-referential closure at one level can facilitate systems' ability to establish selective relations with their irreducibly complex environments and enable their simultaneous openness at other levels, often described as "the principle of openness from closure," identifies a way beyond the current oppositions we use to describe social systems and their interrelations to material and technological lifeworlds. It is social systems theory's aversion to addressing the ontological in any more rigorous way and its absolute injunction against any kind of informational flow across system/environment boundaries that significantly limits its ability to account for the dynamic relations the technicity of the human unfolds. To return to the line of inquiry social systems theory opens onto, if "sociocultural evolution does not proceed" either "from matter to mind" or from mind to matter, but "leads, rather to combinations of corporeality and functionally specific communication,"[52] how exactly do material and discursive, ontological and epistemological bodies and meaning join together, guided by distinct technics, to continually realize recognizably and unrecognizably sexed, gendered, and racialized human subjectivities and to reorient them toward various lifeworlds?

Shelley Jackson's digital hypertext rewriting of Mary Shelley's *Frankenstein*, *Patchwork Girl*, opens up another window on modern technics that leads toward a significantly different understanding of these strange, enactive relations of nonidentity through which material and discursive bodies join forces with a range of subjectivities and social practices. It registers the monstrous agency of physical bodies, of the material world, and of other "media." These are material forces that humanism either disables, disavows, or abjects, that constructivist theories prefer to bracket, and that digital writing technologies seem to bring to the fore with their emergent technics. The work's perspective on enactive relations and, equally, its technique for registering them—its comparative approach to technics, juxtaposing and moving across enactive relations encouraged in print and in emerging digital hypertext writing—is quite valuable to new materialist engagements with technics and to thinking through the comparative media practices introduced in early digital hypertext fiction. These are practices whose influence has since traveled well beyond digital hypertext fiction, yet whose full relevance to human technics remain unregistered.

Modalities of Relation

An irreverent rewriting of Mary Shelley's *Frankenstein* that features the female monster destroyed by Victor Frankenstein as its protagonist, Shelley Jackson's *Patchwork Girl* experiments with digital hypertext to creatively extend Mary Shelley's literary print classic to this digital context. Using Storyspace, the early digital hypertext authoring program designed by Mark Bernstein, Jay Bolter, and Michael Joyce, to create this stand-alone digital hypertext, *Patchwork Girl* reassembles the female monster (last seen in pieces at the bottom of a lake in Mary Shelley's novel) in five different sections. Each section is composed of *lexia*, boxes of text connected by multiple links. As the patchwork girl explains, "My birth takes place more than once. In the plea of a bygone monster; from a muddy hole by corpse light; under the needle; and under the pen; or it took place not at all."[53] The five sections of the work—"story," "graveyard," "crazy quilt," "journal," and "body of text"—correspond to these separate births. Each section assembles the patchwork girl in relation to a particular technological apparatus—print narrative, reconstructive surgery, quilting, handwriting, and digital hypertext respectively—foregrounding the organization, sensory modalities, and interactions made available (or foreclosed as non-sense) through these different media. The character of the patchwork girl emerges in the text through multiple, enactive relations to these media, through the work's juxtaposition and recombination of these distinct technics. The section titled "story," for example, draws on excerpts from Shelley's *Frankenstein*, reconstructing a narrative of the patchwork girl that begins with Dr. Frankenstein's creation of a female monster and continues to the present day. Its links connect sequential text boxes in chronological order, for the most part, moving forward in time like a print narrative, as the section title suggests; "crazy quilt," which privileges the technology of sewing, stitches the patchwork girl together out of quotations from the children's story *The Patchwork Girl of Oz* by L. Frank Baum, from Shelley's text, and from theorists such as Hélène Cixous, Gilles Deleuze, and Félix Guattari.[54] These textual snippets are combined in colored text boxes that take the form of a quilt with links that move, as if stitching, down and across the columns of boxes that function as patches in this "fabric of relations."[55]

The five sections of *Patchwork Girl* foreground the generative influence of different "writing" technologies on subjectivities, highlighting their capacity to provide and secure organizational schemata, spatiotemporal frames, and material affordances that inform the material and discursive, literal and symbolic formation of variously human and nonhuman bodies.[56] Reflecting on these strange, enactive relations of nonidentity between subjectivities and distinct media, the work underscores the variability of their selective modalities and, in combination, the variability of subjectivities as highly specialized, mutually transformative engagements with physical bodies. The patchwork girl is literally an assemblage; her multiple and multiplicit subjectivities, as illustrated in each section, are inextricable from the technics that motivate and materialize specific kinds of legibility, illegibility, intersubjectivity, and desire.

Patchwork Girl inquires into the human's co-production through such technics, as does social systems theory. In this context, its understanding of the relations between cognitive and biological bodies, subjectivities and technological apparati, and meaning and matter deserve close scrutiny. Both approaches to the human's technicity imagine highly contingent structural

Fig. 1. "her" (frontispiece to title page) from *Patchwork Girl by Mary/Shelley and Herself*. Courtesy of Eastgate Systems.

couplings, or enactive relations of nonidentity across these phenomenal domains. Yet *Patchwork Girl* inquires into these processes of materialization and, in doing so, revalues their force. It brings the monstrosity of bodies and physical matter into full play, searching for means to register their agency without, in this very act, symbolically diminishing or taking it away by circumscribing it in meaning. A text box titled "all written," reads, "You could say that all bodies are written bodies, all lives pieces of writing." On a first reading, this appears to conceive of technics as a mode of social inscription, of "writing" on (passive) bodies, in keeping with a constructivist frame.[57] Yet "all written" is linked to a text box, "bodies," which questions this apparent isomorphism between physical and textual bodies, both of which have been conceived in relation to print writing technologies as neutral, passive sites for the inscription of meaning. "bodies" suggests "the body could be said to be the writing of the soul. Its expression, but also and inevitably its misstatement, precisely because it is an expression, and must make use of material signs in all their imperfection, allowing them to garble the pure idea and go home on days off to their own unknowable lives in the kitchen of things. This is if you adhere to the traditional separation of body and soul, form and content."[58] Juxtaposed to its previous formulation, which posits the body as a neutral medium for subjects' self-expression and/or the by-product of social inscriptions, this lexia casts into question the idea that the material body is a neutral medium or passive instrument safe in the hands of symbolic expression. Acknowledging the "imperfection" and "unknowable lives" of the body and other "material signs," which always "garble the pure idea," this passage endows material complexity with an agency that contravenes Cartesian dualisms of body/soul, form/content, medium/meaning.

Aligning physical bodies, textual bodies, and other media with Dr. Frankenstein's creatures, *Patchwork Girl* underscores their wonderful monstrosity, their capacity to compromise and elude instrumental attempts to subjugate them to the ends of cognition or meaning, that is, to the ends of their presumed "creator." These bodies' monstrosity resides in their refusal to be passive, secondary, transparent, or neutral, their refusal to respect the distinction between the content of a story and the medium of expression, for instance, or to conform to the role of mere media. In refiguring the enactive relations of nonidentity that join meaning and medium, cognition to physical bodies, and subjectivities to technological apparati, *Patchwork Girl* refuses to bracket the meaning of discourse from these material forces while it also inquires into distinct modes of engaging and registering those matters. It foregrounds the technics and technical apparati that allow specific kinds of relations to and very selective engagements with material bodies. The work, thus, walks through the door Luhmann leaves open for a nonrepresentational relation to the ontological, yet social systems theory refuses to walk through.

If read in terms of recent new materialist systems thinking, such as Karen Barad's "relational ontology" based on Niels Bohr's quantum physics-philosophy, *Patchwork Girl*'s inquiries into shifting technics can be understood as inquiries into the "intra-actions," through which distinct agencies become perceivable and meaningful under specific technological and discursive conditions.[59] *Patchwork Girl* is similarly concerned to explore the technics or material practices that enact "agential cuts" between subject and object. In Barad's account, it is through that enactive relation or "intra-action" that shifting human and nonhuman boundaries are delineated and that distinct subjects and objects are defined, in contradistinction to a typical conception of interaction occurring between two wholly independent, preexisting entities. Barad develops a concept of "intra-activity," as opposed to interactivity, to describe the ongoing horizon of processes through which "phenomena," in her Bohrian terminology, mutually enact entities that then come to be perceived as distinct subject and objects, or separate phenomenal domains, or to have stable bodily boundaries. These distinctions are realized within the frame of a specific technological, discursive, and material "apparatus" or technics that makes certain properties "determinate" and others indeterminate.[60] Barad bases her "relational ontology," and exploration of the "*differential patterns of mattering*" that are the offspring of such enactive relations, on Niels Bohr's discovery that, depending on the experimental and discursive apparatus, light can be registered as either waves or particles; an indeterminacy at the ontological or operational, rather than only at the epistemological, observational level, in her reading.[61] With this "relational ontology" in mind, she insists that "to write meaning and matter into separate categories, to analyze them relative to separate disciplinary technologies, and to divide complex phenomena into one balkanized enclave or the other is to elide certain aspects by design. On the other hand, considering them together does not mean forcing them together, collapsing important differences between them, or treating them in the same way."[62]

Patchwork Girl's inquiries into the enactive relations of nonidentity that combine matter and meaning in distinct ways balances the interdependence *and* incommensurability that seem to characterize such relations, a balance Barad gestures toward in the passage above. The text reconceives the subject-object distinctions used to differentiate author and text, text and reader, subjects and their technological prostheses, cognition and the nervous system, meaning and matter, explicitly countering the tendency to construe and conflate all of these as oppositional relations of user and tool. Explicitly refusing the distinction between object and subject, "the traditional separation of body and soul, form and content" that "bodies" references, the text box "bodies too" (connected with a link to "bodies") states that "we are inevitably annexed to other bodies: human bodies and bodies of knowledge. We are coupled to constructions of meaning; we are legible, partially; we are cooperative with meanings, but irreducible to any one. The form is not absolutely malleable to the intentions of the author; what may be thought is contingent on the means of expression."[63]

In this passage and elsewhere, *Patchwork Girl* differentiates between material bodies and bodies of knowledge—between biological and physical forces entering into human subjectivities and the socially embedded technics that, through processes of materialization, make the former bodies "partially" meaningful. At the same time, it insists on their co-implication. In this way, *Patchwork Girl* redescribes the relations between cognition and the nervous system, social systems and the organic systems in their environments, subjectivities and various technological apparati as enactive relations of productive difference. Reconceptualizing the relations of nonidentity through which various "subjects" and "objects" emerge as relations that— like a hypertext link, a stitch in sewing, or a scar—both "mark a cut and commemorate a joining,"[64] *Patchwork Girl* provides a competing account of the simultaneous openness and closure of enactive relations that join cognition and the nervous system, meaning and medium, subjectivities and technological apparati in distinct modalities of relation. In contrast to Luhmann's account of structural coupling, *Patchwork Girl*'s theorization of these enactive relations of productive difference respects the noncorrespondence or nonidentity of these co-productive forces while also interrogating their interdependencies; interdependencies that, in the work's view, compromise any attempt to privilege or absolutely differentiate cognition or discursive meaning.

Comparing these enactive relations to the stitches that riddle the patchwork girl's body and the hypertext links that traverse the work, *Patchwork Girl* underscores the selectivity involved in specific technics of human and nonhuman boundary formation, which always entail a cutting away or reduction of material complexity. Simultaneously, it insists that these stitches and links, like psychic systems' and social systems' meaningful attributions, are informed by the bodies and mediums that actualize meaning, that they "commemorate a joining."[65] In this way, *Patchwork Girl* refuses to give cognition or the bodies of knowledge circulating within social systems sole credit for the production of meaning. The text box "it thinks" suggests, "There is a kind of thinking without thinkers. Matter thinks. Language thinks. When we have business with language we are possessed by its dreams and demons, we grow intimate with monsters. We become hybrids, chimeras, centaurs ourselves: steaming flanks and solid redoubtable hoofs galloping under a vaporous machinery."[66] Matter is not secondary to cognition and meaning; it is not simply a medium or tool for the latter because "it thinks." Consequently, material bodies compromise the apparent integrity and purity of the subjects they "possess," transform, and hybridize through such enactive relations, necessarily enlisting subjectivities to ulterior ends. From *Patchwork Girl*'s purview, enactive relations between cognition and the nervous system can neither determine nor disregard the reciprocity that both comprises and differentiates their operations; a reciprocity that generates distinct, dynamic, hybrid, co-productive modalities of relation.

Insisting, in this regard, that matter and meaning are co-implicated in such relations, *Patchwork Girl* does not go quite so far as Barad does in its take on their degree of entanglement.[67] For Barad, phenomena are contingent patterns of mattering that emerge through specific apparatuses that materially configure the world, whereas *Patchwork Girl* more often presumes the operational incommensurability of distinct material and discursive bodies even as it registers their enactive, reciprocal interdependence. Nonetheless, in spite of this key theoretical difference, both *Patchwork Girl* and Barad's work, similarly to other recent systems thinking in new materialist theory, shifts critical inquiry to the *"material (re)configurings of the world through which boundaries, properties, and meanings are differentially enacted,"* and encourages us to register the material consequence of distinct material "intra-actions."[68]

Technics of Gendered Subject Formation

Patchwork Girl's engagement with digital hypertext writing to inquire into the technicity of the human is catalyzed, like other feminist media practices, by its awareness that women and the feminine have historically been aligned with the material world, with media, and with the repetitive, mechanical, inhuman and, thus, monstrous, threatening force of technicity. Juxtaposing digital writing with gendered, feminine practices of sewing and weaving *Patchwork Girl* accentuates key similarities between these "writing practices," while obliquely referencing the Jacquard loom and Ada Lovelace's programming of its weaving patterns using punch cards, an influential nineteenth-century precursor to binary code and its incorporation into digital computational processes. Yet rather than simply claiming digital hypertext writing and other computational practices as decidedly feminine, as many early cyberfeminists did, *Patchwork Girl* pursues the question of how digital technics productively and differently enter into the ongoing processes of subject formation through which gendered and racialized subjectivities emerge.

Its refiguration of instrumental subject-object distinctions as enactive relations of nonidentity modeled on stitching in sewing and quilting and digital hypertext linking, suggests how digital hypertext writing might help elaborate upon and extend feminist critiques of these dualisms and of the masculinist logics of possession and mastery they often sustain. "This crude model of the user and the used," as Sadie Plant argues, "has legitimized . . . scientific projects, colonial adventures, [and] sexual relations," positioning women as media, means of communication, or, to quote Luce Irigaray, as an "'infrastructure' unrecognized as such by our society and our culture" in that the "use, consumption, and circulation of their sexualized bodies underwrite the organization and the reproduction of the social order, in which they have never taken part as 'subjects.'"[69] These oppositions between user and tool, subject and object privilege an implicitly masculine human culture and subjectivity that achieve their integrity and mastery through a symbolic abstraction from physical embodiment and the material world (coded feminine). Their privilege is predicated on and against this supposed infrastructure or medium, a move that reduces the material processes and the feminine to "sameness," to an "originary ground" that is mere medium without meaning. It is against this masculinist, liberal humanist ideal that the work rethinks and revalues a monstrous, embodied, feminine writing realized in relation to digital hypertext writing practices, and questions the former consignment of embodiment and the feminine to a backdrop against which the masculine, instrumental subject and his meaning emerge.

In her counterhistory of communication technologies, *Zeros + Ones: Digital Women + the New Technoculture*, Plant explains the particular relevance of digital media to such feminist critiques. Aligning digital networks such as those on which hypertext relies with weaving and textile production, Plant argues that weaving provides a historical precedent and a model for the inextricability of process and product, of the medium and the meaning, of means and ends. In weaving, Plant suggests, "textile images are never imposed on the surface of the cloth: their patterns are always emergent from an active matrix, implicit in a web which makes them immanent to the processes from which they emerge," thus, "the visible pattern is integral to the process which produced it; the program and the pattern are continuous."[70]

Plant's comparison of digital hypertext writing to weaving suggests, as do the comparisons *Patchwork Girl* draws between hypertext and stitching, that the process of navigating digital hypertext and, in particular, of navigating a work of hypertext fiction such as *Patchwork Girl*, is itself a crucial component of its meaning. Its reading is, to a degree, performative.[71] As the patchwork girl informs the reader in "graveyard," "I am buried here. You can resurrect me, but only piecemeal. If you want to see the whole, you will have to sew me together yourself."[72] Reading digital hypertext fiction is similar to weaving and sewing to the extent that the collaboration between user and medium, reader and text, forms an integral part of the work and its inflections. The reader is involved in choosing the sequence of links in such multilinear works, even if, as Marie-Laure Ryan and others underscore, the interactivity in early digital hypertext fiction primarily impacts the narrative discourse or sequence of reading rather than generating completely new stories on each reading.[73]

Patchwork Girl's reciprocal relays between user and text, text and world, subject and technology, nonetheless, have a significant impact on relations between reader and text, reader and character, and our understanding and experience of this embodied reading process. Foregrounding and celebrating the monstrosity of material bodies and the technics through which we differentially realize, reassemble, and understand them, *Patchwork Girl* self-reflexively engages the medium of digital hypertext and the mechanics of the Storyspace program. It takes advantage of the program's associative linking capabilities, which provide word- or image-based hyperlinks to move laterally from a series of lexia to others or back again, as well as using Storyspace's map-views, which allow the reader to shift from reading one lexia or text box at a time to looking at a visual overview of the spatial arrangement of the boxes of text that are nested within each of the work's five main sections and their subsections. It explicitly elaborates on the potential of this writing technology to reveal how these materially realized processes are integral to the meaning of a digital hypertext fiction. Its five sections, characterized above as distinct segments similar to chapters in a book, are linked by a complex structure that moves unexpectedly from within one section to another, following themes and figures that traverse and thereby subvert the apparent organization of the work by exploiting, to full effect, the multiple, transversal patterns of linking that digital hypertext makes possible. It is for this reason, perhaps, that Jackson claims hypertext's "compositional principle is desire."[74] The meaning of each text box changes depending on the path of links one follows to and from or back to it, as a result of the different interrelations these movements reveal. This instability requires one to take the somewhat variable paths to and from each block of text into account and, although it doesn't generate an infinitely variable textual labyrinth as some early hypertext theorists proclaimed, it does make each reading of the work a divergent act of rewarding and unsettling complicity.

Importantly, while many early hypertext theorists understood these dynamic interrelations between the process of navigating a digital hypertext fiction and its textual product as inextricable, as an "emergent" dynamic in digital hypertext pioneer, Stephanie Strickland's promising terms, in light of more recent generative, computation-based writing it is worth clarifying how *Patchwork Girl* does and does not enlist these dynamic, processual dimensions to digital writing into an ongoing production of emergent textual meaning. This also helps to clarify the work's thinking about these interrelations between reader and digital text, embodied human and computational interface. Alice Bell, in her recent analysis of *Patchwork Girl*, "Ontological Boundaries and Methodological Leaps: The Importance of Possible Worlds Theory for Hypertext Fiction (and Beyond),"[75] identifies a fundamental paradox to Storyspace hypertext fictions such as *Patchwork Girl*. They insistently "foreground the ontological divide" between the reader and the digital text, requiring the reader to actively navigate and decipher the technical interface in light of the works' self-referential gestures and motifs. Yet at the very same time, these digital hypertext fictions reinforce a "consistently material and tactile relationship with the machine that displays the text."[76] Bell stresses that Storyspace digital hypertexts "contain devices that concurrently alienate and embrace the reader so as to simultaneously assert and collapse the ontological boundary that surrounds" their textual worlds.[77] This textual dynamic of digital hypertext fictions can be understood in light of *Patchwork Girl*'s other attempts to think through the complex feedback loops and interrelations between subjectivity, physical bodies, and the different material and discursive technics through which we co-realize their modalities of relation. When read in this way, one is reminded that the work conceives such enactive relations to both "mark a cut and commemorate a joining," as a process of simultaneously differentiating or distancing and in this way bringing into contingent, discrepant, materially realized relation.

In this way, *Patchwork Girl* brings the reader into selective connection with this distinct technological interface, at the level of its reading. Readers' difficulties in stabilizing the work's omnipresent, yet multiple ontological divides (as a result of its transgression of the lines dividing author and text, or text and reader, or body and text) effectively reinforce the distinct enactive relations afforded by this digital hypertext medium and juxtapose those to other media-specific methods that similarly and differently "bring forth a world." In contrast to more interactive and thoroughgoing generative writing practices that have emerged since, *Patchwork Girl* forces recognition onto the distinct technics through which our relations to textuality, to subjectivities, and to material lifeworlds co-emerge through such selective collaborations. Noting in her reading of *Patchwork Girl* how "different ontological levels (character, writer, user) mingle so monstrously in this text," Hayles reads this aspect of *Patchwork Girl* as one example of the "intermediating dynamics" digital writing technologies involve us in.[78] In describing these relations of "intermediation" between subjectivities, embodiment, material technologies, and digital textuality in the work, Hayles's description shifts from a relation described as a "permeable membrane" to "dotted-line connections/divisions" to "fluidly mutating connections between writer, interface, and user," not all of which are akin to the enactive relations of nonidentity I've tried to theorize here.[79] At the same time, I fully endorse her efforts to use this broader concept of intermediation to account for "the recursivity implicit in the coproduction and coevolution of multiple causalities" in such complex, "multilayered interrelations."[80] As she warns, "Privileging any one point as the primary locus of attention," whether writer, interface, or embodied reader, "can easily result in flattening complex interactions back into linear causal chains," which forecloses our ability to work through the complex, distributed, hybrid agencies in which the technicity of the human engages us.[81]

Aligning digital hypertext with weaving and sewing, *Patchwork Girl* self-reflexively engages digital technics and their dynamic, interactive, recombinant material processes as a means of revaluing the modes and materials of communication that have been aligned with the feminine and, together, devalued. As suggested above, its critique of the subject-object distinctions that differentiate the user and tool, the "weaver and the loom, the surfer and the Net"[82] has a revaluation of the contributions of women, as well as the contributions of other "mere" media, in mind. Strategically accepting the historical alignment of the feminine with material processes—both imagined as static, passive, neutral, noncontributing objects or "media"—*Patchwork Girl* engages the material in dynamic terms, theorizing material processes as active and transformative participants in the production of meaning and in the co-realization of variously human and nonhuman intersubjectivities. Strategically extending this debilitating equation, the work joins recent feminist and new materialist efforts to contest this joint reduction of material processes and the feminine to a stable, passive, homogenous ground for (masculine) processes of meaning production and the reproduction of patriarchy.

Drawing on digital hypertext's unruly lateral linking tendencies, its modular capacities for recombination, and its unlikely, collaborative patchwork formations, *Patchwork Girl* aligns the feminine with this changeability and multiplicity of material bodies; a dynamism to material processes that digital media make especially apparent through their computation-based de- and rematerializations, now extending through bioinformatic sciences and associated network technologies. In *Patchwork Girl* and in her lecture "Stitch Bitch: The Patchwork Girl," Jackson identifies the feminine with the "amorphous, indirect, impure, diffuse, multiple, evasive," arguing that this feminine "gets edited out of literature" and "gets exiled from the realm of meaning."[83] Importantly, in describing the feminine as the "banished body,"[84]

Jackson associates material complexity and the feminine with a multiplicity that characterizations of the feminine and of matter as sameness, stasis, and equilibrium must banish or repudiate in order to imagine the masculine and the symbolic aligned in a position of instrumental mastery over the feminine and over material complexity.

In her rethinking and recasting of the feminine as the banished body, Jackson underscores the direct relevance of shifting technics to gendered processes of human subject formation, pointing attention toward the socially and historically contingent processes and apparati through which gendered, sexed, and racialized bodies are allowed or not allowed to mean. In *Patchwork Girl* and her more recent web-based fiction, Jackson inquires into the processes through which human boundary formation comes about and becomes meaningful and to what social and cultural ends. If digital hypertext provides distinct means of registering modes of material agency and intra-acting with them, it queries, then what is the impact of these technics on the category of the feminine as it relates to both the sexual difference and the gender roles and sexualities that are supposed to follow from material bodies?

This is a line of inquiry into the force of sexual difference and other material microagencies that is stopped short by constructivism's insistence on the absolute divide between cultural discourses of gender and the biological actuality of sex, by the sex/gender system, and, more recently, by cyberfeminist and vitalist theories that, in attempting to read material bodies back into theories of the human, posit a return to a more primary or preexisting organic body (albeit a return facilitated through digital technics). In doing so, the latter collapse the distinction or difference between biological or cultural altogether, eliding the specificity of the relations they enact. Sadie Plant, for instance, describes the intermingling of user and used in digital hypertext, like weaving, as a reconnection with material flows, as "a convergence of organic and nonorganic lives, bodies, machines and brains which had once seemed so absolutely separate. Any remaining distinctions between users and used, man and his tools, nature, culture, and technology collapsed into the microprocessings of soft machines spiraling into increasing proximity."[85] In this passage and elsewhere in Plant's work, the difference between organic systems and cognitive systems completely disappears, which leaves no option of inquiring into their differential, dynamic, enactive modes of interrelation. In putting the feminine in touch with a material flow, Plant ignores important differences between these bodies and seemingly positivizes the feminine in its direct relation to material complexity. Understood in terms of its proximity to material flows, the category of the feminine is easily collapsed into and conflated with the female sex. Plant quotes the online cyberfeminist manifesto posted by VNS Matrix, which claims, "'The clitoris is a direct line to the matrix,' a line which refers to both the womb—*matrix* is the Latin term . . .—and the abstract networks of communication which were increasingly assembling themselves," only to reinforce this suggestion, however strategically inflammatory, that female genitalia give direct, privileged access to digital information networks.[86] Positivizing the feminine, figuring it as networked material complexity, Plant's framework overlooks the racial, ethnic, cultural, economic, and biological differences that striate the category of the feminine and of the female sex and forecloses consideration of variable relations between sex and gender, relations that, the transgender movement stresses, are quite common.

Patchwork Girl's understanding of the dynamic, strange relations of nonidentity connecting and separating cognition and material bodies, as well as readers and digital texts, explicitly refuses to collapse the feminine gender with a female sex or to put women in a more primary or unmediated relation to material complexity. While refusing to positivize its conception of the feminine, *Patchwork Girl* nonetheless keeps it in touch with an unruly material force of sexual difference, complicating the absolute sex-gender divide constructivism requires. Inquiring into the processes through which gendered, sex-specific human bodies become meaningful, *Patchwork Girl* pursues the question of how to register the material force of sexual difference, and other apparently nonhuman agencies without figuring them, or otherwise circumscribing and foreclosing their potential meanings or agencies. In light of shifting technics that provide distinct apparati through which we organize, understand, experience, and engage with material bodies, *Patchwork Girl* reimagines the category of the feminine gender that is supposed to follow from the presumed coherence and facticity of the female sex as an ongoing, multiplicit category comprised of, and in conversation with, material bodies and competing microagencies it cannot purify, identify, fully delimit, or evade.

Patchwork Girl is interested in the potential of shifting technics informing digital hypertext writing technologies to enter into processes of gendered and racialized subject formation, and to reelaborate these human boundaries with a difference. It engages digital hypertext writing as a means to register and, thereby, better appreciate the variability resulting from the monstrous force of material bodies and their intrusions into human meaning and experience. In spite of the patchwork girl's momentary aspirations to femininity, it is her failures, her persistent illegibility and multiplicity, which align her with the feminine as this category is reconceptualized in *Patchwork Girl.* Due to the patchwork girl's monstrous stature—her body parts are, after all, borrowed from several women, men, and a cow—she is mistaken for a man, a "man in lady's garb," a disfigured woman, a half man, half woman, a transsexual, a homosexual, and even a trained gorilla in disguise.[87] Her monstrous illegibility is not a product of her striking figure; rather it is a product of binary sex and gender, which conceive the masculine and the feminine, the male and female, and their respective heterosexual orientations as mutually exclusive oppositions, forcing subjects to disavow the discrepancies that make such oppositions and the hinging of dualisms of sex to gender far from absolute. Simultaneously believing that the patchwork girl who "could not possibly be a woman (was therefore a man)" and holding "the conviction that [she] . . . could not possibly be a man (and therefore had to be a woman)," Chancy, a cabin "boy" the patchwork girl befriends during her voyage to America, identifies the oppositional logic of binary sex and gender as the source of the patchwork girl's seeming contradiction.[88] Yet her identity, or lack thereof, is contradictory only in light of these mutually exclusive options, the rules of differentiation that Chancy's refusal of either/ or in favor of both/and attempts to disable.

The ambiguity surrounding the patchwork girl's gender and sex reveals binary gender's reliance on idealized morphologies that subjects, try as they might, are unable to realize. It is an ambiguity that *Patchwork Girl* reconceives as the potential for bodily boundaries, and the gender roles and human subjectivities that follow from them, to be realized differently, facilitated by the lateral, nonoppositional, aggregative compositional methods of digital hypertext. The patchwork girl's failed aspirations to femininity, which she chronicles, commenting that she "was not a success as a lady" but "more like a caricature of one," parallel the plight of all aspirations to a legible, gendered, human identity.[89] Attributing her aspirations to femininity to a "conservative coup" led by her duodenum, the patchwork girl claims that this organ "did not have full dominion over my body. Many organs work in secrecy, uncalibrated by the conscious mind, and in this manner, signs of unrest—twitches, wriggles, smirks—would wedge themselves between one accomplished gesture and the next."[90] Binary gender roles, as this passage suggests, attempt to align material bodies with an oppositional, binary, heterosexual logic, yet binary gender is unable to master the multiplicity of physical bodies. Attempts at mastery instead prompt "signs of unrest," noncompliance, and tics—they merely amplify, rather than manage, this illegibility and the material agencies that underpin it.

The "story" section branches into two accounts of the patchwork girl's experiences that narrate recognizably similar events from quite divergent perspectives, a divergence signaled by links titled "monstrous" and "mistress" that differentiate these two branches. The redoubling of the mistress and the monstrous patchwork girl in this section marks the limits to femininity as a socially mandated ideal that amplifies the very monstrosity that it attempts to stabilize and legislate. The monstrous patchwork girl is constitutive to the mistress, just as the monstrous agency of material bodies is constitutive to subjectivities, a realization that eventually leads the patchwork girl to relinquish her search for coherent univalent feminine identity, to stop clinging to "traditional form with its ordered stanzas."[91] She chooses, instead, to pursue her multiplicity, extending and "inventing a form" as she "went along," accepting certain degrees of illegibility and instability as the cost of rethinking the shape of her life.[92]

The monstrous multiplicity that the "mistress" ideal of nineteenth-century white bourgeois femininity abjects and exiles is in defiance of binary racial categories that code the feminine as white in addition to confounding binary gender roles. The patchwork girl's refusal to sever monstrous bodily agencies from her distinct realization of feminine gender, thus, interrogates these co-implicated processes of racialization and gendering. Body parts taken from numerous corpses give the patchwork girl the "motley effect of patched skin."[93] As Jackson's "Mary Shelley" describes the patchwork girl: "the various sectors of her skin were different hues and textures, no match perfect," "warm brown neighbored blue veined ivory."[94] The patchwork girl's failed aspirations to an implicitly white femininity, modeled on Mary Shelley, foreground, once again, the multiplicity of the feminine. The patchwork girl combines transgendering and transraciality in her "composite, queer, 'multiculti' body, made out of grafts and surgical implants of ethnic or racial features," features characteristic of cyborg identity (since Haraway), as Emily Apter reveals in her analysis of an emergent "postcolonial cyberpunk."[95]

Patchwork Girl cites the multiple exclusions that comprise and compromise specific enactments of gendered and racialized human subjectivity. It underscores how processes of differentially realizing gendered, racialized, and sexed human bodies and associated human subjectivities also entail processes of unmaking, or foreclosing from coherent, tangible human meaning. In this way, processes of human boundary formation lead to the objectification and resulting dispossession of women and other subalterns (i.e., their foreclosure from a liberal humanist subjectivity defined according to a logic of self-possession and self-ownership). Defined by her feminine, multiracial, and

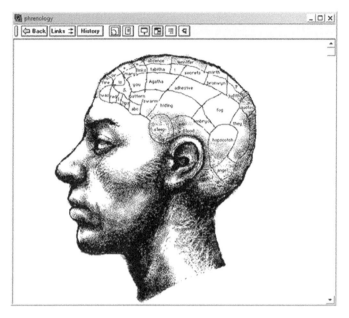

Fig. 2. "phrenology" (frontispiece to the subsection "body of text") from
Patchwork Girl by Mary/Shelley and Herself. Courtesy of Eastgate Systems.

multispecies incoherence, the patchwork girl literally cannot claim ownership
of her borrowed body parts. The section titled "body of text" features an image of a woman's cranium, in profile, titled "phrenology." The image directly
references the scientific discourses key to the racialization and resulting objectification of African Americans, criminals, and other subalterns. This was a
social Darwinist enlistment and scientific description of material attributes to
foreclose select subjects from recognizable human subjectivity. By replacing
the numbered regions of the skull with words that serve as highly associative,
unpredictable hyperlinks, the image ironically deploys this computational
medium to call into question any such effort at quantitatively measuring or
mapping the material forces of the body and presents a countermapping to
register what such mappings necessarily render intangible, nonsensical. The
patchwork girl later claims, "I am never settled. I belong nowhere. This is
not bizarre for my sex, however, *nor* [my italics] is it uncomfortable for us, to
whom belonging has generally meant, belonging TO."[96] Explicitly connecting and differentiating between the modes and methods of rendering women
and subalterns less than human, *Patchwork Girl* further underscores the dif-

Fig. 3. "hercut" (frontispiece to the section "crazy quilt") from *Patchwork Girl by Mary/Shelley and Herself*. Courtesy of Eastgate Systems.

ferences that striate the category of the feminine. In attempting to "become a real woman," the patchwork girl, thus, practices both racialized and gendered modes of passing before she finds another approach.[97]

In Pursuit of Strange Modalities of Relation

Selectively capitalizing on the technological affordances of digital hypertext writing, juxtaposed to a range of print-based technics, *Patchwork Girl* plays out their potential value to feminism, as well as to posthumanist theories of technics more broadly. It exploits the lateral connections traversing different kinds of "bodies," the resulting modular, patchworked assemblages hypertext writing technologies enable, their nonoppositional modes of reproduction, their variable, multilinear texts that emerge through a specific reading, and the reader's simultaneous separation and connection through this writing technology's suturing of human subjects to its computational, code-based processes. In this way it opens onto an alternate understanding of the modalities of relation digital technics might enable among and between subjectivities and material bodies. In particular, the work suggests digital hypertext and the transformative, enactive relations its technics facilitate provide a crucial means to acknowledge the multiplicity within the category of the feminine. This is a multiplicity and dynamism that compromises social systems' and subjectivities' attempts to stabilize a single gendered identity within an oppositional, binary, instrumental framework. Once gendered and racialized subjectivities are acknowledged to be in collusion with material bodies and microagencies, the latter reveal the monstrous limits to any masculinist illusion of instrumental mastery.

Patchwork Girl engages with the material processes that enter into cognition, subject formation, social systems, and digital hypertext reading and writing (among other recursive systems processes) and proceeds to illustrate how such technics help bring to light nonoppositional modalities of relation modeled on these transversal linkages across different domains and sites. As mentioned above, *Patchwork Girl* rethinks the relations between cognition and the physical body, between meaning and medium, and between subjects and their technological prostheses as enactive relations that, like a scar, both "mark a cut and commemorate a joining," and as a "dotted line," such as a basting stitch in sewing, that "indicates difference without cleaving apart for good what it distinguishes."[98] These modalities of relation, as realized through distinct technics, inform subjectivities and, by extension, the intersubjective relations they enable or foreclose. Engaging digital hypertext to enact recombinative relations that do not require the subjugation of difference and a logic of possession that attempts, but inevitably fails, to secure the reproduction of the same, *Patchwork Girl* turns attention toward the intersubjective relations emergent technics might encourage.

The significance of *Patchwork Girl*'s attention to enactive, multiplicit modalities of relation is quite clear in the patchwork girl's intimate relations with women, the most famous of these being Mary Shelley. The patchwork girl's sexual relations with women challenge and rework the oppositional logic of gender dualism in two important respects. They challenge the reduction of the feminine to an undifferentiated matrix or sameness by insisting on the differences between women, differences that a binary logic must disavow. Its attention to the differences between women functions, equally, to trouble the positioning of lesbian sexuality in relation to binary, heterosexual difference as "nonreproductive" and a "risky 'sameness'" because, as Judith Roof has argued, "configurations of the lesbian tend to mark the failures" of this binary, heterosexual system.[99] *Patchwork Girl* is clearly interested in how lesbian relations throw the oppositional sexual economy naturalized in relation to print narrative into relief and open onto alternative, queer modalities of relation. In addition, it perceives the potential of nonoppositional modalities of relation to allow for more complex relations between sex, sexual orientation, identification, and desire.

The patchwork girl's intimacy with a woman named Elsie—though initiated by the patchwork girl's desire for self-possession, her desire to buy Elsie's identity and name and assume it as her own—results in the patchwork girl's remaking (due, in part, to Elsie's eventual refusal of this exchange). In this and other important respects, their relation is rendered as mutually transformative. In "I made myself over / Elsie triumphant," the patchwork girl, who is literally "parting"—with different pieces of her body falling off quite inconveniently and simply going their own way—describes sitting in the bathtub with Elsie. The patchwork girl's stray parts bob in the water around them:

> Elsie was immersed in me, surrounded by fragments, but somehow she held me. I was gathered together loosely in her attention in a way that was interesting to me, for I was all in pieces, yet not apart. I felt permitted. I began to invent something new: a way to hold together without pretending I was whole. Something between higgledy-piggledy and the eternal sphere. I became supple. My furniture parts became mellow as wax and the joints and junctures, long turned to proper purposes, bent past their right angles into impossible obliquities, or found curves not known to their before-uses. . . . All disassembled, I made myself over, forgetting not to remember.[100]

A metaphor for their sexual exchange, their mutual immersion signals the reciprocity of this embrace, in stark contradistinction to a logic of sexual possession in which one assumes the active position and the other a passive position. Comparing her morphology, the organization of her body, to the "joints and junctures" in furniture, the patchwork girl marks this "remaking" as an intervention in the rules of differentiation or technics that not only co-organize her understanding of her body, but in doing so, also partially delimit its "proper purposes," the possible uses of its parts. Discovering "curves not known to their before-uses," her sexual relations with Elsie allow her to acknowledge her literally disparate parts and to imagine a way "to invent something new: a way to hold together without pretending [she] was whole." The patchwork girl finds a way to make these parts meaningful that does not aspire toward a union, conjoinder, or wholeness. It does not resolve or overcome difference; instead, it is an intersubjective relation that gathers together her pieces yet acknowledges her multiplicity and the multiplicity that divides her and Elsie. Characterizing her dispersal in terms of a "diaspora," as in the title of the lexia quoted below, the text links this multiplicity to ethnic de- and reterritorializations, as well as to the patchwork girl's transformation from "a would-be settler to a nomad" within the established territory of a heterosexual, binary sex and gender system.[101] Rejecting the "libidinous dynamic" of sexual mastery—what Roof describes as "an urge to know (to bring parts together)" and to resolve the parts into a meaningful whole—this passage theorizes, instead, a modality of relation that joins disparate parts without mastering their multiple differences.[102]

A skin graft or suture, as "a place where disparate things join," yet a joining or relation that also leaves a scar as testimony to the persistence of the differences that foster this "new growth," serves as one figure for this modality of relation in *Patchwork Girl*. In the words of Mary Shelley quoted above, the patchwork girl's scars "not only mark a cut, they also commemorate a joining."[103] This realization leads Mary to consolidate her sexual intimacy with the patchwork girl by fulfilling her "crazy wish" to cut off a part of her body to give to the patchwork girl to be "a part of her."[104] The patchwork girl and Mary Shelley exchange skin grafts taken from their inner thighs, a reciprocal exchange that marks their joining as well as the differences that result in the story of how Mary "loved a monster and became one," a story that Mary insists, contrary to an instrumental logic of authorship or of sexual possession, is "ours."[105] Operating on two levels, as a sexual joining as well as a textual joining, the graft marks the sexual intimacy between the patchwork girl and Mary Shelley, and the work's textual relation, its status as a joining with, and a graft on Mary Shelley's *Frankenstein*. The metatextual status of their relation foregrounds print narrative's implication in the technics that structure sexual relations in binary, oppositional, heterosexist, instrumental terms, as well as the work's status as a literary print narrative and digital hypertextual hybrid.

In linking print narrative to digital hypertext, *Frankenstein* to *Patchwork Girl*, and Mary Shelley to Shelley Jackson, *Patchwork Girl* effectively reconceives technics of subject formation and the resulting intersubjectivities in light of the lateral, recontextualizing, and stitched, differential relations this digital hypertext fiction establishes with its readers, underscoring their potential to recalibrate liberal humanism's gendered and racialized binaries, and to trouble their presumably stable, hierarchical relation to sexual difference and to other material bodies. It suggests how these emergent technics might help to reconceive distinct modes of material agency, their microagencies, and the intersubjectivities they co-realize. It illustrates how digital hypertext and digital writing technologies that have emerged since can shed new light on these enactive relations, on the processes of embodied action that link material bodies, perception, sensorimotor action, and cognition to larger lifeworlds in specific, recurring, dynamic, differential ways.

In *Patchwork Girl*, these enactive relations are, I'd suggest, envisioned as tactics of the human through which the specific, intersecting differentiations that consolidate the legible sex, gender, and race of human subjectivity and their possibilities for intersubjectivity are sedimented and rerealized over time. Understood as tactics of the human, these relations can be seen to establish highly contingent, yet recurring experiential and materially-realized parameters through which the recognizably human emerges. Tactics are, in Michel de Certeau's sense, everyday practices, "ways of operating," or doing things that entail a strategic borrowing from that which one has selective access to, but, by definition, cannot own or control, in this case, the unrealizable, "proper" place of the human.[106] One is unable to pick or choose these relations and the modalities of the human they open onto as they are already structured through recurring discursive and material relays and embedded in experience; "the place of a tactic belongs to the other."[107] Instead, these relations are the very means through which the boundaries of the human become perceptible and are registered. Nonetheless, the enactive relations joining the human with technics are multistable, open to degrees of manipulation and play and, thus, open to tactical engagement, to reorientations and "makeshift creativity."[108] Engagements with emergent digital writing technologies, such as *Patchwork Girl*, underscore multiple, long-standing, sedimenting and transformative tactics through which the human is co-produced without ever attaining full ownership of the terms of this ongoing coproduction.[109]

Patchwork Girl's attention to the enactive relations through which the human emerges, its engagement with the monstrosity that informs all tactics of the human and renders them subject to change, is radical when read in relation to liberal humanism's instrumental understanding of the human—as absolutely, timelessly, and categorically distinct from his technological prostheses, from material lifeworlds, and from nonhuman animals. Yet it is increasingly clear that in the context of corporate technoscience and late capitalism's practices of "flexible accumulation," simply acknowledging the negotiability of the human and adopting a posthumanist understanding of technicity is inadequate.[110] As numerous critics have noted over the past ten years, late capitalism encourages just such a deconstruction of oppositions in favor of the ongoing generation of more fine-tuned, profitable differentiations. Its own logics now pursue such a dynamic production of difference. For this reason, the text's vision of a dynamic, patchworked, multiplicit, racially and culturally hybrid, "flexible" femininity (capable of being variously assembled, disassembled, and reassembled) can equally be recuperated to serve, not unsettle, instrumental ends and to endorse networked material processes such as those differentially linking women in maquiladora factories just south of the U.S. border with Mexico to wired women in the United States. The latter networked, flexible material processes clearly don't necessarily work to the benefit of women, nor do they facilitate a progressive recognition or revaluation of multiplicit, dynamic femininities. For this reason, it is crucial to expand *Patchwork Girl*'s queries from the level of subjectivities and writing technologies to address digital technics' engagement by larger economic, geopolitical, and cultural formations and their space-making practices, an issue I will explore in the next chapter.

To reiterate my initial claim, it matters not just if, but how materialities reenter such posthumanist accounts of the human's technicity. A broader geopolitical scope reinforces the fact that such efforts to think through dynamic processes of human subject formation, even those new materialist theories that attempt to acknowledge subjectivities' and social systems' reliance on unstable and agential material forces, are not necessarily the basis for radical or even progressive feminist and queer practices and intersubjectivities in the twenty-first century, especially when one attends to the transnational scale on which such technics unfold and establish their infrastructure for future interrelations. In addition to developing such posthumanist perspectives on the human's ongoing multilayered technicity, it is necessary to differentiate between specific modalities of relation enabled by distinct technics, as well as to register the different ways in which these posthumanist understandings of the human in formation are played out in specific macro- and microeconomies.

On this front, *Patchwork Girl*'s comparative technics, moving between print, digital, and other bodily technics introduce a crucial method of inquiring into and registering the distinct human and nonhuman subjectivities and modalities of relation they open onto and foreclose. They provide a potential means of engaging with the formative tactics of the human through which we realize and fail to realize distinct, and distinctly meaningful, bodies and delimit their interrelations. Such comparative technics help identify and exploit shifting and multistable tactics of the human to encourage gendered, sexed, and racialized human boundaries with an enabling and sustaining difference. Engaged as a critical practice, such comparative engagements with technics that trace their unperceived potential and blind spots by transposing them from one medium, genre, or platform to another might allow one to comparatively register the material force and impact of distinct technics, not only on how we realize the boundaries of human subjectivity, but also on how we imagine the gendered, racialized, and queer modalities of relation they make possible and sensible. Through this critical method, texts such as *Patchwork Girl* not only encourage multiple, emergent modalities of femininity that are in conversation with a range of physical bodies, material forces, and nonhuman others, but through cross-media movements between distinct print and digital technologies, they suggest how we can proceed to register material constraints and possibilities these intersubjectivities might afford. The work's insights into technics as tactics of the human reveal how if we can't absolutely differentiate between matter and meaning, ontology and epistemology—in large part because these lines are themselves radically unstable—we might track and take partial responsibility for the different modalities of relation that emerge through distinct technics.

3 / Realizing the Vitality of "Dead" Spaces

> Political work . . . reshapes the very surfaces of bodies and worlds.
> Or we could say that bodies resurface when they turn the tables
> on the world that keeps things in place.
>
> —Sara Ahmed, "Orientations Matter"

When technicity is approached at the qualitatively distinct scale of political economy, geopolitics, and social space, a somewhat different perspective on technics as tactics of the human emerges. What happens to the enactive relays technics establish between subjectivities and distinct material practices, so apparent at the level of digital writing technologies, at this geopolitical scale? This chapter examines technics in their capacity to establish dynamic infrastructures that help sediment or unsettle materially realized social formations. Global economic networks defining late capitalism, and their extraterritorial logics of circulation, production, and consumption, have made the space-making potential of digital technics unavoidable. This poses the question, exactly how do shifting technics transform social relations to material spaces and, in this process, help to solidify or disarticulate social formations and their political power in crucial ways? What, in turn, are the limits and blind spots to late capitalism's efforts to realize computation-based social spaces that further its operations (evading labor unions, environmental regulations, national taxes, and political jurisdiction, to name a few)? And, how do literary texts' comparative media practices attempt to register the material limits to these social spaces and, as importantly, their epistemological blind spots? As I'll suggest below, comparative media practices in print literature as well as in digital media can provide critical cartographies that retrace how technics enter into and sediment distinct space-making processes. In attempting to understand the emergent social spaces digital technics help realize, it is, therefore, key to read such tactical engagements with digital media and their emergent social spaces for what they relay about contemporary modalities and topographies of space-making and power.

The emergence of late capitalism's "informational economy" involved a significant restructuring of capital and its infrastructures since the late 1970s that, according to Manuel Castells and others, relied upon the affordances of digital information technologies in a primary way.[1] This restructuring, though driven by a wider array of social, cultural, and political forces, served to realize distinct new kinds of social space and power. In the early days of the Internet, the space-making abilities of digital technics and their computational processes were often perceived to be creating a secondary, largely separate virtual space layered on top of the existing physical terrain and its social, cultural, and political operations. John Perry Barlow's famous "A Declaration of the Independence of Cyberspace," posted online in 1996, strategically describes the virtual world of the early Internet as a space of "mind" free from the physical constraints of property-based law or gendered and racialized embodiment that so thoroughly circumscribe political and economic and cultural life in face-to-face social spaces.[2] And Sherry Turkle's early accounts of identity play in text-based, online forums were similarly invested in the potential of these spaces to expand the boundaries of subjective identity beyond socially circumscribed gender roles and behaviors, occurring as they do, to some degree, in the alternate space of online multi-user domains, or MUDs.[3] Not surprisingly, these assumptions of a divide between physical and virtual worlds facilitated supraterritorial and somewhat liberatory, if not always distinctly libertarian, readings of computation-based communication spaces. They led theorists to initially overestimate the novelty and assumed difference of information-based social spaces from the social, cultural, material, and economic (not just technological) processes through which they emerge.

It has since become quite clear that the computational processes and infrastructures digital technics instantiate no longer involve, if they ever did, a simple addition of information-based communications and technologies as a distinct, overlying social terrain. Computational processes are not, in fact, confined to computers or to software as self-contained technical objects opening onto distinct spaces beyond the screen; instead they are coming to be "everyware."[4] They coordinate and co-articulate countless spatial dimensions of our everyday physical as well as our virtual life online, now having become so pervasive that we are encouraged to reconceive the spaces we inhabit every day as what critical geographers Rob Kitchin and Martin Dodge redescribe as largely interpenetrating "code/spaces," as social spaces and practices realized to differing degrees by their reliance on computational technologies and infrastructure.[5] If this sounds like an overstatement, try to imagine going through a single day without recourse to a technological object (alarm clock, cell phone, computer), or reliance on an infrastructure (GPS, weather satellites, surveillance, radio, product scanning, transportation, digitally designed and fabricated buildings, financial accounts) that involves some kind of digital computation and/or computational information network. Code and space mutually, if dynamically, inform each other and differentially inform social life for distinct subjects.

While the field of ubiquitous computing explicitly aims to integrate computing into the fabric of our lives so that it remains largely unseen, critical geographers exploring contemporary social space, such as Nigel Thrift, note the prevalence of a much wider range of social and technological spatial practices supported by computational technologies that remain unseen, a "technological unconscious."[6] It is a technological unconscious, notably, that we experience at some level yet are explicitly encouraged to "unsee" in that the code-based processes generating these spatial practices and their supporting configurations are largely designed to remain opaque, hidden from view so that they become an accepted, habitual part of our environment, interactions, modes of communication, and political life.[7] While coming to terms with the distinct impact of digital technics and their pervasive computation on contemporary social and economic practices and lived space is essential, this co-imbrication of computation-based technical infrastructure with lived physical and symbolic social spaces also encourages careful consideration of preexisting, predigital practices of space-making and their technically enabled processes of augmenting reality to both materially and symbolically orient different bodies to each other and to the world.

Returning to early theories and elaborations on the "informational economies" of late capitalism and the emergent social spaces and practices, or "network societies" they introduced, I reconsider and counter underlying assumptions about late capitalist technics that encourage theorists such as Manuel Castells to overemphasize the uniqueness, novelty, and self-originating character of the computation-based practices and social spaces digital technologies enable. This leads them to overlook their continuities with previous social spaces and practices of space-making. Several common assumptions about how technics enter into spatial practices and social relations reinforce this continuing habit of overlooking and underestimating the co-imbrication and coexistence of various digital and analog social practices. These habits of thinking about digital technics and emergent social spaces are particularly detrimental when it comes to assessing the ongoing interrelations between emergent, networked economic spaces and preexisting, industrial capitalist economic spaces and their social consequences.

Reading Castells's extensive analysis of digital technics' impact on contemporary spatial relations and social space from the perspective of Leslie Marmon Silko's 1991 print novel *Almanac of the Dead*, I illustrate the value of comparatively reconsidering emergent late capitalist space-making processes both within *and* beyond this particular techno-economic frame.[8] The novel provides a *spatiotemporal* remapping of capitalism's information-based digital networks that situates them alongside long-standing, dynamic, though presumably low-tech networks of circulation, production, and consumption, which have sustained the spatial practices integral to colonialism and imperialism in the Americas over the past five hundred years. These processes of spatial differentiation are integral to the racialization, gendering, and economic differentiation of bodies and populations that, thus, come to differentially inhabit and move through hegemonic spaces. Connecting spatial transformations to the "biopolitical"[9] imperatives of both nation-states and transnational capitalist networks, the novel examines these emergent, computation-based, networking logics and spatial practices as they *both* extend and depart from colonialist and imperialist precedents.

As the novel illustrates, grappling with the material processes through which digital technics co-realize social formations and their social spaces in light of this broader historical, technological, material, and cultural context is key to understanding the reproduction and contestation of contemporary forms of social power, not just their novelty. The novel reconsiders how digital technics impact and enter into contemporary social spaces and attends to their distinct modes of engaging with existing material spaces to realize culturally and historically specific social formations. These are social spaces that reinstantiate certain epistemologies and reinforce their privilege. *Almanac of the Dead* reconsiders the more complexly reciprocal, socially and culturally embedded and embedding dimensions to digitally enabled processes of space-making in twentieth- and early twenty-first-century American culture. Rather than accepting late capitalist techno-economic networks' self-description as a universal, unstoppable, self-sustaining, natural force, the novel acknowledges the mutually transformative dimensions to ongoing encounters between late capitalist networks and the social agents intent on redescribing, if not redirecting, their "exploits."[10] This reciprocal view of space-making processes complicates the unicausal assumptions that require that *either* material place engenders social spaces *or* late capitalist social networks are entirely responsible for unfolding social spaces through their creative destruction of preexisting material places.

In turn, this attention to the co-imbrication of lived, material place and emergent, computationally enabled social space enables careful reconsideration of ongoing, unequal contests over social space as shifting technics serve to solidify or de- and rearticulate select social formations and their sustaining lifeworlds. Taking these co-productive interrelations between technics, material spaces, and social formations into account, this chapter examines social contests over different understandings of space and time. These contests over the material and symbolic co-production of social spaces remain crucial to the emergence and sustenance of contemporary social and spatial formations. In establishing itself as the New World Order, late capitalism's informational restructuring and networked social space has also, unwittingly, drawn attention to industrial capitalism's methods of establishing social spaces and political forms that secure its uneven, differential circumscription of subjectivities and social life. Late capitalist digital networks' ability to realize simultaneous global spatial connections in real time has, for instance, largely compromised modernity's three worlds system, which differentiated the spaces of the world temporally according to a single, hierarchical Eurocentric timeline with Europe and the United States occupying the modern present.[11] Although this latest spatial transformation facilitates an increasingly fine segmentation and differentiation of the "markets" of the former three worlds, and is not itself politically progressive, it does undermine the spatial logic supporting the colonial difference between "first" and "third" worlds. It provides one example of how late capitalism's emergent spaces unwittingly catalyze critical reconsiderations of the colonialist and imperialist spatiotemporal logics and epistemologies that have consolidated, and, in somewhat altered guise continue to consolidate spatially differentiated, gendered, racialized, and (even more) economically stratified social formations.[12]

This line of inquiry into a wider range of space-making agencies and processes than are usually admitted into readings of late capitalist political economy and its spatial geographies has recently been pursued in the field of critical geography. This chapter elaborates on influential work on postmodern space and critical geography by Castells, Doreen Massey, and Nigel Thrift to illustrate what their perspectives reveal about how technics enter into materially realized late capitalist social spaces and how, in turn, these preexisting and emergent social spaces and agents influence these ongoing processes of space-making. As I argue, their work is extended by a range of "new materialisms" and "critical materialisms" that are similarly attentive to the dynamic reciprocity of material and social practices in the ongoing unfolding of social space. Attending to both preexisting and emergent material practices and understandings of space-making, these approaches are, perhaps, more appropriately described as "renewed" or "critical material-isms," rather than "new" materialisms even if they respond, in part, to recent pressures introduced by digital technics and recent scientific developments in physics and genetics. As I mentioned in the introduction to the book, they join in opening "new" lines of inquiry into established understand-ings and practices of materiality, that is, in reapproaching these fundamental questions from the vantage of present-day sciences, digital technologies, and their privileged modes of economic and cultural transmission, yet one must also read the "new" as an interrogative stance towards materialisms today and a sustained inquiry into their apparent novelty. Critical geography and new materialisms' shared attention to the influence of social and material forces on social spaces, in addition to the techno-economic ones often privi-leged in political economy, distinguishes their efforts to rethink the material practices unfolding in and through emergent social spaces.

Read alongside *Almanac of the Dead*, this work's attention to the materi-ality, historicity, and heterogeneity of social spaces allows me to recommend that we reconceive such processes of space-making as processes of *reorienta-tion*.[13] Complicating the more prevalent, reductive view of emergent social spaces as wholly superseding existing social spaces or creating utterly dis-tinct, unique ones out of thin air, the concept of reorientation underscores how spatial practices that engage technics and their formative infrastructures to establish new social spaces and spatial relations necessarily draw upon ex-isting, materially realized spatial relations and social life, even as they work to reorient them in significant ways. Developing this concept to address contemporary late capitalist social spaces as they emerge with and against and, thus, reorient industrial capitalist spaces and affiliated political forms such as the nation-state, among other social formations, I extend Ahmed's insightful, "critical materialist" examinations of the complex interplay be-tween practices and experiences of space, the physical matter of places and bodies, and the social relations they help to sediment and habituate.[14] When

social spaces are understood in their capacity to orchestrate spatial orientations, lived bodily experience, experiences of space, and the social relations
these jointly facilitate and habituate, then technics of space-making come
to be understood as processes of reorientation that introduce new ways of
relating bodies, and of physically and epistemologically orienting individual
and collective social bodies.

To the extent that "the social depends in part on agreement about how
we measure space and time," as Ahmed stresses," it is necessary, in light
of spatial transformations accompanying late capitalist networks, to query
the ongoing contests over social spaces and their modes of orientating and
hinging bodies and cultures to material worlds and, thus, circumscribing
how they matter.[15] New or "critical materialisms" such as that recommended
by Ahmed, with this unpredictable, dynamic reciprocity to spatial practices
in mind, reapproach material spaces as simultaneously physical and physically realized through distinct material practices and technics; inextricably
social in their attempted realization of particular, culturally informed spatial
imaginaries; and necessarily plural as moments in ongoing, transformative
processes in which humans are not the only agents. Such new materialist
engagements with space confront the pervasive influence of an emergent
technical apparatus on spatiotemporal frames for action, existing lifeworlds,
and other social spaces, and, contrary to many theories of postmodern space,
they also explore how the reciprocal force of multiple, competing spatiotemporal frames, lifeworlds, and social spaces counters and complicates those
emergent technics and their privileged social formations. This interaction
makes new sense of shifts in global political economy and their impact on
spatiotemporal practices in the United States and throughout the Americas.
Further, it recognizes and reconceives the vitality of material spaces, the fact
that "space is the sphere of multiplicity, the product of social relations, and
those relations are real material practices, and always ongoing," which means
that "space can never be closed, there will always be loose ends, always relations with the beyond, always potential elements of chance."[16] These engagements with *material spaces*, in refusing to accept or be confined by the
opposition of *place* (as local, territorial, historically meaningful) and *space* (as
global, abstract and immaterial, functional), raise the question of how, and
in what distinct, multiple ways, one aligns and allies oneself with and against
such space-making processes.[17]

Redescribing late capitalist economic networks just as their informational turn was becoming apparent, *Almanac of the Dead* grapples with the
spatiotemporal logics of these emergent network processes and the socio-

spatial formations they were just beginning to realize. Insisting on the material embeddedness, historicity, and lived dimensions to technically realized spatial formations, the novel's comparative, print-based understanding of how digital technics facilitate space-making processes reveals how social space-making unfolds as a material and symbolic process of reorienting, not superseding, the material places, social formations, and the individual and collective orientations to the world that precede these emergent social spaces. The novel anticipates and helps to clarify how late capitalist networks, as we've since come to realize, rearticulate and coexist with, even profit off of, the territorial, modern logics of power and industrial capitalist methods they reengineer. It underscores how the restructurings of social spaces accomplished through late capitalist networks intensify quite familiar practices of differentiating social space and bodies along intersecting racialized, gendered, cultural, and economic lines, while also introducing new turns to these logics and elaborating unique methods for their realization.

From the vantage of the novel's indigenous Americans and other subalterns, it is quite clear that these emergent social spaces reinstitute, even intensify, colonialist spatial and bodily orientations that take privileged discourses and practices of whiteness and heterosexist masculinity as an unacknowledged given. In turn, these networks' emergent spatial practices delimit the scope of other cultural discourses and the mobility of differently racialized, gendered, and classed bodies in definitive, deadly ways. The novel explores how late capitalist networks and the biopolitics they enable *both* unsettle and realign distinctions between the vital and the dead, and underlying ideas about the dynamism of time and stasis of space integral to U.S. colonialism and state power. Identifying this pivotal distinction as it delimits people, animals, places, and things according to varying degrees and modalities of liveliness and stasis, the novel reorients such material space-making and spatializing practices and rejects the unquestioned spatial imaginaries on which they rely.

Almanac of the Dead unfolds its comparative approach to networks as a means to tactically reorient such hegemonic social spaces and, thus, to register emergent late capitalist technics and their topographies of power. It pursues the political consequences of its rethinking of networks and the alternate, historically and cross-culturally contextualized vantage on late capitalist, digital information networks this provides. In addition, the novel depicts a series of tactical reengagements of hegemonic spatial formations to ulterior, subaltern ends that are informed by the "almanac of the dead," the generative indigenous text that materially and symbolically sustains these social networks. The novel's own literary print narrative is similarly reconceived as a dynamic part of these larger spatiotemporal networks, as a materially embedded text that participates in social space-making through its, at once, material and symbolic circulation.

Almanac of the Dead anticipates tactical media practices in digital media, which, I argue, are similarly interested in registering the complex relays between material space, embodied experience, computational processes, and social discourse and in exploiting them to different ends, even momentarily. Considered together, the tactical media practices they propose and undertake reveal crucial shifts in hegemonic social formations and their relation to material worlds that are accompanying digital technics. Drawing on Rita Raley's analysis of tactical media practices emerging in new media art, I will foreground several defining traits of the novel's and more recent tactical media practices to explore how they both register and respond to the social and spatial transformations accompanying digital technics.[18] The novel's proposed multileveled, open-ended, heterogeneous, and site-specific political tactics are easily critiqued for many of the same reasons more recent networked tactical media practices such as those deployed in the Occupy movement have been. *Almanac of the Dead* helps to underscore, in light of Native American and indigenous American knowledges and a longer history of anticolonial and anti-imperialist subaltern tactics of 'table-turning" or "writing in reverse," how these media tactics not only serve to reorient hegemonic social spaces, they also allow one to bring to the fore the epistemological assumptions and social privilege these spatial practices and sedimenting spaces realize.[19]

The novel's materialist tactics for engaging the historicity and heterogeneity of material spaces, in particular, draw attention to tactical media practices' ability to retrace and render tangible the unseen relays between digital technologies, culturally distinct epistemologies, symbolic spaces, subjectivities, and materially realized social spaces. It encourages a reconsideration of the relations to material spaces such tactical spatial practices and their critical cartographic methods open onto, underscoring their relevance to how we think about cultural politics and geopolitics. Realizing the vitality of "dead" spaces in *Almanac of the Dead* involves reorienting global capitalist networks and their deadly, stultifying, standardizing Cartesian spatiotemporal logics *and* reckoning with the dimensions and meaning of a wider range of social and spatial practices that have been consigned, through the former's spatializations, to a supposedly "dead" space outside modern time.

Refusing the absolute differentiation between living and dead, temporal and spatial, meaning and matter, animate and inanimate so central to late capitalist social spaces and political life, the novel opens onto an understanding of material practices and their cultural agency that reorients the spatializing logics of U.S. biopower and, thereby, suggests what may be the most necessary politics of all.

Material Practices of Space-Making as a Social Medium

Recent work on postmodern space in the field of critical geography has gone to great lengths to understand material practices' transformative force and their formative role in establishing physical and symbolic parameters for social life. Working just prior to global capitalist restructurings, Henri Lefebvre, in *The Production of Space*, had already developed an account of capitalism's "social space" as a dynamic "matrix of social action" that, in addition to providing an infrastructure or background for social relations, is itself the *medium* of material practices within which social relationships are realized.[20] Subsequent spatial transformations have since generated a growing body of critical work on processes of geographical knowledge-production and its relation to power: Ed Soja's *Postmodern Geographies*, David Harvey's *The Condition of Postmodernity*, Doreen Massey's *Space, Place, and Gender*, Jon May and Nigel Thrift's work *Timespace: Geographies of Temporality*, and Manuel Castells's three-volume work *The Information Age: Economy, Society, Culture* are prominent examples. This work, in thinking through how technologically enabled material practices and infrastructure impact experiences, understandings, and movements within a variety of social spaces, underscores the material, productive work of social formation and its forceful influence. It opens new doors for critical geographies to track and, it is hoped, unsettle modes of social power realized through these materially situated, dynamic networks.

Approaching social space as it emerges in relation to the networks of production, exchange, and consumption within industrial and now global capitalist political economy, much of the work on social space has understandably centered on capital's impressive capacities for "creative destruction," for re-creating and materially realizing social spaces in its image so that we come to take them both as a kind of "second nature," in Lefebvre's terms.[21] As a result of this emphasis, theories of late capitalist social space, subsequent to Lefebvre's, frequently attribute shifts in spatiotemporal practices and experience accompanying the introduction of communication and transportation technologies (such as the telegraph and the railroad in the nineteenth century), and those accompanying digital information technologies and communication networks in the twentieth and early twenty-first centuries to emergent, technologically enabled *economic* practices, though these theorists are clearly invested in their broader social and cultural impact.

More recent work on social space in critical geography now acknowledges that this focus can lead to an overestimation of the power of late capitalist economic practices to override and wholly recode existing economic, social, and physical spaces. Due to this exclusive focus on the late capitalist economic networks impacting the production of space, such processes and resulting spaces come to be seen as much more monolithic, uniform, and determined from above than they may actually be.[22] David Harvey's theory of "time-space compression," for instance, perhaps the most famous account of how capitalist political economy impacts contemporary experiences of modern space and time, generates the impression that global capitalist practices have transformed all social spaces and are experienced similarly by all subjects regardless of gender, race, ethnicity, class, religion, sexual orientation.[23] Such theories' emphasis on shifting economic practices' ability to recreate the world in their image is often predicated on their tendency to see space-making processes in unicausal terms, as the effect of technologically enabled economic practices driven by capital. This understanding of how technics and other material practices produce social space overlooks the more complex processes through which material practices, guided by economic, technological, *and* other forces, interact with existing culturally distinct social formations that reciprocally inform and transform these emergent techno-economic practices.

As Doreen Massey stresses in "Power-Geometry and a Progressive Sense of Place," it is not capital alone that generates our sense of space: "There are many other things that clearly influence that experience, for instance, ethnicity and gender."[24] Taking into consideration the complex, multiple, even conflicting practices that influence our relation to material spaces, Massey redescribes materialism, refusing to reduce it to what she describes as an impoverished "economism."[25] This economism, as I intimate above, relies on a reductive understanding of how technics vie with social and material practices. What I've described as the socially embedded and embedding relays into which emergent technics must enter help explain why a radical and total disjuncture between existing industrial and emergent postindustrial economies and the social practices they realize, such as that Manuel

Castells offers in his early theorization of an informational "space of flows" wholly overriding existing place based relations in modernity's "space of places," is now considered inaccurate, not just unfinished.[26] If one acknowledges that existing technics and the apparati that support them are always already embedded in social relations, infrastructure, and material practices and that emergent technics must enter into, as well as partially transform, those practices and sedimented architectures, then it begins to make more sense why information technologies and the material spaces and cultural knowledges they realize are not single-handedly superseding or completely recoding existing material practices and social spaces, leaving previous social spaces completely in the dust. Instead, as I'll go on to illustrate, it might be worth following Massey's new materialist lead and reconceiving such space-making, at multiple levels, as processes of reorientation that cannot be reduced to a single, Euro-American, techno-economic timeline.

By acknowledging the more complex socially embedding and embedded force of technics as material practices, one becomes responsive to the power-geometry that catalyzes shifting technics and the purposefully uneven topographies they encourage. As Massey explains this term, "Different social groups and different individuals are placed in very distinct ways in relation to these flows and interconnections," which is all "about power in relation to the flows and the movement."[27] Complicating current understandings of the material practices that enter into late capitalist socio-spatial formations allows for a consideration of the multilayered processes and multiple agents and agencies through which shifting experiences and understandings of social spaces emerge, revealing the power-geometries apparently determined by late capitalist networks and their privileged material practices and agents to be both more complex and uncertain.

In the introduction to their edited collection *TimeSpace: Geographies of Temporality*, Jon May and Nigel Thrift stress that "the nature and experience of social time is multiple and heterogeneous," as is "its manner of construction."[28] They go on to identify (at least) four interrelated levels at which our sense of space and time is differently shaped: (1) at the level of the material world's bodily, tidal, and seasonal rhythms; (2) at the level of the social through disciplines of clock, calendar, domestic arrangements, religious and cultural practices, and economic practices; (3) through our relationships to a variety of instruments and devices; and (4) through texts that give meaning to new conceptualizations of space and time.[29] Exploring the overlapping interrelations between these distinct kinds of material practices, May and Thrift's new materialism, like Massey's, credits multiple, human and nonhuman contributors to the space-times we continually realize, inhabit, and often take for granted. Importantly, the materialisms emerging out of Massey's and May and Thrift's work include the material world as an active, ongoing, dynamic contributor to contemporary experiences and practices of space-times, not a mere object or passive resource in the hands of capitalism.

Such attention to the processes through which material practices sediment social spaces and, through them, uneven social relations allows one to explore how differently sedimented social relations enter into and erode hegemonic, late capitalist social relations in expected and unexpected ways through their tactical engagements with distinct material spaces and the practices they open onto (though these are, by definition and strategy, vastly unequal forces). As Ed Soja stresses, spatiality and social relations are "simultaneously contingent and conditioning," an unpredictable "outcome and medium for the making of history."[30]

Almanac of the Dead stages its own critical reencounter with the material practices and processes engendering social spaces. The novel's perspective on material practices as a social medium, while explicitly drawing upon Marx's work and historical materialism, undercuts and contravenes dominant readings of digital, information-based networks and late capitalist space in key respects. It diverges, in particular, with regard to its understanding of the processes of social and technological change that enter into material practices and spaces. The novel redescribes space-making as an emergent, generative material practice, a view in conversation with Native American, indigenous American, and other subaltern knowledges and, equally, one cognizant of recent information-based shifts in late capitalism's materially realized spatial practices. It reveals the difference materialisms re-attuned to the force of material spaces and the social differentiation they realize—as are Massey's efforts to rethink materialism from a feminist perspective, or materialisms developed through Native American studies and subaltern studies—are able to make as they confront crucial blind spots in accounts of contemporary network societies and their understanding of the difference digital technics make through these "novel" social spaces.[31]

Almanac of the Dead opens with the "Almanac of the Dead Five Hundred Year Map" that encapsulates and encodes events that prefigure and those that unfold in the novel. Centered on the city of Tucson, its dotted lines depict the primary movements of the novel's characters and of commodities—such as cocaine, military arms, aircraft, and illicit videotapes—across the border between the United States and Mexico. The edges of the map gesture beyond this central node to the far reaches of the Americas with arrows heading south toward the Caribbean, Central and South America, north to Alaska, and east to the coast of New Jersey. What readers of the novel slowly come to understand is that this transnational "Almanac of the Dead Five Hundred Year Map" encodes a dynamic network of materially realized, intersecting *spatiotemporal* social relations. It is modeled on several surviving Azteca codices that figure time and space as inextricable, with events figured as dotted lines linking geographic places. Its temporal plot is, notably, read through the tracking of such spatial itineraries. In addition, rather than imagining the narrative's relation to a specific place, that is, its material geography, as a static backdrop to its temporal unfolding, this transnational network of social relations is located within a five-hundred-year geopolitical history that continues to actively inform these socio-spatial networks in their ongoing social and material transformation. One of four "keys" to the map is a text box titled "The Indian Connection," which reads,

> Sixty million Native Americans died between 1500 and 1600. The defiance and resistance to all things European continue unabated. The Indian Wars have never ended in the Americas. Native Americans acknowledge no borders; they seek nothing less than the return of all tribal lands.

Another text box titled "Prophecy" gestures both back in time and forward to the novel's near future, stating,

> When Europeans arrived, the Maya, Azteca, Inca cultures had already built great cities and vast networks of roads. Ancient prophecies foretold the arrival of Europeans in the Americas. The ancient prophecies also foretell the disappearance of all things European.

The plot of the novel works to realize this prophecy, concluding in 1991 (nearly five hundred years after Cristóbal Colón arrived in the Americas) at which time the end to the five-hundred-year system appears imminent, but the outcome unclear. It tracks the movements of its large cast of characters to and from Tucson, movements that ultimately converge into an uprising led by a subaltern coalition of Native Americans and indigenous Americans, African Americans, Mexicans, Mexican Americans, a Korean hacker, Eco-warriors, homeless men, and Vietnam veterans to "retake the land" that has been stolen from them. Notably, this event just begins to unfold in the final section of the novel, titled "One World, Many Tribes."[32]

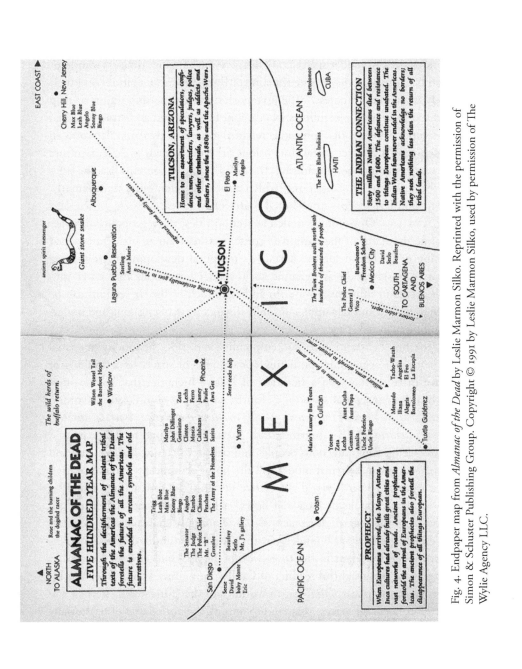

Fig. 4. Endpaper map from *Almanac of the Dead* by Leslie Marmon Silko. Reprinted with the permission of Simon & Schuster Publishing Group. Copyright © 1991 by Leslie Marmon Silko, used by permission of The Wylie Agency LLC.

Envisioning social relations as materially realized, yet dynamic, embodied networks unfolding in and transforming historical time, the map is one of several strategies the novel uses to recast and refuse the gendered Cartesian distinction between space and time, which has worked in the modern world system to render space as an abstract, unchanging, timeless setting or dead backdrop for the unique timeline of Euro-American cultures and their lively masculine "progress." The juxtaposition and superimposition of map and narrative itself recombines what might be perceived as distinctly spatial or temporal modes of expression, refiguring both as dynamic networks in which spatial and temporal dimensions are intertwined, as Azteca culture perceived them to be. In addition, the novel's table of contents lists the titles of the first four of six sections, which appear to refer, quite transparently, to geopolitical spaces—the United States of America, Mexico, Africa, and the Americas. Once foregrounded as section titles, these geopolitical spaces assume the status of the narrative's content rather than an unacknowledged setting or backdrop for the narrative's temporal development, prompting their reconsideration as dynamic socio-spatial formations that enter into plot events in substantial ways. In addition, each of the six sections can be seen to unfold and rely upon culturally distinct ways of engaging and understanding material spaces.

The novel's attention to the temporality and, thus, historicity of spatial formations foregrounds conflicting conceptions of space. Its rethinking of space in time draws on a tradition of Native literature that locates itself within the conceptual space of a "fourth world," as chronicled in Gordon Brotherston's *Book of the Fourth World: Reading the Native Americas through Their Literature*.[33] The "fourth world" is commonly used to designate and acknowledge the indigenous peoples and cultures that are dearticulated and displaced by a nationalist model, yet the novel complicates this conception of a separate, "fourth world" of Native literature by articulating it in relation to late capitalism's "space of flows," which it designates as "The Fifth World." In this regard, *Almanac of the Dead* not only challenges the "particular concept of space as bounded territory" that is naturalized by the "nationalist model dominant in the three-worlds theory," but also, as Tom Foster suggests in his insightful reading of Guillermo Gómez-Peña's "Five-Worlds Theory," co-implicates the "fourth world" and the "fifth world" in their status as "conceptual spaces" that tend to rethink the boundaries of territorially defined, geopolitical space "in terms of motion, flux, and relationality."[34]

Deploying place-names as section and book titles, taking these places as its subject, rather than taking them for granted as its setting, the novel flags its interest in the production of geo-political spaces, unsettling the transparency they assume when taken as stable, innocuous territorial designations. The abstraction of space from time has functioned to secure the geopolitical distinctions of the modern world system, to mask the ongoing production of this geopolitical system in and over time. It has enabled the spatialization of women, Native Americans, indigenous people, black Americans and many others coded nonwhite by aligning them with an unchanging space outside modern time. The view of space as stasis, as "fixed and unproblematic in its identity," which Massey thoroughly critiques in her groundbreaking work *Space, Place, and Gender*, enabled the modern world system to project its own temporal distinctions, with Europe as the point of arrival or present, on the world and, subsequently, to disavow the productive work this and other modes of colonialist and nationalist mapping entail.[35] When their participation in processes of historical transformation is acknowledged, the seeming transparency of geopolitical spaces such as the United States, their apparent innocence in designating a geographic territory or securing a bounded cultural identity that preexists that denotation, is revealed to be a product of this and other nation-states' ability to impose and enforce, to materially and symbolically instantiate, this social space.

Almanac of the Dead counters this view of space as stasis, and the gendered nationalist and colonialist social hegemony it supports, with its *spatiotemporal* mapping of the Americas. On the map and within the novel, the movements of characters comprise a mapping of these spaces, materializing a network of social relations that cross-cuts and, in other respects, undermines the primacy of the geopolitical distinctions between nations such as the United States and Mexico. Far from existing outside the social or existing as a mere backdrop to the social, outside time, these geopolitical spaces are, the map suggests, irrevocably tied to the hegemonic and nonhegemonic social relations that inform and transform them. As mentioned above, the narrative is divided into sections such as "The United States of America," "Mexico," "Africa," and "The Americas," section titles that do not simply correspond to the geographical location of the events figured within them or serve as place-names denoting a preexisting, geographic space. Instead, these place-names introduce sections that chart the dynamic movements of characters—their overlapping trajectories and mutual participation in several key events. Through these print-based strategies of "spatial" or "environmental storytelling," the novel indicates how these characters' movements work to call into question the homogeneity, integrity, and coherence of national space by realizing competing spatial imaginaries through a range of material practices.[36]

The characters' movements enact an alternative geography based on competing understandings and complex renegotiations of materially realized social spaces. For instance, the third section, titled "Africa," includes books titled "New Jersey," "Arizona," and "El Paso," which are intertwined with, not contained within, Africa, as the section title might appear to suggest. In this section readers first encounter Clinton, a now homeless black Indian and Vietnam veteran living in Tucson whose life story and teachings in black history register the ongoing, transformative influence of diasporic African cultures throughout the Americas. "Slavery joined forever the histories of the tribal people of the Americas with the histories of the tribal people of Africa," Clinton stresses in one of his "liberation radio broadcasts."[37] Reconceptualizing movements across these geopolitical spaces, *Almanac of the Dead* not only troubles the illusion that these geopolitical place-names designate an abstract, preexisting, uncontested space, it demands recognition of the ongoing deformation and rerealization of these spaces on the part of a wide variety of social actors. As a "Five Hundred Year Map" this entails a recognition of the contributions of social actors in the past as well as the present, a recognition of the communities and cultural identities that agents of colonization attempted, but never wholly succeeded in "razing" in Mary Pat Brady's terms.[38]

The novel's spatiotemporal remapping of the Americas in terms of dynamic, materially realized practices of networking anatomizes and intervenes in processes of spatial de- and rearticulation that have been central to U.S. nationalism and colonization in the Americas. The characters' realization of an alternate geography through their movements, as suggested by the Almanac of the Dead Five Hundred Year Map, is the first indication of the novel's rethinking of such social networks and the material practices through which they are realized as emergent, "ontogenetic" material practices, as dynamic engagements with existing spaces that realize, through a set of epistemologically informed material practices, specific relations to and modes of being in the world, a reconceptualization of materiality that will be explored in greater depth below. As Nigel Thrift describes the effect of similarly "ontogenetic processes" in digital spaces, the "logic of the system, as it becomes both necessary and general, will gradually become the logic of the world," receding "from human perception, becoming a part of the landscape which the body 'naturally' adjusts to."[39]

The Novelty of Networks

Almanac of the Dead's literary print critique of U.S. colonialism and imperialism in the Americas is a direct response to and a concerted, critical remapping of the shifts introduced through late capitalism and its digital technics and computation-based spatial practices. Though it was written well before the full scope and character of emergent capitalist networks were apparent, its competing account of networks is designed to make the continuities between existing print-based, national, territorial spatial logics and the emergent, deterritorializing logics of late capitalist, transnational economic networks apparent, contesting the assumption that these digitally enabled social spaces are either spatially or temporally distinct. Emerging transnational networks and the dramatic socio-spatial transformations accompanying them might appear to make the novel's critique of abstract, static, naturalized space unnecessary by rendering late capitalist networks' dynamic, productive power and participation in material processes and practices of history undeniable, yet *Almanac of the Dead* underscores troubling continuities between industrial and late capitalist spatial practices that encourage us to reconsider how these distinct relations to and understandings of space are linked by unacknowledged, underlying similarities. In addition, it illustrates how these different socio-spatial practices often work surprisingly well together in spite of some notable differences. The novel engages the spatial form of a network to reveal the ongoing, willing, profitable erasures accomplished through both of these predominant spatiotemporal logics. Developing a competing logic and practice of networking, it illustrates the potential and continued need to recognize and pursue material practices that presume and open onto the heterogeneity and historicity of social spaces. This responds directly to a predominant tendency to overestimate the productive, space-making power of hegemonic social formations and their fetishized technics, as late capitalism's self-description and much political economy encourage us to do.

As mentioned above, research on postmodern space, political economy, and critical geography, attentive to the productive power of emerging neoliberal late capitalist practices to create spaces facilitating its flows of capital, commodities, and labor, continues to emphasize the striking novelty of these socio-spatial formations. Modernity's temporal organization of the spaces of the world is fractured by the simultaneity of global capitalist networks, which link places around the world so that they are now working together in real time, as evidenced in the finance markets, for instance. As theorists have worked to understand the vast social and cultural consequences of these shifts, their initial emphasis on the differences between these spatial logics and the latter's novelty, though, has led to a significant overestimation and misconstrual of these transformations. Sociologist Manuel Castells's account in *The Rise of the Network Society*, part of his three-volume work *The Information Age: Economy, Society, and Culture*, remains one of the most extensive and exacting accounts of recent late capitalist spatial transformations. It provides crucial insight into the difference digital technics and their late capitalist social formations introduce, while it also illustrates how an emphasis on the productive power of economic practices and their computation-based, digital technics generates a particular, somewhat limiting view of such transformations.

Castells's account of the emerging social space realized by postindustrial capitalist economic networks credits new informational technologies that provide the "material, technological basis of economic activity and social organization" in what he describes as an emerging "network society."[40] He proposes that the global restructuring of capitalism in the late 1970s and early 1980s, and resulting global interdependence of economies throughout the world, introduces "a new form of relationship between economy, state, and society, in a system of variable geometry."[41] He attributes these reconfigurations to the "informational" mode of development enabled by new technologies, which is transforming the material basis of our experience and reforming it according to the spatial logic of its information networks. In his view, the space of historically rooted, territorial economic, social, and political forms, the "space of places," is being superseded by the new spatial logic realized through the techno-economic networks of informational capitalism, the "space of flows."

Castells understands the emergent "space of flows" as "*the material organization of time-sharing social practices that work through flows,*" underscoring the material and conceptual dimensions to these social practices even though they are not "*self-contained within the boundaries of physical contiguity,*" not historically rooted to a particular, meaningful locale as they are in the existing "space of places."[42] He argues that the dominant spatial logic, the "space of flows" supersedes the "space of places" by disembedding and reintegrating historically specific territories and social actors into a functional network. As the figure of a network suggests, the "space of flows" establishes a highly dynamic set of relations between these places, places that are abstracted from their former historical and geographical meaning and redefined solely in terms of their position and function within the structure of this instrumental network. By deterritorializing places and reterritorializing them according to its own functional logic, the "space of flows" ensures its flexibility and adaptability. It exploits the specific resources of any one node or site and simultaneously renders that node, in its very specificity, secondary to the network's organization; any specific site can be replaced by another equally capable of fulfilling this function. For this reason, the "space of flows is not placeless, although its structural logic is."[43] Due to the flexibility of its networks, which depend on the heightened mobility of new communications technologies, the "space of flows" surpasses previous limits imposed by geographic distance. It surpasses territorial limits in another important respect in that its networks can more easily evade "territorially-based institutions of society," the mechanisms of social control that might impede its circulation of capital, information, and technologies, its flows.[44]

Late capitalism's "networking logic" further privileges the abstract, spatial dimensions of social relations and elides their necessary temporal dimensions with its synchronous, "timeless time," which is how Castells describes the emphasis on simultaneity and timelessness, an "ever-present" now that results from these networks' use of technologies to flexibly manage time as a resource. One of the key differences between the current global economy and a world economy that has been in place since the sixteenth century is that the former's "*core components have the institutional, organizational, and technological capacity to work as a unit in real time, or in chosen time, on a planetary scale.*"[45] "Globally integrated financial markets working in real time for the first time in history" are, in Castells's view, "the backbone of the new global economy."[46] He describes these flows of capital, information, technology, images, sounds, and symbols as "the expression of processes *dominating* our economic, political, and symbolic life" as "the network of communication is the fundamental spatial configuration: places do not disappear, but their logic and their meaning become absorbed in the network."[47]

While Castells carefully and thoughtfully identifies distinguishing features of the "space of flows" that have since become legend and brings attention to some of the pressing social, cultural, political, and economic problems this emergent spatial logic poses, his initial, defining assumption of the novelty of these materially realized social spaces and his belief in their ability to supersede and override existing socio-spatial formations generates some problematic blind spots that remain with us. Beginning with the assumption that these implacable flows of capital, information, and technology are *dominating* our economic, political, and symbolic life, Castells leaves no alternatives to capitalist modernity's territorial, place-based logics and late capitalism's space of flows (though he does advocate creatively recombining them) and risks reducing the world to this single, economic time line. Another consequence of his emphasis on the novelty of late capitalist networks is that it blinds his theory to the interdependence and interaction between these industrial and postindustrial capitalist spatial logics, in spite of, or even in light of, their differences. This leads him to assume that these spatial transformations, and the supersession of the "space of places" by the "space of flows," is incomplete and not a strategically unequal restructuring, as were many industrial capitalist spatial transformations. What Castells initially describes as exceptions to the rule of late capitalist spaces, instead, if read against the grain of this economist framework several years later, "undermine the story" late capitalism "tells about itself," and reveal the most unavoidable similarity between late capitalist networks and industrial capitalist territorial places to be that both are, to use Massey's words, "imaginative geographies which *legitimise* their own production" and, in this way, disregard their "own real spatiality."[48]

The telling exceptions to the rule, exceptions with which Castells, to his credit, remains preoccupied, yet which his assumption of novelty makes it so hard for him to theorize are the complex interdependencies between these networking logics and the existing spatial logic of territorially bounded political and cultural forms. He acknowledges that while the "space of flows" expresses the dominant spatial logic of a global economy, this economy "does not embrace all economic processes in the planet, it does not include all territories, and it does not include all people in its workings, although it does affect directly or indirectly the livelihood of all humankind."[49] The globalization realized through the "space of flows" has been highly selective not only in its strategic inclusion and exclusion of places, but also in the very nature of its engagement of those places lucky enough to be of use. Those places lucky enough to be worth exploiting, as Castells describes their double-edged status, suffer the consequences of a loss of their cultural, historical, geographic meaning as they are reintegrated into global, functional networks.[50] Even more detrimental is the economic system's "highly dynamic, highly selective, highly exclusionary, and highly unstable" incorporation of certain localities, which reinforces a "fundamental asymmetry" between developed and developing countries, allowing its key sites and an elite managerial class to reap the benefits of, and share the mobility of, its information, capital, and other resources at the expense of those excluded from its networks.[51]

Taking into account the efficacy of the "space of flows" in extending and elaborating on existing patterns of domination and forms of dependency, the differences between these spatial logics and the novelty of the networks that sustain the "space of flows" quickly diminish in importance. The "space of flows" and its "variable geometry" enables a *heightened* sensitivity in the processes used to differentiate the world's economies, resources, and labor, which means that the apparent flexibility, fluidity, and open-ended mutability of these networks function in the service of increasing segmentation and differentiation at unprecedented degrees. As Castells himself notes:

> On the one hand, valuable segments of territories and people are linked in the global networks of value making and wealth appropriation. On the other hand, everything, and everyone, which does not have value, according to what is valued in the networks, or ceases to have value, is switched off the networks, and ultimately discarded.[52]

Under closer scrutiny the continuities between the social spaces of the modern world system's "space of places" and the "space of flows," as the latter exacerbates and extends existing logics and practices of economic segmentation, begin to tell a different story. As Castells acknowledges, "Most production, employment, and firms are, and will remain, local and regional" and there is evidence to suggest that global capitalism profits from precisely such a discrepancy between increasingly global flows of capital and unskilled labor forces that are "restricted by national barriers."[53] In more recent work, further pursuing the question of *Communication Power*, Castells now acknowledges that many of these strategic differences between the spatial logic of the "space of flows" and the "space of places" are systemic.[54] They are integral to the current functioning of global capitalist networks, not residual. Nonetheless, as a result of his (techno)economism he remains less willing to acknowledge material spatial practices that are anything other than reactive to this dominant and dominating economic spatial logic.

Networks as Means of "Channeling Energy"

Contrary to theories of late capitalist space that are catalyzed by and founder on the apparent, unqualified *novelty* of late capitalism's transnational, information-based networks, *Almanac of the Dead*'s multileveled engagement with networks counters this defining assumption, among others. The novel recontextualizes late capitalist networks, enabled through digital information networks such as the Internet, and satellite television and weather broadcasting, and other digital communications technologies. It locates them alongside existing and competing, "low-tech," spatiotemporal networks such as those materially realized through practices such as migration, long-standing practices of smuggling and drug-trafficking, and the circulation of cultural texts such as its own indigenous text, the "almanac of the dead," partially modeled upon the Azteca codices. Once juxtaposed to existing materially realized spatial formations such as these, late capitalism's uniquely transnational, supposedly deterritorialized "space of flows" is revealed to be equally reliant on a material geography, co-realized through material practices, and to participate in transformative, continually contested, unpredictable historical processes.

Reading late capitalist networks against its own understanding of spatiotemporal networks as ongoing, materially realized, dynamic, transformative socio-spatial relations, *Almanac of the Dead* refuses the former networks' suppression of historical time, what Castells describes as these networks' "timeless time." Reactivating the spatial *and* temporal (i.e., historical) dimensions of social relations, it relocates and implicates late capitalist networks within a five-hundred-year system of colonial and imperial expansion, which foregrounds continuities between these spatial practices as they further colonialist and imperialist modes of spatial and cultural de- and rearticulation. In the novel, El Grupo Gun Club, a conglomerate of politicians, judges, governors, military and ex-military, a former ambassador, friends of the CIA, and police chiefs on both sides of the border between the United States and Mexico, exhibit many of the tendencies of global capitalist networks and their flow-based, transnational logics. Considering themselves "chief executives of the future," these representatives of the state disregard territorial and political distinctions between the United States and Mexico, circulating money and cocaine north into Tucson, where they exchange the drugs for arms and military aircraft and invest in real estate.[55] The weapons are used to stifle "political" unrest that threatens to interfere with their business interests throughout the Americas.[56] As Menardo, whose company, Universal Insurance, manages the private security force that protects the group's business interests insists, "Politics had no place in their common cause, which was survival, whatever their minor political differences."[57]

In addition to marking the tendency of late capitalist networks and the economic interests they further to override national jurisdictions, the corruption of these figures of the state flags the inextricability of national political interests and economic interests, locating both within a long-standing history of U.S. imperialism. Late capitalist flows may striate the geopolitical space of the nation-state, the novel suggests, but such processes of segmentation perpetuate, rather than pose a challenge to, the privilege accorded to these figures of the state. El Grupo Gun Club's members are, in several important respects, no different from the "speculators, confidence men, embezzlers, lawyers, judges, police and other criminals as well as addicts and pushers" that have made Tucson their home since the "1880's and the Apache Wars."[58] Menardo, thus, may have good reason to believe the "'new world' could belong to them just as the old one had."[59]

The novel also registers distinct new turns in what it, otherwise, perceives to be quite familiar transnational, colonialist, nationalist, and imperialist spatial practices circulating information, commodities, people, and knowledges to materially realize and sustain specific social formations. El Grupo Gun Club's activities in the novel, like late capitalism's "space of flows," reveal the formative power of social relations to de- and rearticulate the spaces of the world. Their activities also underscore key discrepancies between the socioeconomic relations furthered by global capitalist networks and those realized by the geopolitical space of the nation-state. Taking its critique of space-making power one crucial step further, the novel illustrates how competing material and social forces always enter into, recode, reorient, and survive such spatial transformations with unexpected, transformative consequences: a critical insight that its counterhistory of networks as means of channeling energy makes tangible.

The novel's remapping of late capitalist networks reconceives both high- and low-tech networks in terms of their shared, underlying status as means of channeling energy. With its own spatiotemporal networking logic, the novel foregrounds essential limits to the productive power of late capitalist networks, which are frequently understood to function supraterritorially, to wholly rearticulate the spaces of the world in accordance with their placeless, variable geometry. The novel illustrates how late capitalist networks effectively suppress material and historical dimensions to their social practices, refusing to acknowledge their participation in a historical process with more than one kind of agency. It contravenes such efforts by illustrating how these networks do not, in fact, transcend those material and historical dimensions to social practices or escape the consequences of their ongoing, unpredictable co-realization in space and time.

Located alongside other socio-spatial networks within a five-hundred-year system, late capitalism's "space of flows" is read as the latest manifestation of, and elaboration on, modernity's Eurocentric, rational management of the world-system. From this vantage, modernity's spatiotemporal networks come to be seen as materially situated and culturally motivated spatial practices that, through the "discovery, conquest, colonization and integration (subsumption) of Amerindia," were able to gain a definitive "*comparative advantage* with respect to the Ottoman-Muslim world, India, and China."[60] Offering what Enrique Dussel describes as a "planetary" re-description of modernity as "the culture of the *center* of the 'world system'" rather than as the product of an independent Europe, the novel underscores the economic advantages resulting from (neo)colonial, imperial, and other systematic economic and environmental exploitation, which (continue to) enable late capitalist networks to impose their abstractions on the world.[61] Late capitalism's spatiotemporal networks, it suggests, channel these material resources and, in doing so, solidify their socio-spatial formations, epistemologies, and power. Their complete, continued reliance on material resources, and on the cultural and economic imperialism required to secure these resources, is something Eurocentric descriptions of modernity prefer not to acknowledge.

The novel's insistence on socio-spatial networks' sustaining, ongoing ties to material energies (physical materials, electricity, and labor, among others) insightfully resituates capitalist and neoliberal late capitalist networks and their practices of "channeling energy" in another way, as well, by refusing their claims to universality. Reconceiving spatiotemporal, technological, and economic networks as means of channeling energy, *Almanac of the Dead* underscores the cultural specificity of the Cartesian spatiotemporal logics so central to Euro-American aspirations to Enlightenment rationality. The latter come to be perceived in the novel as only one of many ways to engage and understand the social and its potential relations to material spaces, and, thereby, to attempt to realize "the possibilities" in the world.[62]

In the novel, the by-product of Europeans' Enlightenment rationality, the five-hundred-year system, is known as "Reign of the Death-Eye Dog" and "Reign of the Fire-Eye Macaw" because "the sun had begun to burn with a deadly light, and the heat of this burning eye looking down on all the wretched humans and plants and animals had caused the earth to speed up too."[63] The "burning eye" evokes the bird's-eye view of Cartesian objectivity and its fiery, scopic "enlightenment" taken to destructive extremes, once magnified in the hands of capitalism. Descartes's definition of matter as "corporeal substance constituted of length, breadth, and thickness; as extended, uniform, and inert . . . provided the basis for modern ideas of nature as quantifiable and measurable" and facilitated the absolute space of Euclidean geometry and the mechanical, linear causality of Newtonian physics.[64]

According to the novel, the five-hundred-year system capitalizes on just such objectifying, Cartesian abstractions, which speed up the circulation of commodities and people commodified as labor by reducing the world to a set of general equivalents. It may appear that this system speeds up circulation through standardization and profits from this accelerated "progress." Yet the apparent triumph of such processes of abstraction over material complexity, their ability to facilitate speedy exchange and circulation through standardization, is only a triumph if one overlooks the destructive simplification and reduction that the system's wholly shortsighted engagement with the world as objectified thing requires. Calabazas, a Yaqui Indian who operates a smuggling network through Tucson, insists that, in actual fact, the simplifying reductions that define Europeans' spatial understanding represent "a sort of blindness to the world," noting that to Europeans, "a 'rock' was just a 'rock' wherever they found it, despite obvious differences in shape, density, color, or the position of the rock relative to all things around it."[65] The problem, in his view, is that "once the whites had a name for a thing, they seemed unable ever again to recognize the thing itself."[66] As he suggests, such understandings and deployments of abstraction—as a result of their Cartesian separation of material and symbolic, inanimate and animate, spatial and temporal—fail to see or value the ongoing processes of social and spatial enactment or realization, the emergent, generative dimensions to materiality that enter into and reciprocally inform and exceed the greatly reduced, objectified "thing itself" that emerges through ongoing, materially realized processes of meaning and space-making.

Calabazas's critique draws attention to the heterogeneity of material spaces that is suppressed and negated when the world is approached only in terms of its uses, uses that are specified in advance by this spatiotemporal logic. The latter understanding of absolute space objectifies material processes and spatial practices, and, in doing so, it also positions the human to perceive and interact with the world as if it is a passive resource or object, categorically distinct from his conscious life. Calabazas refuses the unidirectional, wholesale substitutions required by this fetishistic logic of abstraction and, instead, recommends acknowledging how socio-spatial practices involve us in ongoing, though necessarily selective, spatially and temporally contingent, engagements with the energy and force of the material world. Calabazas actively rejects the word "*identical* . . . There is no such thing. Nowhere. At no time. All you have to do is stop and think. Stop and take a look."[67] His references to "nowhere" and "at no time" stress capitalist standardization's selective suppression of the contingencies of space and time.

Calabazas and several other characters indicate how this spatiotemporal logic, and the epistemologies it helps realize, also extends through to Euro-Americans' understanding of subjectivity and bodily space. The conception of subjectivity as a similarly abstract, unchanging, "identity" secured through a possessive individualist notion of self-ownership is another outrageous by-product of this spatial imaginary, in the novel's view. Calabazas's name, citing the pumpkins he used to make his break in smuggling networks between the United States and Mexico, is one of many he adopts, in defiance of this understanding of identity as bounded possession or as sameness across space and time. His friend and collaborator, Lecha, similarly realizes "she had never seen any person, animal, place, or thing look the same twice" and acknowledges that she finds herself greeting subtly different faces in the mirror each morning.[68] The former modes of abstraction, the novel stresses, facilitate certain kinds of circulation, such as those realized through the "space of flows," but this circulation is paradoxically premised on stasis and sameness, and, therefore, within the novel flows that function according to a capitalist logic of abstraction are equated with destruction and death, with a "worldwide network of Destroyers who fed off energy released by destruction."[69]

Recasting the spatial logics furthered by late capitalist networks in this way, the novel underscores the continued centrality of this spatial imaginary as it underpins and sets the terms for hegemonic understandings of subjectivity, cultural identity, nation, and even the literary's symbolic and material space. As Calabazas and others suggest by recasting these spatiotemporal logics as a "blindness to the world," these practices and their cultural and political imaginaries are unable to render social spaces impervious to time, a realization late capitalist networks' emergent spatial practices facilitate, as does growing environmental awareness.

Realizing the Vitality of Dead Spaces

An immanent mode of subaltern resistance follows from *Almanac of the Dead*'s understanding of networks as means of channeling energy and its view of space-making practices as processes of reorientation. The way to counter the particular kind of death realized by the five-hundred-year system's "space of flows" and its "blindness to the world," it suggests, is to rerealize the emergent, generative potential of spatial practices and, thereby, to revitalize material spaces otherwise consigned to stasis and sameness and, thus, significantly, restrictively immobilized. Sections titled "Eskimo Television" and "Tundra Spirits" begin to illustrate how one might, in this way, engage material spaces in their complex heterogeneity and dynamic potentiality and strategically counter the instrumental single vision of late capitalism's socio-spatial formations. Once networks are reconceived as means of channeling energy, as material practices that help to realize distinct socio-spatial formations, it becomes clear how materially realized spatial configurations and material spaces can also resist, elude, and transform, as well as further sediment, social relations.

Insisting on reciprocal, dynamic relays between socio-spatial formations and the material spaces they inhabit and work to realize, *Almanac of the Dead* enlists material spaces and, importantly, the people, cultures, and knowledges that have been disarticulated through an alignment with material space, in the service of transforming existing social relations. The novel, similarly to recent new materialisms, rejects the gendered, Cartesian logic of stasis to which a feminized and spatialized material world has been consigned. Its rethinking of material spaces is designed, in particular, to contest the gendered and racializing spatializations that confine Native American and other indigenous cultures, as well as the natural world, within the realm of the dead. These spatializations, in projecting indigenous people to a space outside modern historical time, attempt to consign distinct "populations" to a shared status as material resource, object, or static backdrop to the progressive time of modernity. In sections titled "Tundra Spirits" and "Eskimo Television," Yupik townspeople in Bethel, Alaska gather in "the village meeting hall where government experiments with satellites had brought the people old movies and broadcasts from the University of Alaska."[70] While marking the Yupik Eskimos' positioning as an audience to, or object of, transmissions enabled by government experiments—weather broadcasts and programs such as *Love, American Style*—these sections introduce an old Yupik woman and her younger accomplice, Rose, who have "realized the possibilities in the white man's gadgets."[71] As the TV screen flashes "satellite weather maps one after another," the old woman slides her finger across the glass, gathering

great surges of energy out of the atmosphere, by summoning spirit beings through recitations of the stories that were also indictments of the greedy destroyers of the land. With the stories the old woman was able to assemble powerful forces flowing from the spirits of the ancestors.[72]

Using "natural electricity. Fields of forces," her "plane-crashing spell" redirects these weather satellite transmissions to scramble the magnetic compasses on petroleum exploration companies' planes, causing them to crash.[73] "White people could fly circling objects in the sky that sent messages and images of nightmares and dreams, but the old woman knew how to turn the destruction back on its senders."[74]

"Eskimo Television" figures a networked communication technology and takes full advantage of the openness or "multistability" of technics[75] as well as of the heterogeneity of material spaces through which these technics are realized. It refuses the positioning of the Yupik Eskimos as a passive audience or object of these transmissions and the simultaneous objectification of the Alaskan tundra, which is described by an insurance adjuster working for the petroleum companies as "frozen wastes" with "no life," "nothing of value except what might be under the crust of snow and earth"—"oil, gas, uranium, and gold."[76] The narrator's reference to "circling objects in the sky" invokes the technological infrastructure that includes the speculators' planes, the communications satellites, the satellite weather maps on TV, and, more poignantly, their reliance on a deterritorializing logic of abstraction that instrumentalizes the spaces of the world. The old Yupik woman's "plane-crashing spell" challenges the former logic's claims to dematerialized abstraction by highlighting the continued reliance of the "circling objects" on electromagnetic energy (and, indirectly, on the petroleum these speculators are hoping to extract). It reveals that as material flows, these satellite transmissions, like other materially realized socio-spatial networks, cannot be controlled, canceled, or reduced to mere objects or a means to an end. Always exceeding their momentary instrumentalization, they remain material transmissions with untapped, unpredictable potentialities, as well.

Realizing that white Americans' computation-based satellite networks are not immaterial and realizing possibilities in their materiality unrealized by these capitalist flows, the old Yupik woman intercepts and channels the electromagnetic waves on which these satellite transmissions rely. Her understanding of material spaces as immanently generative and multipotent draws from the "tundra spirits," from Yupik knowledges and historical experience to realize unperceived "possibilities in the white man's gadgets." Aligning this unnamed Yupik woman with the untapped heterogeneity of material spaces, which she ingeniously exploits, "Eskimo Television" illustrates that material spaces are not mere "outcomes" of social relations with "no material effect" because the social is spatially constructed too, which means that material spaces have "unexpected consequences," and "effects on subsequent events that alter the future course of the very histories which have produced" them, as Massey describes the reiterative processes that underlie what she terms the "emergent powers" of the spatial.[77] The ongoing co-realization of socio-spatial networks in and through material spaces means that these networks are always subject to embedded histories and the dynamic, multiplicit force of materiality and other human and nonhuman agencies that enter into and work with and against specific cultural practices.

Subaltern Tactics of Reorientation

The "plane-crashing spell" in "Eskimo Television" is one of a series of material practices the novel depicts as subaltern strategies for reorienting and reimagining hegemonic material spaces and spatial practices that otherwise position those subjects as subordinate, as subaltern. The novel shares Ahmed's and other critical and new materialisms' interest in attending to spatial practices and the differential spatialization of bodies as lived "orientations" that are epistemologically *and* physically circumscribed and circumscribing. Ahmed stresses that "if we think of bodies and spaces as oriented, then we re-animate the very concept of space" and can take measure of its influence on both how we reside in space and how we perceive other subjects and our lifeworlds through the resulting material spaces and spatial differentiation.[78] Attentive to the productive work and influence of spatial practices on lived experience and physical movement in the world, Ahmed's postcolonial and queer engagement with a phenomenological conception of "orientation," as lived experience, addresses both "how spatial perceptions come to matter and be directed as matter."[79] Ahmed stresses that established "'orientations' depend on taking points of view as given," which foregrounds that the reorientation accomplished through emergent social spaces involves the recalibration and redirection of some of those habitual modes of relating to material spaces and to other subjects who co-realize those social spaces.[80] Space-making, therefore, involves what she describes as a "disorientation and reorientation" of the preexisting social space, of spatial understandings realized through technics, lived experience, and the social relations to which they habituate us.[81]

She underscores that those who are rendered "out of place" in hegemonic social spaces, such as the Yupik woman and many other subalterns in the novel, "have to secure a place that is not already given."[82] Such political work, which often entails using materially realized social space as "a disorientation device," "turn[s] the tables on the world that keeps things in place," "making things lose their place, which means the loss of coherence of a certain world."[83] From this perspective, it is possible to read "Eskimo Television" and see the Yupik woman's tactical reorientation of digital communication networks, which introduces electromagnetic interference or noise into the petroleum surveyor's flight compass, as reasserting the agency of the Yupik people and their knowledges and as a quite valuable "disorientation" of hegemonic, white American, spatially realized cultural values and material lifeworlds. It is a disorientation that changes understandings of how these "bodies" and cultures respectively "matter" within this social space. Notably, this section of the novel is one of several featuring violent ends to characters who exploit social spaces, spatial practices, material life, and other subjects to their own ruthless benefit, underscoring the novel's awareness of the high stakes, at once material and symbolic, in such radically unequal contests over material spaces and the sustenance they provide.

"Turning the destruction back on its senders" involves the introduction of some kind of interference into the very sociopolitical networks that otherwise reproduce biopower, networked spatial practices that are, thus, far from innocent or unmotivated. Reading this scene as a practice of "whiteout, a terrifying diffusion, or deterritorialization of whiteness," Eva Cherniavsky underscores how the old woman's practice can be understood to cast into relief hegemonic American spaces and the cultural and epistemological whiteness they help realize.[84] She argues that such methods of rendering whiteness and its cultural and epistemological specificity more tangible could serve as an important means to generate more critical perspectives on whiteness, stressing the value of such dis-orientations.

Since the September 11 attacks, these episodes in the novel and what I'm describing as tactics of disorientation likely raise new questions for readers. The distinction I draw between such tactics of disorientation and those of terrorism is that contrary to terrorist acts that attempt to generate unthinking terror and often target innocent civilians and inflict bodily harm, tactics of disorientation aim to prompt, however drastically and even traumatically, new perceptual and cognitive ways of seeing the world. This distinction is complicated by the growing variety of political acts currently described as terrorism, which, according to Title 22 of the U.S. Code, Section 2656f(d), involves "premeditated, politically motivated violence perpetrated against noncombatant targets by subnational groups or clandestine agents," and is, therefore, applied to widely varying political acts.[85] Though addressing the novel's view of all such political acts or the U.S. state's shifting legal designation of terrorism is beyond the scope of this chapter, it is important to note that the novel, in several ways, circumvents the reactionary, *oppositional* politics that drive much contemporary terrorism and also, frequently, many of the U.S. state's efforts to combat terrorism. In addition to the novel's diagnosis of hegemonic white America as a primary obstacle, there are white characters, such as Seese, a drug addict who loses her baby, and Root, who suffers a motorcycle accident that leads to his estrangement from his family, who undergo a "disorientation" due to these life traumas. Their "disorientations" eventually open onto a critical perspective on whiteness and neoliberal biopolitics, which leads them to realize the limits to those epistemological orientations in valuable ways, though not without a loss of their privileged social positioning.

The novel's key protagonists have all been, quite distinctly and diversely, rendered "out of place" in hegemonic social spaces spanning the American continent. They are, therefore, well described as subaltern, which is a category that is the by-product of subordinating practices, which confine a range of subjects to a relational, structural category that encompasses "the general attribute of subordination . . . whether this is expressed in terms of class, age, gender, or office, or in any other way," as Ranajit Guha of the Subaltern Studies Group defines this structural, not identitarian, term.[86] The novel's politics of subaltern "table-turning" involve a series of tactics of reorientation that change the way these cultures, epistemologies, and subjects "matter" within hegemonic social spaces. Their tactics all serve to disorient these dominant national and transnational socio-spatial formations by making the material processes and epistemological assumptions they rely on apparent and by exploiting their unacknowledged limits, thus realizing the vitality of variously "dead" spaces in this way.

As mentioned above, those subjects rendered "out of place," have to secure a place that is not already given through a tactical reorientation of hegemonic social space. The subaltern tactics of reorientation the novel proposes, like more recent tactical media practices in new media, involve "creative and/or subversive uses of communication technologies by those who don't usually get access to them," which serves as a "table-turning instance of drawing attention to power and its concocting language."[87] Importantly, when understood in light of this postcolonial context, such "table-turning" practices clarify how reorienting late capitalism's material spaces often serves to make the productive, ongoing, spatiotemporal power of its networks apparent. By situating hegemonic knowledges and socio-spatial practices both culturally and geographically, these tactical reorientations make hegemonic late capitalist spatial practices tangible and can help demarcate their un-acknowledged material, historical, and cultural limits. The latter move, I'd stress, provides important means to disorient hegemonic social and spatial practices and opens onto different ways of seeing and living and relating in the world for subalternized subjects and for those who join them to reorient key social spaces and spatial practices.

It is important to underscore that such "table-turning" challenges the very terms of materially realized social discourses and spatial practices rather than demanding recognition or directly opposing those discourses on their own terms. It is for this reason that Ahmed suggests that the table, in such instances, becomes a "disorientation device." Such tactics are comparable to what subaltern studies describes as an anticolonial practice of "writing in reverse" that is, notably, "inscribed in elite discourse."[88] By inverting hege-monic knowledges, or in Guha's terms, "writing in reverse," John Beverley stresses, "The subaltern represents the dominant subject to itself, and thus unsettles that subject in the form of a negation or displacement."[89] This is a practice that is interested, as is subaltern studies, in both "retrieving the presence of a subaltern subject and deconstructing the discourses that con-stitute the subaltern as such."[90] Importantly, such tactical "table-turning" and "writing in reverse," such as Calabazas's unsettling of the unquestioned value system supporting Eurocentric instrumental rationality by recasting it as "a blindness to the world," is both a demand for subalterns' social, po-litical, and economic recognition *and* an ingenious critique of (and hence refusal of) the very social, political, and economic terms within which that recognition and the rights that accompany it are imagined. Subalternity, the novel stresses, demands and requires that *the very terms* of the dominant discourses, which establish the category of a subaltern whose actual speech is disallowed, in Gayatri Spivak's terms, must be reoriented.[91] In the process, it is hoped, specific, hegemonic, spatially realized views of the world will be disoriented and perceived, even momentarily, to no longer cohere. *Almanac of the Dead*'s subaltern tactics of reorientation explicitly focus attention onto the spatial imaginaries and technic-based social spaces that set the terms for, and materially realize, the discourses and practices that position certain subjectivities as subaltern and others as elite, contributing to "a continual deconstruction of power relations" through such multileveled, tactical en-gagements with material spaces.[92]

Rather than representing the subaltern within the terms set in place by hegemonic discourses and their material spaces, such practices unsettle the very spatial imaginaries and affiliated epistemologies that, otherwise, resolidify distinctions between subaltern and elite, or dead and vital. The aim of "writing in reverse" is, thus, an unwriting of hegemonic knowledges and spatial orientations that underscores their contours, rhetorics, and infra-structure, by juxtaposition, and, thus, reveals their fatal limits and inability to encompass all the possibilities in the world. As practices of reorientation, these subaltern tactical media practices open onto other possibilities not ex-hausted through hegemonic discourses and material practices, insinuating this multistable potential, however ingeniously, into social systems that rely on subalterns' subordination and enforced silence and immobility.

Pre-occupied with Power

In the final section of the novel, "One World, Many Tribes," a coalition of subalterns assembles to "retake the land that had been stolen from them." The subalterns include tribal internationalists from across the Americas who join forces with an Army of the poor and homeless and ecowarriors to bomb a dam and, thereby, to cut off the supply of electrical power that sustains the economic and political infrastructure of the southwestern United States.[93] In the words of Awa Gee, the Korean hacker who infiltrates the information networks to accomplish the electrical shutdown, "the giants had become de-luded about their power. Because the giants were endlessly vulnerable, from their air traffic control systems to their interstate power-transmission lines. Turn off the lights and see what they'd do."[94] Somewhat spontaneously, these subalterns join together in a series of actions that contest their positioning as subordinate and its consequences. Many of the participants in this coali-tion share the experience of colonization, what Cherniavsky describes in an article that locates "Subaltern Studies in a U.S. Frame" as the United States' "systematic displacement of indigenous peoples and non-white labor."[95] Yet in spite of the differences in their modes of disenfranchisement, they see important commonalities that cross the categories of race, ethnicity, nation-ality, gender, class, religion, and distinct political platforms. These common-alities bring them together to confront the five-hundred-year system with the consequences of its socio-spatial networks: "the ecological destruction of the planet"; "the destruction of humanity itself" by poverty; and "the impos-sibility of the subsumption of populations, economies, nations, and cultures that it has been attacking since its origin and has excluded from its horizon and cornered into poverty."[96]

The novel's subalterns share key similarities with contemporary transnational networks of resistance, the "unexpected currents of opposition" emerging "from the transformed conditions created by transnationalization," as well as with more recent tactical media practices in new media.[97] In *Cyber-Marx: Cycles and Circuits of Struggle in High-Technology Capitalism*, Nick Dyer-Witheford notes that "capital's very success in creating for itself a worldwide latitude of action is dissolving some of the barriers that separated oppositional movements geographically," introducing "forms of work, dispossession, and struggle that were previously segregated."[98] In addition to the far from desirable "commonalities" resulting from "the global imposition of neoliberal policies," "capital's own diffusion of the means of communication has" "in creating the pathways for its own transnational circuit . . . unintentionally opened the routes for a global contraflow of news, dialogue, controversy, and support between movements in different parts of the planet."[99]

Importantly, one of the first groups to take tactical advantage of these emergent networks were the Zapatistas, now considered "the first information guerilla movement."[100] In 1994, the Zapatista Army of National Liberation staged an uprising against the Mexican government, deploying communications networks such as Peacenet and Usenet and the Internet to denounce "capitalist globalization as the culmination of a centuries-long dispossession of the people of Chiapas."[101] Silko herself speaks to the connections between her 1991 novel and the Zapatista uprising in 1994 in the essay "An Expression of Profound Gratitude to the Maya Zapatistas, January 1, 1994," in which she thanks the Zapatistas for realizing, within clear limits, the prophecies in her novel.[102] Since then, the Critical Art Ensemble and hacktivists such as the Electronic Disturbance Theater (EDT) have continued to use the Internet to disrupt government and corporate digital spaces using their FloodNet software to carry out denial-of-service attacks, some still targeting the Mexican government on behalf of the Zapatista movement. In her book on tactical media practices in new media art, Rita Raley analyzes how new media tactics respond to "the neoliberal condition in all its aspects (political, cultural, economic)," suggesting that "[a]ctivism and dissent, in turn, must, and do enter the network."[103]

The similarities between the novel's subaltern tactics of reorientation and what have since been defined as "tactical media practices" reveal how these shared political methods explicitly respond to recent shifts in capitalism's technics and topographies of power, although tactical methods also have a much longer history. The term "tactical media" was defined by the Next

Five Minutes (N5M) group to include "'all forms of old and new, both lucid and sophisticated media.'"[104] As Raley stresses, "tactical media" remains a "mutable category"; in "its most expansive articulation, tactical media signifies the intervention and disruption of a dominant semiotic regime, the temporary creation of a situation in which signs, messages, and narratives are set into play and critical thinking becomes possible."[105] Clearly quite consistent with the aims of the subaltern reorientating tactics envisioned in *Almanac of the Dead*, it is possible to identify quite a few additional similarities between the novel's and more recent tactical media practices. Addressing these notable overlaps underscores the role tactical engagements with digital technics and social spaces can play in opening up, quite literally unfolding, critical vantages on late capitalist social space and its contemporary modes of power, facilitating political disorientations (albeit with distinct methods, aims, and duration). It also clarifies the distinct contributions the novel's subaltern tactics of reorientation provide to this broader set of activities. *Almanac of the Dead* encourages the use of tactical media practices that provide crucial insight into how these dynamic, epistemologically and technologically informed relays, in fact, bring materiality and symbolic social practices together in distinct ways to realize social space and its lived orientations. The novel's and other comparative methods to tactically reorient the relations solidified by existing media practices and the social space they help realize might, in this way, help bring to the fore crucial dimensions to the material and technological unconscious of late capitalist space-making.

It is by exploiting their *misrecognition* or apparent nonidentity—a fortuitous product of white Europeans' "blindness to the world"—that the novel's subalterns are able to tactically reorient hegemonic material spaces and, thus, unsettle the spatiotemporal networks and power relations they secure. An "International Holistic Healers Convention," attended by several of the novel's key protagonists, is one of multiple tactical events leading up to their joint efforts to orchestrate the shutdown of the U.S. electrical grid. The convention, which provides commodified "tribal" wares to white, New Age yuppies, features several characters in stereotypical, racialized roles as indigenous "healers" and "spiritualists." Yet they also meet separately and redirect their revenues from late capitalist economic networks and material spaces, like the convention, to their own covert political project. Lecha and Zeta, Yaqui Indian mixed-blood twin sisters born in Sonora, Mexico, and now living outside Phoenix, willingly profit off their misrecognition, realizing that asserting a single, stable, positive cultural, racial, or ethnic identity feeds into the convention's late capitalist networks, which are only too eager to commodify historical experience and aestheticize "ethnic" identities for others' ideological and economic profit.

These subaltern tactics of reorientation are notably nonoppositional and explicitly refuse to put forward a particular identity or countermessage. Instead, these tactics of reorientation register the fact that contemporary modes of power are largely *immanent* to these digital technics and materially realized, networked social spaces. For this reason, these political methods are, themselves, devised to be immanent to the very socio-spatial practices they intend to reorient. These tactics, therefore, involve using these very emergent, late capitalist socio-spatial networks and other hegemonic social spaces to remap these same system processes and open onto other possibilities, however open-ended, short-lived, or aggregative their political acts may be. Similarly to more recent tactical media practices, such as the influential Occupy movements with their diverse coalitions only identified as the 99 percent, these tactical reorientations of material spaces serve to make the social, cultural, and epistemological agenda of the 1 percent tangible and visible. The Internet-based Occupy movements' momentary reclamation of public, material spaces serves to make apparent the resources and political power that has been stolen from the diverse, unnamed 99 percent, making the exclusion of the bulk of the U.S. population from the full benefits of this social space literal and tangible at these site-specific encampments. While the lack of a concrete, shared political program is often the basis for sustained critique of these political methods, it is worth reconsidering what the nonidentity of the 99 percent and the open-endedness of their platform, similarly to other recent tactical media practices, reveal about the nonoppositional workings of power in late capitalist, U.S. social spaces and what this suggests about political methods well-suited to this terrain. The nonidentity of the 99 percent significantly transformed the discourse and, likely, the results of the 2013 U.S. presidential election, while the encampments, long since relinquished to city officials and the ordinances they designed to prohibit such public gatherings, now appear to have been equally symbolic, yet no less forceful reverse "occupations."

The novel's diagnosis of late capitalist modalities and topographies of power anticipates these more recent tactical media practices: their immanence to the hegemonic code/spaces they intend to materially and symbolically reorient; the nonoppositional "table-turning" of spatially sedimented power they instigate; and the momentary, open-ended character of their political methods. The novel ends, for instance, before the results of the subaltern coalition's reorientation of the electrical grid unfold, reinforcing the ephemeral, uncertain, speculative aims and outcomes of tactical political methods that are often aimed at the "Next Five Minutes" (N5M), as the name of the Dutch group who coined the term "tactical media" foregrounds.

More importantly, perhaps, *Almanac of the Dead*'s own tactical media practices cast into relief the different, epistemologically and culturally distinct ways of connecting material and symbolic practices and spaces, and, thereby, of understanding and responding to late capitalism's ongoing re- and deterritorializing of social spaces, symbolic practices, and bodily space. Its close attention to the spatial logics that inform late capitalist networks suggests how tactical engagements with the technically facilitated relays between material places, social space, and physical bodies that, otherwise, serve to reinforce culturally and historically distinct epistemologies and to materially realize social power can encourage and allow us to comparatively register the epistemologies and social interests they serve and some of their blind spots. As mentioned in the introduction, *Almanac of the Dead* raises the question of how to align and ally ourselves with such space-making processes. It answers, in part, by underscoring what tactical media practices of reorientation can do when they take up and take on the relays linking material spaces, figurative practices, representational spaces, and networked social relations. It suggests that tactical media practices, in this way, can facilitate the perception of space-making and spatial practices as modes of material and symbolic orientation, thus opening onto other possibilities, other orientations, knowledges, and experiences of lived space.

In this way, the novel encourages the recognition and critical analysis of materialisms. It encourages readers to reexamine the relays residual and emergent technics establish between material spaces, social practices and their, at once, physical and symbolic lifeworlds for what they might require us to understand about materialities and social space. An encounter with discrepant materialisms is explicitly staged in the novel's depiction of Angelita La Éscapia, a Maya tribal leader, through her vexed relations to international Marxism (just prior to her participation with sisters Lecha and Zeta, the hacker Awa Gee, Clinton, and many others in a larger coalition to "retake the land"). Before joining forces with the other subalterns, Angelita practices her own tactic of reorienting hegemonic socio-spatial networks. She draws money from a network of international Marxist donors whom she wholly ironically calls "Friends of the Indians," to support her indigenous tribe's fight for the return of their land, rather than to promote international Marxism. She soon realizes that Bartolomeo, a Cuban Marxist leader, and his party have no interest in indigenous peoples' history or in returning their land. For this reason, Angelita eventually severs the tribe's ties to the Marxists and helps convince them to hang Bartolomeo for his "crimes against history," though she maintains their relations with the "friends of the Indians" so that they can surreptitiously buy weapons to protect the indigenous people on their march north to demand the return of their land.

This section of the novel encourages readers to distinguish between materialisms, which, if understood as culturally, technologically, and epistemologically distinct means of channeling energy, engender distinct kinds of spatiotemporal "networking" and social space. It underscores a crucial point of overlap and a distinction between Angelita and her tribe's and Marx's understanding of, and investment in, materially realized historical processes. Angelita explains that she respects Karl Marx, the man, who "had understood that the stories or 'histories' are sacred; that within 'history' reside relentless forces, powerful spirits, vengeful, relentlessly seeking justice," though she insists that "Marx got his notions of egalitarian communism" "from here . . . Marx stole his ideas from us, the Native Americans" and only imperfectly understood these ideas.[106] Angelita's materialism insists on the material *and* cultural historicity of spatial practices, the embedded cultural and geographical dimensions to the dynamic material processes that Marx was so adept at diagnosing. Reasserting the tribal history and geographically embedded cultural history that, she argues, remains unacknowledged by international Marxist understandings of dynamic, materially realized historical processes, Angelita redescribes her indigenous people's army as "tribal internationalists."[107]

Angelita's materialism underscores the spatial and historical oversights of a Eurocentric historical materialism that, in privileging time and differentiating it from space, facilitates the frequent reduction of the world to a single, apparently universal economic time line. In this way, the novel stresses that assumptions about materiality and its relation to social space directly enter into and impact our understanding of the *political* life these materially realized social and spatial relations might afford and foreclose. Aware of the political consequence of her tribe's understanding of materialism, Angelita's designation of the tribe as "tribal internationalists" links them to a distinct historical and material geography, while it also insists that, as internationalists, they remain open to the heterogeneity of material spaces, human cultures and practices, and nonhuman agencies. In this way, Angelita and the novel contravene the opposition between modern place and postmodern space that limits the social's relation to material places and its cultural meaning to these two, equally unsatisfactory options of (local) place and (global) space.

Underscoring how late capitalism and other hegemonic social spaces thrive off their narrow delimitation of the possible relations between cultural and material life, their hinging of cultural meaning and material spaces to realize specific relations, and not others, the novel's materialism allows it to redescribe and refuse the ideological link between people and territorial place consolidated in relation to the nation-state. The latter local, place-based identities often rely on essentialized, transhistorical cultural and/or ethnic identities.[108] Yet the novel also refuses late capitalism's abstraction of social relations from any necessary relation to historically or culturally meaningful material spaces, the supposed unhinging of late capitalist networks from material spaces in its "space of flows." Angelita's conception of "tribal internationalists," thus, reorients these two competing, similarly oppositional understandings of the relation between cultural and material life, which currently provoke all kinds of reactionary oscillations and interdependent desires for and against various kinds of global flows and local meaning, one of the problems Castells's work astutely identifies. This thread in the novel underscores how distinct materialisms inform social relations and resulting conceptions of the political, and circumscribe our recognition and appreciation of political agency (and who or what might yield it).

In this episode and elsewhere, the novel underscores the centrality of assessing the epistemological assumptions and spatiotemporal logics realized and furthered through dynamic material processes in late capitalist geographies. Insisting on the historicity, agency, and heterogeneity of material spaces, in particular, the novel's materialism reminds readers that rendering material bodies, life, and lived spaces dynamic, as late capitalist, U.S. biopower is so inclined to do, can extend, not critically disrupt, colonialist and imperialist spatial logics. Networking practices currently unfolding through bioinformatic sciences, for instance, animate material space at the scales both of lived bodies and of populations, yet they are frequently guided by logics of objectivity and mastery that continue to manipulate those spaces and people as a resource to the benefit of a very few. Animating space, seeing it as involved in a dynamic, materially realized temporal process, is not enough if it disregards the historicity and heterogeneity and agency of material bodies and physical geographies. Rendering material spaces and bodies more dynamic, as late capitalist technics and the disassembling and reassembling circulations preferred in the space of flows tend to do, in fact, can clearly feed directly into an intensified instrumentalization of these lived spaces. The risks involved in facilitating the latter, late capitalist de- and rematerializing tendencies, which intensify industrial capitalism's Cartesian spatial imaginaries and their biopolitical objectification and quantification of material life, is made quite clear in the novel by the company Biomaterials, Inc. The business is devised by a wealthy paraplegic, Trigg, who hopes to use it to further and fund scientific research that might enable him to regain the ability to walk. Getting impatient waiting for donors, Trigg decides to take matters into his own hands, killing homeless and poor people who, according to hegemonic, biopolitical logics, are already less "vital" to the U.S. nation and its social and economic interests, having already, actively been reduced to what Giorgio Agamben describes as "bare life."[109] Rendered liminal and subject to state-sponsored death, these people are easily perceived as biomaterial "objects" or resources that can serve to support the life of a lucky few. Such biopolitical practices reimagine material life as dynamic, manipulable, and unfolding in time, yet these flexible, late capitalist practices that secure U.S. biopower open onto a more thoroughgoing instrumentalization of lived spaces, not a recognition of the agency or complexity of life.

The "almanac of the dead" as/and an Enactive, Materially Realized Literary System

The novel's exacting juxtaposition of these competing materialisms in their capacity to realize lived experience and the possibilities of the world in distinct ways reveals the importance of devising methods able to comparatively register and reckon with the epistemologies that inform distinct material processes of space-making. The novel itself can be understood as a comparative media practice designed to tactically reorient the novel as a symbolic space of literary figuration in relation to the Native American, indigenous American, and subaltern social spaces, national political forms, symbolic and material imaginaries, material lifeworlds, and bodily experience print novels help to co-realize. *Almanac of the Dead* illustrates that such comparative media practices serve as one invaluable means to recognize these socio-spatial, biopolitical orientations and the material and social relations they open onto and actively foreclose. The novel's primary and most compelling answer to the question of how one might align and ally oneself with such materially realized space-making processes is provided by the "almanac of the dead" it both doubles and figures.

In explicitly linking its featured "almanac of the dead," as a figurative space, to the socio-spatial, subaltern networks this dynamic text helps solidify and realize, the novel reminds us that the literary system is itself already involved in space-making processes. Literary and other figurative spaces are crucial to imagining and materially embodying a sense of cultural and geographic, as well as textual, space. *Almanac of the Dead* tactically reorients its own novelistic, literary print narrative, reimagining its narrative as a spatio-temporal network that enters into and is transformed by these dynamic, materially embedded social relations. *Almanac of the Dead*'s engagements with extraliterary, social space-based material practices share key features with recent literary practices, such as locative media narratives, that are similarly distributed across physical and virtual and embodied physical spaces. The novel, in this way, reimagines the literary as a crucial means to reorient the very colonialist and imperialist spatiotemporal logics and social spaces the literary print novel frequently works to resolidify.

The "almanac of the dead" is a notebook of writings and glyphs containing the stories of all "the days and years" of the tribes of the Americas. The almanac comes to be understood as a dynamic means of channeling energy, as a material network that does much more than passively figure these social relations. The pages of the almanac are believed to hold "many forces within them, countless *physical* and spiritual properties to guide the people and make them strong."[110] Journeying north with four young Indian slaves fleeing European slavery, this "bundle of pages and scraps of paper with notes in Latin and Spanish" eventually makes its way to Lecha and Zeta's grandmother, old Yoeme, who then leaves it in their care.[111] The circulation of the ancient almanac, its spatiotemporal movement, helps consolidate a network of social relations. The almanac's journeying evidences a logic of flows or exchange that is premised on the mutual transformation of the almanac and the social relations it embeds rather than a circulation premised on the stability or essential identity of the almanac. The almanac bears witness to its material and figurative transformation as a result of these spatiotemporal movements. It is torn, illegible in places, there are notes scribbled in the margins, and "whole sections had been stolen from other books and from the proliferation of 'farmer's almanacs' published by patent drug companies."[112] Also, "There was evidence that substantial portions of the original manuscript had been lost or condensed into odd narratives which operated like codes."[113] The narratives act as codes that must be transcribed by Lecha and Zeta, who are typing the pages of the almanac into the computer. Importantly, this process of transcription is a process of transformation. Adding the first entry in English and a number of highly idiosyncratic personal notes, Lecha reinterprets the almanac from her own spatiotemporal perspective and, thereby, transforms the almanac or, more precisely, resituates it in the present just as she rematerializes the almanac by typing it into the computer.

This process of transcription, like other immanent, generative practices in the novel, is imagined as a means of channeling energy and explicitly likened to Lecha's abilities as a psychic. Originally believing that the power she had to locate the bodies of the dead, abilities she exploits with great success on the television talk show circuit, is as an "intermediary," Lecha soon realizes that "the concept of intermediary and messenger was too simple."[114] She cannot "cut off the channel" of the flows of energy that link her to the dead, yet she is not a mere medium, either.[115] When a cable-television producer's girlfriend enlists Lecha to exact revenge against her former lover, she begins

> to see patterns in the lives of the cinematographer and his immediate family. Their lives were stories-in-progress, as Lecha saw them, and . . . she would realize possible deadly turns the lives of the cinematographer and his close relatives might naturally take.[116]

As a process of identifying patterns in their lives, storytelling comes to be seen as an enactive means of realizing possibilities in the world, not passively or neutrally recording them.

Lecha notes that her grandmother, old Yoeme, and others believed that the almanac had a "living power within it, a power that would bring all the tribal people of the Americas together to retake the land," a prophecy that the subalterns in the novel appear to realize.[117] The almanac is vital in that it relies on, draws from, and both materially and physically extends the networks of socio-spatial relations that it materially instantiates and, thereby, refigures. "Those old almanacs," Lecha insists, "don't just tell you when to plant or harvest, they tell you about the days to come—drought or flood, plague, civil war or invasion. . . . Once the notebooks are transcribed, I will figure out how to use the old almanac. Then we will foresee the months and years to come—everything.[118] The almanac's narrative is, thus, a catalyst for Lecha and Zeta's ongoing, dynamic process of rearticulating their relation to the past, which enables their construction of a future that is, as the Five Hundred Year Map suggests, "encoded in arcane symbols and old narratives."[119] This is a generative process through which these cultural networks and their material spaces are rerealized and continually, if subtly, reoriented. The novel itself continues this reiterative process through its addition of a wide range of subaltern and elite characters' notebooks, journals, diaries, and histories, which have, apparently, made their way through the almanac's narrative and transformed it.

Reimagining storytelling as a means of channeling energy spatiotemporally, as a socio-spatial network that produces an understanding of material space and materially instantiates the epistemologies and spatial relations it figures through its figurative space and its circulation, "the almanac of the dead" counters Eurocentric print cultures and the colonialist, imperialist, and masculinist spatial imaginaries they resolidify. It rejects representational understandings of mimesis as a secondary, subsequent, merely symbolic imitation of the "real," which severs these ongoing, co-productive relays between material and symbolic spaces, medium and meaning, space and time. It refuses this view of texts as spatially and temporally separate from the social and historical processes in which they participate, associating that representational logic with European hegemony.[120]

Modeled on three surviving Azteca codices, the almanac's spatial form instead operationalizes its spatial and temporal dimensions equally, somewhat as a calendar does. Described as "loose squares of the old manuscript" bundled together with pages of notes, the unbound pages of the almanac function as a multiplicity of spaces that are not subjugated to a single narrative chronology or temporal progression. Acknowledging a multiplicity of spaces, the almanac's spatial form does not subjugate the spatiality of the text to a universalized, abstract, figurative meaning. Yet its spatial form does not solidify these spaces as absolute locations and, thus, disavow their temporality, either. Each page's meaning is a product of spatial relations that change as the almanac is transcribed and reinterpreted. The almanac operates, in other words, according to a logic of transcription that is constrained and enabled by existing spaces, by the material existence of the pages, but not determined by them. Yoeme tells Lecha and Zeta that "nothing must be added [to the almanac] that was not already there. Only repairs are allowed," which seems a blatant contradiction when we find out Yoeme included an account of her survival of the influenza epidemic of 1918 within the almanac's pages.[121] Yet her insistence on "repairs only" foregrounds the almanac's logic of transcription, which requires that one draw from, rather than blindly add onto, the existing pages, respecting the historicity of the social relations embedded and unfolding from there.

The networked, subaltern coalition that emerges at the end of the novel in "One World, Many Tribes" rerealizes the recombinatory spatial imaginary the almanac and its material space encode. This subaltern coalition emerges through an ongoing encounter between distinct and overlapping cultural networks—such as the "tribal internationalists," the "Army of the Poor and Homeless," and "ecowarriors"—that are spatiotemporally situated and materially embedded in, but not determined by, material spaces. Acknowledging space as "a sphere of coexisting heterogeneity," these social relations, like the pages of the almanac, are perceived to participate in a continual process of reelaborating their relations to material spaces and the cultural consequence of these relations, and of responding to the heterogeneity they there encounter.[122] The transformation of material spaces and the social formations they realize is imagined as a process that draws from and reworks existing socio-spatial formations, as a process that is materially enabled and constrained, though not determined by its history.

Playing out the potential of generative space-making technics and the kinds of cross-cultural relations and engagements with the heterogeneity of material spaces they might allow, *Almanac of the Dead* reveals how tactically allying ourselves with space-making processes and registering the distinct relays between material spaces, cultural practices, and subjectivities they realize provides a crucial means to intervene in hegemonic material spaces and the power geometries they would like to rerealize. Through this oblique angle on late capitalism's dynamic, computation-based networks and social spaces, the vital is redescribed as this very reciprocity between what are more often defined, differentiated, and capitalized upon in oppositional terms as living and dead, material and symbolic, spatial and temporal, animate and inanimate.

In response to the question of how to align and ally oneself with such space-making processes and to what ends, the novel's tactics of reorientation encourage greater attention be paid to the epistemologies informing and rerealized through shifting technics and their practices of re- and dematerializing social spaces. Its tactic of networking suggests how these technics of space-making might also open onto alternative epistemologies and understandings of materialities and their relation to social life. The subalterns' reorienting practices register dynamic, generative processes of space-making and, thus, open up the possibility of materially situated, yet dynamic cultural practices that might exploit these co-productive relations between material and cultural to different ends than late capitalist networks. The novel's tactical networking practices, conceived as means of channeling energy, reveal that space-making processes are processes of *re*orientation as the material forces that social formations engage always precede and exceed such processes. "Human life spans weren't much," Calabazas's old aunt Mahawala notes before she passes on.[123] These subaltern tactics to reorient hegemonic, late capitalist socio-spatial formations according to multiple, alternate, even discrepant spatiotemporal cultural imaginaries and practices underscores the potential and importance of recognizing the lively and deadly material and social dimensions of space-making realized through distinct technics. Once space-making processes are understood and engaged as ongoing, materially realized, open-ended socio-spatial practices, they might enable social formations that are cognizant of, and ultimately more responsive to, the varied consequences and potentialities of the material and historical processes in which they participate. Such dynamic, yet historically and materially situated social networks might enable one to register and revalue the ongoing contests taking place through spaces and to understand the changing "power geometries" that work through material spaces as they regularly, however subtly, shift. It is important to remember that these radically unequal contests are frequently characterized by what Anna Tsing describes as "friction: the awkward, unequal, unstable, and creative qualities of interconnection across difference," "heterogeneous and unequal encounters [that] can lead to new arrangements of culture and power."[124] Understanding digital technics, as they enter into and recode material spaces, as entailing processes of reorientation and disorientation reveals their potential to hinge material and cultural praxis in other ways and might serve to acknowledge the processes through which cultural meaning is embedded and transformed through its material histories.

The "almanac of the dead" is imagined, I suggest, as a kind of distributed, materially realized, enactive literary system, not wholly unlike more recent locative media narratives and augmented reality storytelling that unfold their site-specific, computation-based narratives through highly contingent relays between specific material and social spaces, individual and collaborative bodily experiences, and computational processes. Locative media artist and theorist Teri Rueb describes the emergence of "narrative works in locative media . . . that begin to explore storytelling forms and conventions that specifically exploit the highly indeterminate interaction of place, time, narrative, and the mobile body of the participant," in direct contrast to the more usual [augmented-reality] audio tour in which "place is understood as a noun"[125] Quite similarly to the "almanac of the dead," Rueb's and other place-based narratives often "approach 'place' as a verb, 'movement' as a highly indeterminate choreography, and 'point of view' as radically multiplied, fragmented, fluid, and unstable."[126] Rueb stresses how "the narrative and its structure and meaning emerge from and are dependent on the interaction of participant, place, time, and social context." In this way, locative media narratives are similarly well poised to tactically explore orientations toward lived space at multiple, interrelated, material and symbolic levels. In fact, distributed locative narratives using mobile digital media to explore socio-spatial orientations and lived bodily space paradoxically rely on GPS-based technologies and their absolute, Cartesian space. One might, therefore, argue that when these GPS-based digital media are used to develop alternate understandings and perceptions of spatiotemporal, multimodal, and culturally and experientially thick understandings and experiences of social space and its spatiotemporal orientations, they are similarly enlisted in a kind of tactical reorientation. At the very least, it is worth inquiring into the potential of such enactive, materially realized literary systems to cast lived spaces into relief.

Within this unfolding context, *Almanac of the Dead* recommends tactical engagements with past and present media as a crucial means to comparatively track emergent and familiar relays between material spaces, embodied orientations, computational processes, social discourses, and their imaginaries. Its renewed materialism, in turn, encourages close attention is paid to the heterogeneity of material spaces, not in their productive, valued, instrumentalized "life" but in their vexing multipotentiality, resistance, lively historicity, and other, unpredictable, at times deadly agencies. Its politics requires such ongoing grappling with this multipotentiality of the world, reflection on and ethical responsibility for the possibilities for engaging material spaces realized and unrealized, as well as an awareness of larger historical and material processes of which humans are only a minor part. As I've tried to suggest, this both enables and requires a reconsideration of the relations to material spaces and to intersubjective social relations such literary and other tactical spatial practices open onto and their consequence to how we might think about politics and agency as they enter into and are transformed through these long-standing networks.

4 / Counting on Affect: Engaging Micropractices of the U.S. Nation

This chapter continues to consider how emergent digital technics, as material practices, impact spatiotemporal understandings of, and orientations to the U.S. nation-state and its lived space. It shifts its focus and scale, slightly, to address digital technics that are as crucial to national reproduction as are the networked social formations and social spaces in the previous chapter, yet less noticeable as they enter into the most everyday "bodily" life of the nation: micropractices of farming, eating, cooking, sexuality, family planning, and reproductive technology. While these material micropractices are transformed by many of the same transnational, biotechnological networking practices of late capitalism scrutinized by *Almanac of the Dead*, they raise a slightly different set of questions and insights into how technics are materially realized through the nation's lived space and how the U.S. nation-state is impacted by these emergent practices. In particular, the transformative impact of bioinformatic sciences' combination of information science, mathematics, and genetics on what has been conceived as the private, interior life of the body politic—on its domestic spaces, its families, its citizens' and non-citizens' bodies—underscores the continued implication of these private, domestic, feminized bodily spaces in the supposedly distinct, public circulations of capital and closely affiliated U.S. state power.

As suggested in the previous chapter, U.S. nationalism is directly involved in an ongoing co-production of the boundaries between private and public spaces and between a series of associated bodily, geographic, and imaginary boundaries between insides and outsides that inform the nation's preferred modes of interrelation. In fact, far from guarding or protecting the sanctity of what are often perceived to be preexisting private spaces, U.S. nationalism has been continually, though differently, concerned with managing these private, interior spaces. Since the 1980s, for instance, we've witnessed the emergence of a terribly lively "intimate public sphere," as Lauren Berlant argues.[1] This is just one moment in a much longer history of sentimental nationalist discourses, which reveal that domestic space, sexuality, and American citizens' "private" familial and emotional life are explicitly co-realized through distinct state formations, nationalist imaginaries, and flows of capital, not outside them.

What is the impact, then, of shifting technicities and their technical recalibration of the biological at this micro scale? How do these material practices enter into the processes the nation-state uses to differentiate between a series of gendered and racialized bodily and discursive insides and outsides at the level of subjects, family, community, and national bodies? At first glance, late capitalism's flexible, transnational networks and biotechnologies of food production, distribution, and reproductive sciences apparently contravene U.S. nationalism's colonialist practices. The nation-state relies on the continual, absolute differentiation between the nation's inside and outside at geopolitical, imaginary, subjective, and physical levels and has preferred to imagine the nation as a self-contained space impervious (at least symbolically) to time. In contrast, emergent digital technicities have been both celebrated and bemoaned since the 1990s for their tendencies to disregard such national political and geographic territories, opening onto transnational modes of belonging and political action and new kinds and degrees of capitalist exploitation due to their dynamic information-based networks and remarkable reach. Less obviously, at the micropractical scale, emergent digital technics also facilitate traffic across the nation's designated insides and outsides. Biotechnologies and biomedicine traverse former boundaries between human and animal in their use of genetic sciences and information sciences to modify organisms to facilitate food production (genetically modified and transgenic organisms or tissue-cultured meats, for instance); in their "enhancements" of both animal and human reproduction through biotechnological interventions of multiple kinds (synthetic hormones, cloning, in vitro fertilization); and in their transfer of organs, genetic materials, and other biological products across what were previously thought to be unpassable racial or species lines. The distinctions between human and nonhuman, nevertheless, remain central to U.S. nationalist rhetorics and practices, which continue to rely on the inclusion and exclusion of nonhuman animals and to deploy those differences in gendering and racializing human subjects by aligning them (in distinct ways) with the liminal space along this charged border between human and nonhuman animals.

Influential strains of cultural theory, grappling with new practices and modalities of power, stress that neoliberal capitalism is absolutely intent on overriding modern, oppositional, colonialist dualisms of inside and outside, human and nonhuman animal in favor of a relentless, dynamic pursuit and production of increasingly fine degrees and experiences of difference on which it intends to capitalize. In light of capital's own penchant for deconstructing oppositional dualisms, such theories suggest the need to recalibrate our political methods. As Jeffrey Nealon argues, in the contemporary "post-postmodern" moment, cultural theorists' deconstruction of oppositions seems to be largely beside the point as those methods seemingly play right into late capitalism's preferred circulatory logics.[2] Yet one catch in this line of thinking is the remarkable persistence, if not intensification, of somewhat modified colonialist and imperialist logics and practices of delineating insides and outsides in the operations of the U.S. nation-state. How are we to understand the apparent disconnect between the nation-state's political and material forms of reproduction and the late capitalist material practices in which they are, equally, implicated?

It seems crucial to inquire into this question to consider how U.S. nationalism, in fact, recalibrates its colonialist, oppositional material practices and discourses of national insides and outsides, belonging and exclusion in direct relation to material micropractices realized through emergent, biotechnologies and broader late capitalist networks. This apparent disconnect of U.S. nationalism's oppositional logics from late capitalism's dynamic transnational flows can be usefully reformulated by a systems-theoretical perspective that attends to the *processes* through which U.S. nation-states engage such emergent material technics to co-realize a series of bodily boundaries. A systems-theoretical, posthumanist perspective, as mentioned in chapter 2, attends to the recursive, ongoing processes through which self-contained subjects, objects, and other spatiotemporal relations are co-produced and, in this way, circumscribed and rendered legible. This approach reminds us that such oppositional distinctions are, nonetheless, all about system *relations*. A demarcation of the nation's imagined community's inside and outside, for instance, not only serves to solidify the boundaries defining and, thus, separating subjects and objects, insides or outsides, or social systems and their nonhuman environments. In fact, once these distinctions are understood as ongoing, recursive processes of differentiation, it is possible to see how political systems such as the nation-state perform such distinctions both to instantiate a degree of closure and, simultaneously, to circumscribe the distinct kinds of openness, interconnections, or circulations that are possible in light of that distinction or circumscribed closure. Processes of objectification, for instance, carry out a distinction and circumscription (differentiating object from subject, for instance), yet this distinction serves to *facilitate* an openness to certain kinds of exchange, circulation, and substitution and to foreclose other kinds of movements and interactions rather than simply identifying or delineating a stable boundary or thing. This perspective usefully shifts questions away from the relative closure or openness of these shifting national, familial, and individual bodies to, instead, attend to how material technics *both* circumscribe and interconnect nations, intersubjectivities, and human and nonhuman animals' bodily life at multiple scales. U.S. nationalism's processes of circumscribing the nation's bodily life since the end of the twentieth century, I will suggest, are far from novel, yet its specific modes of dynamically redifferentiating a series of bodily insides and outsides and, thus, facilitating certain kinds of interaction, recognition, consumption, circulation, and belonging while actively discouraging or disavowing others are well worth registering.

To pursue the questions raised by late twentieth- and early twenty-first-century U.S. nationalisms, I draw on Ruth L. Ozeki's influential 1998 novel, *My Year of Meats*,[3] which directly addresses shifts in U.S. nationalism accompanying transnational digital technics and insightfully encourages close attention be paid to the material micropractices or "meat" of the U.S. nation's ongoing colonialist and imperialist reproduction. The novel's inquiries into materially realized, emergent technics informing micropractices of food production and consumption, reproduction, sexuality, and human and nonhuman animal relations are directly linked to several closely interrelated shifts at multiple scales in the U.S. nation-state and its political economy. The novel explores these shifting technicities by registering their direct, disturbing impact on the nation's bodily life, the private, interior, feminized spaces of its citizens and their family life and the physical environment and nonhuman animals on which the former lived spaces rely. The novel, thus, insists that these broader geopolitical and biotechnological shifts play themselves out at this most intimate space of people's everyday life with particularly strong effects on the bodies and lives of women and differently minoritized subjects who are often already positioned as the objects, labor, or medium for carrying out the nation's material practices and, thus, enabling its reproduction.

The narrative's key protagonist is Jane Takagi-Little, a Japanese American filmmaker hired to help a U.S. beef company with their television series, *My American Wife!* The television show is designed to sell American beef to a Japanese audience by aligning it with American abundance and pure, wholesome values.[4] The immediate historical context for such transnational beef exports was the removal, in 1991, of Japan's quota on U.S. beef imports, and shifting U.S.-Japanese relations at this time that, as Emily Cheng stresses in her analysis of the novel, attempted to open new inroads into Japanese markets for the transnational circulation of American products and values, amid continuing American anxieties about the growing power of Japan's, among other Asian countries', economic growth.[5] The novel directly connects this shift in U.S. transnational hegemony and the U.S. beef industry's material practices of production and consumption to the biotechnological innovations enabling the emergence of confined feedlot and factory farms that vastly increased the number of cattle that could be produced in a small space through the use of antibiotics and other mid to late twentieth-century biotech, such as the synthetic, man-made nonsteroidal estrogen, diethylstilbestrol (DES). DES played a related, transformative role in facilitating factory farms and their massive production of cattle by fattening them up more quickly and chemically castrating the males (at least those not chosen for their reproductive value). This same hormone was prescribed to pregnant American women in the post–World War II era, after scientists at the Harvard Medical School published research claiming it could prevent miscarriages, which led to the widespread use of DES to "facilitate" pregnancy. It was not until 1971 that it was banned from this use after in utero exposure to DES was linked to a rare form of vaginal cancer in these women's children.[6] The novel explicitly aligns this reproductive biotechnology, given to both pregnant American women and cattle, to the emergent transnational capitalist digital networks of production and consumption within which Jane's television program, her life, Japanese American relations, and the sustenance and health of their nations' citizens are complexly intertwined.

Living with the consequences of her Japanese American mother having been prescribed DES, which led to Jane's uterine troubles and apparent infertility, Jane devises a feminist, Japanese American, and multicultural project to query and intervene in shifting biotechnological micropractices of the nation as they both reproduce and unsettle former colonialist modes of U.S. nationalism. She attempts to use the "BEEF-EX" television program, and its transnational networks of beef production and consumption, to challenge and recast the gendered and racialized logics the U.S. nation uses to differentiate between "authentic" and "inauthentic" Americans. Jane intends to rescript their positioning of women as the "meat," that is, as the literally and symbolically passive medium of national reproduction. Over the course of the novel, Jane seeks out these and other means to tactically reorient emergent, transnational capitalist networks of production and consumption, taking political advantage of late capitalism's apparent embrace of cultural, racial, and ethnic difference, while redirecting it to her own ends. She intends to divert late capitalism's nonoppositional logics to reimagine the U.S. nation in multicultural, feminist terms that are willing to register and value the very cultural, ethnic, and racial difference that is one outgrowth of the U.S. nation-state's violent colonial and imperial history.

Through this emphasis on material micropractices such as farming, eating, cooking, reproductive and family planning, sexuality, music, and personal narrative, the novel attempts to register the role that everyday material technics play in reproducing citizens' and the nation's lived space. The novel explores the influence of shifting biotechnology and its global flows on the nation's realization of gendered and racialized bodies, family, sexuality, community, and other lived spaces. Interested in how the spatial orientations and lived spaces U.S. nationalism realizes might be encouraged to play themselves out differently, the novel aligns itself with other contemporary transnational feminisms and what Françoise Lionnet and Shu-Mei Shih describe as "minor transnationalisms."[7] Minor transnationalisms, they suggest, pursue global capitalist networks' potential to facilitate new modes of international solidarity, activism, and information-sharing across national boundaries, while they are also fully aware of the highly problematic neoliberal economic practices on which these networks thrive. *My Year of Meats* underscores some of the risks in transnational feminist practices, which can unwittingly reduplicate the colonialist and imperialist logics of the former networks, especially when they uncritically rely on nationalist discourses of love and belonging.

My Year of Meats reapproaches these global capitalist networks as they play themselves out in the most minor of everyday micropractices. It locates the influence and power of these micropractices in their ability to embed and rerealize material technics that play a central, often unnoticed role in generating and reinforcing distinct forms and categories of life. Such micropractices, at this minor scale, help to realize spatial relations that, in Sara Ahmed's terms, instantiate physical, epistemological, and social "orientations" to the world. The novel illustrates how everyday micropractices rely on *and* actively rerealize, through their technics, distinct interrelations between the "subjects," "objects," and "worlds" these practices recursively circumscribe. Importantly, these processes are largely unrecognized and un-derappreciated, unfolding as they do as a kind of embedded and embedding "paratext" that subtends the resulting categories of life and their spatiotem-poral and social relations, which we, then, come to take for granted. Nigel Thrift develops his concept of paratexts in the context of his work on the "background time-spaces" of electronic networks and their computational modes of address.[8] He uses the concept to address the "world of 'pre'-ideas," the "utterly mundane frameworks that move 'subjects' and 'objects' about," describing paratexts as "'invisible' forms which structure how we write the world but which generally no longer receive attention because of their utter familiarity. Like the set up of the page, indexes, footnotes, and the rest of the paraphernalia of written thinking, they have become a kind of epistemic wallpaper."[9]

Conceiving materially realized technics at this scale as paratextual appa-rati, I intend to address how the technics informing and realizing the U.S. nation's micropractices serve as an embedded and embedding substrate for its ongoing reproduction and calculation of distinct forms and modes of life and their intermingling, over and against a much more complex set of potentialities. Micropractices of U.S. national reproduction, such as farm-ing, cooking, eating, family planning, and sexuality, from this perspective, participate in the "utter mundanity of this second nature which is also an inescapability: these items . . . [,] through their recursivity guarantee the re-cursivity of the world," though they also, notably, "require continuous effort to keep going."[10] Similarly to the television program *My American Wife!* that Jane directs, the persuasive power of paratextual apparati is in their enactive performance as much as in their explicitly stated meaning or content, per se. Jane ironically comments on the television show's lack of content other than as an advertisement for the beef industry, stating, "Meat is the Mes-sage."[11] As the novel progresses, Jane's riff on Marshall McLuhan's phrase "the Medium is the Message"[12] is further elaborated upon to suggest that the ideological and material force of micropractices of farming, cooking, eating, and sexuality is solidified and realized through their performance. In other words, these materially realized technics operate as embedded paratextual apparati that preform the way the world is engaged by circumscribing and realizing distinct categories of life and their perceived similarities and dif-ferences, and the social relations and actions open to various subjects and objects in this micropolitical second nature of the nation-state.

My Year of Meats explores the influence of distinct material mic256prac-tices as paratextual apparati that are central to U.S. nationalism's differentiation and categorization of populations, forms, and modes of life and their acceptable and unacceptable interrelations. It suggests that the spatiotemporal distinctions realized through these paratextual technics are materially embedded in practices of food production, cooking, consumption, sexuality, family, and narrativity, as well as in more obvious, official institutions of national life such as economic networks, communications, or novels. Comparatively working to document a range of U.S. nationalism's unacknowledged paratextual practices, the novel explores how such processes, at the level of material bodies and lived space, technically realize boundaries that encourage certain kinds of identification and disidentification, belonging and exclusion, proximity and distance, love and aversion. Once reconceived as paratextual practices, the nation-state's material technics begin to be understood as crucial relays reinforcing the nation's affective economies—the national love, ambivalence, and hate that render boundaries between a variety of insides and outsides quite distinctly charged and, which work hard to encourage and discourage distinct kinds of interrelation through their reinforcement of specific species, gender, and racial lines. In her early work on *The Cultural Politics of Emotion*, Sara Ahmed underscores that "feelings do not reside in subjects and objects, but are produced as effects of circulation."[13] Her work describes how the emotions of national love or hate circulated through such affective economies "create the very effect of the surfaces and boundaries that allow us to distinguish an inside and outside in the first place," reconsolidating or contesting the boundaries of the national body and its gendered, racialized, and classed insiders and Others.[14]

Drawing on *My Year of Meats*'s inquiries and extending the prior chapter's perspective on how technics, as material practices, help to coordinate and co-realize social relations in and through lived space, I will consider how U.S. nationalism's material micropractices embed a set of material, discursive, and affective orientations into the nation's lived space at the micro scale of people's and nonhuman animal's bodily life and communities. Ways of farming, eating, having sex, cooking, communicating, and reproducing family life are affectively charged sites at which national discourses and practices engender certain kinds of interrelations and establish key distinctions between forms and modes of life, directing desire or ambivalence toward certain objects or kinds and away from others and, thus, materially reinforcing a sense of belonging through shared practices and proximity, or one of exclusion or incommensurable difference through a distancing and disgust. As a crucial site at which the boundaries of the human are materially realized and co-articulated with nationalism's hegemonic epistemologies and modes of categorizing life, material micropractices are primary to understanding the impact of digital technics on modern nationalism's gendered and racialized distinctions between inside and outside, human and nonhuman, private and public and the kinds of intersubjective relations they implicitly authorize and rerealize.

My Year of Meats documents the micropractices subtending the U.S. nation-state's affective economy of national belonging and desire, paying close attention to the paratextual logics and orientations they rerealize. The novel identifies material micropractices as a site to register shifting technicities and modes of nationalist belonging *and* as a site from which it might be possible to rescript and reorient U.S. nationalism and, in this way, to open onto other categories of life and modes of interrelating and belonging. It is interested in the micropolitical potential of corporeal intimacies of eating, sex, family life, and interspecies relations—as a result of their embodied, visceral, affective force—as sites at which American nationalism might be unsettled and redirected, not just resolidified.

Similarly to the aims of other recent Asian American "novels," as Lisa Lowe describes them, *My Year of Meats* rethinks the hegemonic national cultural form of the novel as a means to search out and "explore other modes of telling, revealing, and spatializing history."[15] It redeploys the genre of the novel, and affiliated paratextual technics essential to the U.S. nation's colonialist and imperialist categorizations of Asian and other nonwhite subjects, to reveal their grisly, violent underside from the perspective of Jane, her mother, and other Asian Americans, Mexican Americans, and black Americans in the novel. It stresses how the paratextual logics informing the most everyday micropractices of eating, cooking, sex, reproduction, or novel-reading can implicitly circumscribe and realize certain kinds of "life" and social relations at the expense of others whose losses remain unregistered by official national discourses. The novel, in turn, experiments with a series of alternate, paratextual technics revealing "the possibility of alternate modes for historical retrieval and recollection at the very level of the form in which they are written and conceived," an opportunity and pursuit Lowe aligns with other recent Asian American novels.[16] As I'll suggest, *My Year of Meats* carries out its rewriting of U.S. national history from the bottom up, from the perspective of women and nonelites, quite literally aiming its interventions at the material practices and paratextual technics key to U.S. nationalism, including its own paratextual operations as a novel.

Close attention to the novel's own idiosyncratic paratexts, in addition to its central narrative, complicates readers' views on Jane's initial feminist and multicultural project of reorienting global capitalist networks through her strategically feminist, queer, and multicultural TV program. The immigration of one of Jane's Japanese female viewers, Akiko, to America near the close of the novel initially appears to signal a triumphant, transnational feminist reorientation of late capitalist networks. Instead, I'll suggest Jane's initial project might best be viewed as a failed, perhaps aborted project in the novel's view in that it falls prey to transnational American feminism's underscrutinized engagements with multicultural, national love. The novel was initially embraced and/or strongly critiqued for its vision of transnational feminist networks between the United States and Japan, networks that are fueled in the novel by a distinctly multicultural American national love. Readings of the novel such as David Palumbo-Liu's impressive "Rational and Irrational Choices: Form, Affect, and Ethics" identify its concern with affect and global capitalist networks, yet overlook the significance of the novel's rethinking of and engagement with other visceral, intercorporeal intermingling and intimacies between bodies, not simply this privileged narrative of multicultural feminist love.[17] As I'll suggest, *My Year of Meats* places noticeable attention on the affectively charged, bloody, disturbing dimensions to Jane's experience, which exceed and linger over her attempts to narrativize the complex interrelations between U.S. nationalism, meat, race, women, and nonhuman animals.

These relays between U.S. nationalism, shifting material technics, and affect shed light on the novel's insights into the more complex, thoroughgoing, and troubling relays through which late capitalist networks and the shifts they introduce into biotechnological practices such as industrial food production and reproductive technologies and communication technologies viscerally impact micropractices of eating, sex, racialization, gendering, family, and desire. As I'll illustrate, *My Year of Meats* explores shifting technics as a means to reorient American nationalism's dominant affective economy and, in this way, to generate new modes of living, new ways of linking and inhabiting bodies, texts, human and nonhuman animals, lifeworlds, and national and transnational communities. It attempts to align American nationalism's affective economies of desire with a significantly different, multicultural, multiracial, queer national and transnational sense and to direct disgust toward nationalism's patriarchal, racist, heterosexist, meat-eating imaginary. As crucially, it raises unanswered, haunting questions about any such project to direct bodily life and its affective charge toward immediate political ends, any such attempt to count on affect to circumscribe and recapture life.

Registering the visceral impact of technics on individual, social, and national bodies and their modes of relation, *My Year of Meats* raises the question of how feminist minor transnationalisms can register and engage emergent national and transnational micropractices to open onto more ethical and enjoyable modes of life. It identifies affectively charged micropractices of eating, sex, family, and interspecies relations as sites where we might register emergent modes of life, and, potentially, alter the paratextual practices that guide relations between, and ethical understandings of, these. It also forces a consideration of what limits there may be to playing on nationalist logics of desire and disgust, underscoring the continued need to critically examine these charged relays between U.S. nationalism, technics, affect, and their gendered, racialized, and speciesist elaborations on forms of life and their intermingling.

Minor Transnationalisms

Focusing on the relations between Jane Takagi-Little, a biracial television producer, her abhorrent Japanese superior, Joichi Ueno, and his wife, Akiko, *My Year of Meats* aligns itself with and explores the "creative interventions that networks of minoritized cultures produce within and across national boundaries," what Françoise Lionnet and Shu-Mei Shih describe as a "minor transnationalism," a tactical "transnationalism from below."[18] The novel considers the potential for a feminist, minor transnationalism to redirect global capitalist television, advertising and, in this case, beef production industries toward more enabling, feminist, multicultural, and environmentally sustainable ends. Its "minor transnationalism" makes visible "the multiple relations between the national and transnational," acknowledging how differently minoritized cultures and subjects are distinctly positioned in relation to these shifts.[19] It also reinforces Lionnet and Shih's sense that this is a "mode in which the traumas of colonial, imperial, and global hegemonies as well as the affective dimensions of transcolonial solidarities continue to work themselves out and produce new possibilities."[20]

As the novel opens, Jane is living in the East Village, circa 1991, an aspiring documentary filmmaker. Completely broke, she is thrilled when her former boss, from a study abroad stint in Tokyo, hires her to produce a Japanese television series titled *My American Wife!*[21] The television series, which scouts and then showcases a different American "wife" preparing her favorite meat recipe each week, is sponsored by the American beef industry's export and trade syndicate, BEEF-EX.[22] It is designed to "bring the 'heartland of America into the homes of Japan'" and, most importantly, to sell the female, Japanese audience "wholesome" American meats.[23] Through her exposure to these global capitalist television production, advertising, meat-production and export networks, Jane comes to realize their multifaceted, visceral, grisly, dehumanizing, racist and sexist impact on American and Japanese consumers, a system she is deeply implicated in despite her efforts to redirect these transnational networks toward an understanding of, and desire for, a feminist and multicultural American love.

My Year of Meats documents a specifically Asian American minor transnationalism, referencing Asian Americans' distinct positioning in relation to contemporary national and transnational social formations. Jane describes herself as a "go-between, a cultural pimp, selling off the vast illusion of America to a cramped population on that small string of Pacific islands."[24] She pragmatically acknowledges, "Being racially 'half'—neither here nor there—I was uniquely suited to the niche I was to occupy in the television industry."[25] Casting Jane as a self-acknowledged "cultural pimp" hired for her linguistic, cross-cultural skills, multiracial identity, and presumed ability to persuade her Japanese audience, the novel is painfully aware of the ways in which Asian American subjects are repositioned in relation to global capitalist flows and the highly differentiated and complexly classed and racialized "latitudes of citizenship" these flows realize.[26] Asian American cultural formations evidence and interrogate what Lisa Lowe describes as the contradictions of "the international within the national."[27] In addition to marking "the history of Asian alterity to the modern nation-state," which "highlights the convergence of [American] nationalism with racial exclusions, gendered social stratification, and labor exploitation," Asian immigrants in the United States since World War II have come to represent

> a particularly complicated double front of threat and encroachment: on the one hand, Asian states have become prominent as external rivals in overseas war and in the global economy; on the other hand, Asian immigrants are still a necessary racialized labor force within the domestic national economy.[28]

Situated both inside and outside American cultural, political, or economic spaces, Asian Americans, as Lowe stresses, often take on a metaphorical "doubleness" and "unfixed liminality" in American national discourses.[29] The novel references this positioning, noting that Jane is "neither here nor there" and underscoring her perceived tendency to vacillate, according to her mother. Jane herself references the questions her cultural, racial, and gender hybridity seem to pose to the culturally and racially homogenous American and Japanese national discourses and their oppositional, intertwining logics of national culture, race, and gender. Yet she actively rescripts this colonialist, oppositional frame, recasting her "polysexual, polyracial, perverse" identity, as a "prototype" for the hybrid, multicultural future of "this blessed, ever-shrinking world," insisting she is complexly multiple, not contradictory (as the former oppositions suggest).[30]

In this and other ways, *My Year of Meats* cites the traumatizing exclusion of Asian Americans from full citizenship and membership along racial lines, offering a trenchant critique of processes of gendered racialization and class-based discrimination in the United States. It directly connects that critique to its consideration of how such processes are rearticulated in relation to transnational global capitalist flows and is particularly interested in how late capitalist networks might unwittingly enable new modes of critique and transcolonial solidarity between women. The alliances it imagines between its female Japanese American and Japanese characters strategically refigure the international within the national, rescripting American national discourse to acknowledge the nation's historical reliance on immigrant labor and its uneven extension of citizenship rights and symbolic membership in America to Asian immigrants and other racialized subjects. The novel pursues the potential of transnational networks to enable Asian Americans and other minoritized American subjects to intervene in this and other colonialist oppositions the nation uses to secure boundaries between the nation's inside and outside.

As mentioned above, the novel reapproaches the emergent digital technics realized through transnational networks of production, consumption, and communication from below, particularly in its focus on how they play themselves out on and through the minor micropractices of nation's and people's everyday life. This serves not only to rescript U.S. nationalist discourses from below, but also to query their means and methods of reproduction at this micro scale. It is in this regard that we can understand the novel, Jane, and her Japanese acquaintance Akiko as "documentarians" and "thieves" seeking out narrative methods, among other material means, to reorient the U.S. nation-state's ongoing deployment of a series of oppositions between inside and outside that, otherwise, reproduce familiar, gendered and racialized populations and other colonialist categories of life.

The epigraphs opening the novel immediately cue readers in to its concern with micropractices of narrative, bodily, family, and community life and their ability to embed and rerealize paratextual logics key to the U.S. nation-state. A quote taken from *The Pillow Book,* or occasional writings, of Sei Shōnagon,[31] the "great female documentarian" of the Japanese Heian Court (which ruled from the eighth to the twelfth centuries) is juxtaposed to a quote taken from a geography textbook, *Frye's Grammar School Geography.* The latter text uses an abstract, "objective," third-person narration to describe how the "white race in the Old World lies between the lands of the black and the yellow people." Its categorization of the world's people into three races also explains and justifies the growth and expansion of the white race, which "roamed about in search of new homes, where they could find pastures for their cattle," apparently anticipating American discourses of "manifest destiny" as well as cattle farming. Once read as a paratext, the performative force of such a narrative technique to categorize life and circumscribe its modes of circulation and, thus, to symbolically reinforce certain cultural and spatiotemporal assumptions is quite clear. Its detached, omniscient voice and matter-of-factness is key to its persuasive power, orienting readers to the world and to its racialized populations in ways that performatively circumscribe these categories of life and their potential interrelations.

Juxtaposing this excerpt to Sei Shōnagon's description of how she began to write her *Pillow Book,* the novel flags its own and its main characters' comparable efforts to devise alternate paratextual methods to document and rerealize quite divergent modes of life and orientations to the world. The latter efforts are rendered imperceptible, contradictory, impossible, or illogical by the former colonialist and masculinist paratextual logics. Shōnagon, writing in the "subjective" first person, describes how she tactically appropriates the paper for her own, unconventional, and idiosyncratic purposes of writing, claiming she plans to use it as a pillow for sleeping. If this passage is read as embedding a kind of paratext for materially realizing a set of assumptions about the categories of life and their modes of interrelation, it becomes clear that her paratextual technique is nonhierarchical, "often including the most trivial material," and organized according to what she finds "charming and splendid," such as trees and plants, birds and insects. This more materially based, bottom-up "geography" of the world equally and differently engenders a sense of the "order of things" and, thus, shapes its author's and readers' orientation to the world. All of her subsequent entries, which open each chaper of the novel, are organized according to "the months of the year," suggesting the close intertwining of human social interactions with the material world and its cycles. *My Year of Meats* organizes its own "chapters" according to her "months of the year," indicating its own effort to seek out alternate, embedded paratextual techniques to unsettle the novel, among other colonialist modes of knowledge, representation, and lived space and to open onto alternate ways of counting, organizing, and rerealizing material life and its complex interrelations through its narrative practices.

In the Meat

Jane's first words in the novel are "Meat is the Message." Meat, as mentioned above, and American beef, in particular, is quite literally the sole content or message of the television program *My American Wife!* that she has been asked to help direct. As Jane states, "It's the meat (not the Mrs.) who's the star of our show! Of course, the 'Wife of the Week' is important too. She must be attractive, appetizing, and all-American. She is the Meat Made Manifest: ample, robust, yet never tough or hard to digest."[32] The slogan "Meat is the Message" underscores the television program's primary function as an advertisement for meat, its wholesale preoccupation with consumption. It also, not so subtly, references the way in which the meat and the wives, or "meat made manifest," as Jane notes with her characteristic irony, circulate as similarly commodified objects of consumption within these global capitalist networks of beef and television production, defined by their social "use" (i.e., meat, not cattle, and wives, not women). When cattle are transformed into beef and women are transformed into wives, they circulate as privileged symbols of American national virility, affluence, and purity.

American nationalist discourses and affiliated neoliberal economic networks rely on these saturated symbols to elicit national and transnational desire and they are also materially reliant on meat and wives as essential "mediums" through which national life is literally reproduced. Meat and wives provide physical sustenance for the nation in the form of food and in the bearing of offspring and through their labor. The novel considers how emergent technics entering into global capitalist networks of communication, biotechnologies of food production, and reproductive science rely on and materially reproduce themselves through micropractices that help instantiate complex interrelations between wives, racialized subjects, consumers, and meat. In "A Conversation with Ruth Ozeki," at the end of the novel, Ozeki describes "the metaphorical resonance" of the meat, women, and consumers as "a gag."[33] Susan McHugh references this comment in her reading of the novel in relation to other animal stories that cross species lines, insightfully stressing "the inadequacy of metaphor to represent the relations between the people and animals" in the novel, in large part because both women and cattle in the United States are revealed to have been given the same animal hormone, DES, a more literal intermingling between women, cattle, and reproductive practices.[34] As Ozeki concurs later in the prior conversation, "Women weren't just like cows" because they were given the same drug. She suggests here that the meaning of such overlapping micropractices is not simply metaphorical, as women and cows are linked here to the same biotechnological relays attempting to maximize reproduction. If close attention is paid to Ozeki's use of the word "gag" in the quote above, it becomes quite clear that there are more visceral, direct, practical (not simply metaphorical), interrelations between wives, meat, and consumers that are materially realized through such practices.

The novel here and elsewhere points attention toward the U.S. nation-state's investment in symbolically and materially reproducing these distinct categories of life and in designating their acceptable and unacceptable modes of interrelating and circulating. In a footnote Jane appends to the novel, she cites Webster's *New World Dictionary*, which, in light of its alignment with the "New World," evokes the colonialist mode of discourse already encountered in the excerpt from *Frye's Grammar School Geography*. She quotes its definitions and brief etymologies of "Capital," "Stock," and "Cattle," but also proceeds to mark the symbolic slippages between the categories through which official paratexts, such as those underpinning this dictionary, encourage us to understand and relate to "capital," "stock," "cattle" (a variant of "chattel"), and associated human and animal collectives, derogatorily termed the masses.[35] Jane's unpacking of these definitions reveals how these categorizations attempt to hierarchize, as well as differentiate, forms of "life." She notes capital's etymological association with the "head" and cattle with "farm animals collectively" and "people in the mass: contemptuous term."[36] Crucially, her gloss on these entries underscores these categories' *inability* to disentangle these "objects," their interrelations, or their interrelated meanings: "stock" refers to "a human line, or type, as of a group of animals or plants" and "any of the major subdivisions of the human race," as well as "livestock" and "capital," and one troubling variant of cattle, "chattel."[37]

Scrutinizing such categorizations of material life in American national culture as key paratexts guiding and resolidifying its material practices of reproduction, the novel problematizes these particular modes of calculated differentiation. In particular, it questions the kinds of substitutions encouraged and enabled by the reduction of one "form of life" to another. In calculating life in this way, such paratexts facilitate and open onto distinct modes of circulation and relating. While ironically addressing and unpacking the equations, both literal and symbolic, between women and cattle and their positioning in these U.S. national, late capitalist networks, *My Year of Meats* underscores what gets left out and lost through such reductive equations rather than accepting these substitutions. Importantly, the novel refuses to accept this schemata for categorizing life, which serves to equate the commodification and objectification of animals with the treatment of women or racialized others. In this way, the novel departs from Carol Adams, who reinforces this equation in her reading in *The Sexual Politics of Meat: A Feminist-Vegetarian Critical Theory*, arguing that eating meat is sexist and sexism necessarily entails anthropocentric speciesism.[38] Instead, *My Year of Meats* traces literal, symbolic, and affective interconnections, interminglings, and key divergences between life-forms technically categorized as wives, cattle, stock, chattel, and beef. In this way it documents how capitalist circuits and American national culture attempt to reduce these to a similar status as forms of life defined in highly objectified terms, as property, yet may unwittingly reveal other lines of interconnection and identification. Here and elsewhere, *My Year of Meats* explicitly points toward what gets overlooked and lost through these familiar modes of differentiation, troubling the reductions they regularize.

The novel is interested in the embedded paratextual practices that guide and performatively rerealize interrelations between and the intermingling of these forms of life at semantic, material, and affective levels. These are paratextual technics, materially realized "pre-ideas" that circulate in dictionaries and textbooks and, equally, paratextual technics realized through food production and reproductive sciences and the interrelations and circulations they rely on and open onto. As "frameworks that move 'subjects' and 'objects' about," yet are unperceived due to their "utter familiarity"[39] they position material bodies and constrain their potential interrelations within nationalist discourses and the space of the nation in distinct ways.

Ozeki's references to the relations between meat, consumers, and women as "metaphorical, a gag, if you will" is, thus, a sign of the novel's overarching challenge to American nationalist discourses of incorporation, altogether. The novel's own "gag," connoting both a joke and, less humorously, a choke, registers the visceral threat unauthorized, intercorporeal connections and intermingling between gendered, racialized, and sexed forms of life pose to nationalism's purifying, masculinist, racist, classist, and speciesist logics. U.S. nationalism attempts to incorporate and, thus, symbolically and materially "swallow" a range of embodied Others through such technically assisted classifications and material practices, yet they also fail, the novel suggests, if one takes the time and finds the methods to register the material and symbolic complexity these operations attempt and fail to circumscribe.

In addition to anatomizing the U.S. nation-state's visceral, incorporative paratextual methods for solidifying key distinctions between bodily and community insides and outsides, *My Year of Meats* proceeds to elicit and redirect disgust toward homogenous, "wholesome," patriarchal, racist American national discourses and, thereby, to reorient American nationalism's desires. Referencing the renowned murder of a Japanese high school student, Yoshihiro Hattori, who was shot when he knocked on the door of a Winn-Dixie meatpacker, Dwayne Peairs, in Louisiana to ask for directions, Jane redescribes the wholesome, authentic, viril, patriarchal message of meat in American national culture, stating, "Guns, race, meat, and Manifest Destiny all collided in a single explosion of violent, dehumanized activity."[40] Her claim that "we are a grisly nation" connects this "frontier culture" to a history of imperial expansion and conquest, to the objectification and abjection of racialized others, and to practices that rely on the objectification of nonhuman animals and lifeworlds, as epitomized in the mass production of American beef.

In the process of "documenting" the truth of the American nation to her Japanese viewers, which involves traveling throughout rural America with a Japanese film crew in search of "wholesome" American wives to feature on the program, Jane persistently runs up against nationalist discourses of authenticity and purity. Confronted by a World War II veteran at a VFW hall in Arkansas who wants to know where she's from, Jane gives her birthplace, Quam, Minnesota, which leads him to reassert his vision of a racially homogenous American nation, asking, "No, no . . . *What* are you?" to which she replies, "*I . . . am . . . a . . . fucking . . . . *AMERICAN!"[41] Authenticity and purity are crucial to nationalisms and they function as an "othering machine for the minor," serving as a means to deny nonhegemonic subjects full access, rights, and status within the nation-state.[42] They are also a crucial means through which women are positioned within modern nation-states in a mythic, absolute, unchanging space or landscape, confined by a "tradition" located outside the masculine, progressive, modern time of the nation.

Jane actively exploits and redeploys the late capitalist circuits involved in the production of the television show to *undermine* the patriarchal, nationalist discourses of American purity and authenticity, as embodied in wholesome beef and wives, that she is explicitly charged with exporting to

Japanese audiences. She does this through affectively charged imagery and language, revealing their grisly, dehumanizing, racist, sexist, toxic, and often quite literally noxious core through this excessive language. Jane's Japanese boss, Joichi Ueno, whose self-chosen nickname, "John Wayno," as well as his penchant for Texas strippers, reveals his wholesale embrace of hegemonic American national "frontier" culture, is described in viscerally noxious terms from the start: "Ueno was a large, soft-bodied man, with smooth, damp skin and a stunningly profound halitosis, indicative of serious digestive problems, which rose, vaporlike, from the twists of his bowels."[43] In this early scene, Jane resorts to "counting categories," including "Hateful, Unsuitable, Depressing, Annoying" and "Things that Give a Pathetic Impression," to "put enough distance" between herself and Joichi, mimicking her idol, Sei Shōnagon, author of the *Pillow Book* and fellow counterarchivist, who similarly generates idiosyncratic lists and "approves of what others abhor and detests the things they like." This scene vividly illustrates Jane's and Shōnagon's shared status as counterarchivists, attempting to trace and rerealize bodily relations and social life according to logics that contravene the official, masculine nationalist discourses. It also underscores the novel's interest in how paratextual technics such as counting and listing, as they materially realize a distinct mode of categorizing the order of things, influence our sense of how close or how far away they seem, which, in turn, impacts how we both relate to and feel about these categorized life-forms, whether we approach or repel, register or refuse them.

Jane attributes both her involvement with the medium of television and her desire to "be different" to Sei Shōnagon. Jane's status as an aspiring archivist, as mentioned above, links her to Sei Shōnagon. As importantly, her status as a documentarian links her to her Japanese boss's wife, Akiko, as well. Akiko is herself an aspiring archivist. Prior to her marriage she wrote gory comic book copy in a *manga* publishing house, and she continues, under the influence of Shōnagon's *Pillow Book*, to write as a diarist and fledgling poet. All three documentarians are characterized as "thieves," reinforcing their efforts to tactically reorient hegemonic, masculinist national discourses and the paratexts that subtend their production of certain kinds and modes of life. Devising alternate modes of counting, listing, and calculating and, thus, writing life into distinct categories and encouraging and discouraging distinct kinds of interrelations through their redirection of bodily affect, they repurpose distinct micropractices to put their alternate understandings and practices of eating, family, sexual intimacy, community, and nation into circulation. Their tactics, Jane's especially, raise ethical questions about all such practices of archivization, and how they relate to and rely on the "meat" or micropractices through which they realize their "message." Characterized as "thefts," they involve a tactical borrowing from hegemonic nationalist discourses and subjects, while they also raise questions about who or what else might be lost in these transformative relays between technics and the interrelations and meanings they realize and derealize.

My Year of Meats is particularly interested in the different kinds of intimacy and distance specific paratextual technics materially realize. Exploring emergent technologies used in the factory farming of cattle and its transnational networks of production and consumption, reproductive and family planning biotechnologies, and the material affordances and paratexts of television, transnational communication networks, documentary film, and novels, *My Year of Meats* queries whether they might otherwise transform the nation's affective orientations, and the kinds of relations between racially, nationally, and economically differentiated women, men, and nonhuman animals they currently work to rerealize.

The novel situates the late capitalist networks that bring together Jane and Akiko (who is an avid audience member of *My American Wife!* and the wife of Jane's boss, Joichi) alongside a wide range of unofficial, feminine, vernacular paratextual methods such as Shōnagon's diary, written using Chinese characters that were, at that time, considered masculine language in Japan, Akiko's poetry, Jane's documentary film, and a series of the "wives'" recipes. Comparatively moving across a wide range of official and unofficial paratextual practices and their materially realized modes of classification and national archivization, the novel stresses their distinct role in engendering and rendering physically, epistemologically, and affectively perceivable orientations to the world and circumscribing forms of life. In doing so, it underscores the necessary limitations to any specific mode of calculating and its attempted categorization of life, the slippage and seepage that accompanies all such efforts, querying the ethical consequences of these losses.

Its slogan "Meat is the message" plays, as mentioned above, on media theorist Marshall McLuhan's catchphrase, "The medium is the message," which suggests that media are often self-referentially, even myopically, focused on reproducing their specific epistemologies and modes of representation and communication, and nothing else, that is, that media are largely about their status as media. Moving across and directly citing a noticeably wide range of media to underscore their distinct paratextual methods, the novel comparatively forces attention onto the literal "meat" or lived meaning and experience that each of the technics, in its own way, conveys or obscures due to its chosen modes of categorization and circulation. The novel singles out and privileges paratextual micropractices that remain more closely tied and explicitly concerned with the medium and materials through which and against which they are realized, that is, the unofficial, minor, and vernacular paratextual methods such as Sei Shōnogan's pillow book, recipes submitted by each of the television program's featured wives, Lara and Dyann, the lesbian couple's DIY approach to artificial insemination (i.e., a turkey baster), and Jane's independent documentary, which is a reediting of one particularly disturbing television episode she shot at a factory farm exposing American beef production practices' illegal use of animal hormones, such as DES, and antibiotics, and their devastating effects on humans, animals, and the environment.

Micropractices as/and Embodied National Archives

The episodes of *My American Wife!* that Jane directs are intended to provide a counterarchive of the American nation in which women's cultural, racial, sexual, and class diversity are valued and in which to showcase these ordinary women's active political interventions in reproduction, family, sex, cooking, gender, ethnic and cultural identity, community, and nation. Their contributions are largely undertaken at the level of micropractices that are unacknowledged, yet absolutely primary to national life. Jane searches out women whose own lives and family, like her own, evidence cross-cultural, multiracial, and/or diverse familial and sexual relations, drawing attention to the ongoing transformation and hybridization of national culture over time. As she stresses, not even cows and cowboys are indigenous to America; they were introduced into America by the Spanish. Instead,

> All over the world, native species are migrating, if not disappearing, and in the next millennium the idea of an indigenous person or plant or culture will just seem quaint.
> Being half, I am evidence that race, too, will become relic. Eventually we're all going to be brown, sort of. Some days when I'm feeling grand, I feel brand-new—like a prototype.[44]

In this and other passages, Jane imagines herself (in noticeably capitalist terms) as a "prototype" for a multicultural and multiracial America, the America she works hard to document, celebrate, and circulate in the television show, against the wishes of her supervisors. One episode features Lara and Dyann, a biracial lesbian couple who are vegetarians with two children conceived using reproductive technologies. Another focuses on the Beaudroux family in Louisiana, who decide to adopt children from other countries, and actively embrace their adopted children's diverse racial and cultural histories.

Jane's deployment of the television program as a national counterarchive with its own, however alternately imagined, insides and outsides, unravels as she realizes her own implication in the lives she is documenting, the fact that she is not outside her televisual archive. After filming the show featuring Lara and Dyann, who are fervent vegetarians, Jane describes the program in abstract, almost generic terms as "uplifting, a powerful affirmation of difference, of race and gender and the many faces of motherhood."[45] She also admits that her "moral certitude" is undermined by the realization that she never told the women about the show's sponsor, well aware of their politically motivated vegetarianism.[46]

Realizing that, in spite of their abstracting and deterritorializing tendencies, these global capitalist networks linking American and Japanese women and global beef production are embodied and affect real lives, including her own, Jane comes to a new understanding of the slogan "Meat is the message" and reconceives her documentary project. The slogan begins to convey the message that women, animals, and other forms of life, even when reduced to their use value, that is, as meat, maintain their embodied, fleshy irreducibility, their material and affective force, and their ability to transform and contravene the increasingly abstract, deterritorializing social and technical networks in which they are implicated and through which they circulate. The slogan begins to express Jane's growing awareness of the diverse women and other "meats" she has been trafficking as people.

Refusing the reduction of women to their use-value in global capitalist circuits and nationalist discourses, *My Year of Meats* redescribes what are often perceived to be disembodied, deterritorialized, abstract, functional economic networks, insisting on tracing them back to the embodied forms of life that maintain, sustain, and transform these transnational networks. "Meat is the message," in this regard, evokes the fleshy complexity and specificity that these networks, which realize and reinforce a capitalist logic of general equivalence, attempt but ultimately fail to direct and circumscribe.

Jane's new realization that "meat is the message" in this sense of an embodied set of relations between women, global capitalist networks, and the irreducible forms of life they are enmeshed with comes to a climax when she is contacted by one of her most avid audience members, Akiko. Akiko has watched *My American Wife!* with interest, providing her husband, Jane's boss, Joichi Ueno, with "authenticity" ratings of each program, cooking the meats featured in each meal, and eating the beef to placate Joichi, who believes that red meat will improve her health and fertility and their chances at reproduction. The conflict between Akiko and Joichi grows as he discovers that she is bulimic and not only throws up the meat she eats, but that this has led to the cessation of her periods and stands in the way of their successful reproduction. His psychological and physical abuse of Akiko escalates until it results in a brutal rape. After watching Lara and Dyann, the lesbian, vegetarian couple on *My American Wife!* Akiko realizes that she does not love her husband, that she wants a child, and may herself be sexually attracted to women. Akiko contacts Jane and tells her that she plans to come to America to meet her favorite American wives and, perhaps, find her own American wife.

Contacted and then confronted by Akiko in person, Jane realizes her unwitting allegiance in her work as an aspiring documentarian to the paratextual apparati in-forming the beef industry and its specific capitalist modes of calculating and counting forms of life—as producers, products, and consumers. She thinks,

> Akiko's fax threw me for a loop. Maybe it was because my shows were broadcast in Japan, on the other side of the globe, but up until now I'd never really imagined my audience before. She was an abstract concept: at most, a stereotypical housewife, limited in experience but eager to learn, to be inspired by my programs and my American wives; at the very least, a demographic statistic, a percentage point I'd hungered after, to run in a pesky executive's face. . . . Now it hit me: what an arrogant and chauvinistic attitude this was. While I'd been worried about the well-being of the American women I filmed as subjects, suddenly here was the audience, embodied in Akiko, with a name and a vulnerable identity.[47]

The passage marks Jane's realization of her own implication in the life histories she's documenting and, as importantly, her reciprocal transformation as a result of these transnational networks. It adds a whole new dimension to Jane's counterarchive of multicultural American love, a counterarchive that attempts, yet ultimately fails, to register the dynamic, embodied, differential, power-laden interrelations between women without attempting to symbolically capitalize on or instrumentalize their representations to "loving" nationalist ends.

Moving outside the frame of the television program, Jane's real-world encounter with Akiko requires her to confront the differences between the two of them and her "chauvinistic" assumptions about her audience. Yet Jane's encounter with Akiko, and through her, with the cultural and economic differences and embodied specificity of those circulating through these late capitalist networks stops short of a full acknowledgment of cultural, political, and economic differences between women. Fleeing her abusive husband, Akiko comes to America and enthusiastically embraces its multicultural imperative to "love difference," ironically becoming, in this respect, quite like Jane. Pregnant with a child, Akiko explains to her nurse and friend, Tomoko, that she's going to America so that her daughter can "be an American citizen. So she can grow up to become an American Wife," noting that "It doesn't matter so much for a son, but since she's a girl . . ."[48] Once in America, Akiko is astounded by the "generosity, this amplitude of feeling and the openness" of her American hosts' life.[49] Traveling by train out of New Orleans, Akiko meets Maurice, an Amtrak coach attendant, who invites her to join the other black American passengers in eating fried chicken and singing a song together. Akiko thinks,

> This would never happen on the train in Hokkaido! For the second time since she left Japan, she shivered with excitement. She'd felt it at the dinner table at Thanksgiving, and now, again, even stronger—as if somehow she'd been absorbed into a massive body that had taken over the functions of her own, and now it was infusing her small heart with the superabundance of its feeling, teaching her taut belly to swell, stretching her rib cage, and pumping spurts of happy life into her fetus.
>
> *This is America!* She thought. She clapped her hands and then hugged herself with delight.[50]

Importantly, it is through micropractices of eating and song that Akiko gains access to American culture and an excessive, pleasurable sense of her fertility in this passage. While the passage explicitly describes Akiko's and America's embrace of cultural, racial, and alimentary difference, the incorporative language of Akiko's absorption "into a massive body that had taken over the functions of her own" should give pause. In becoming American, Akiko is

largely remade in Jane's Western liberal humanist feminist image and hegemonic U.S. nationalism's imperialist claims to "superabundance," "fertility,"
and unique freedoms for women and girls are reinstalled, though no longer
associated with the meat, homophobia, or purity of prior modes of patriarchal U.S. nationalism.

The collapse of Akiko into the embrace of a feminist and multicultural
American love in this passage is quite problematic. In her discussion of nationalist affective economies, "In the Name of Love," Sara Ahmed describes
how contemporary British multiculturalisms frequently operationalize a national ideal "posited as 'being' plural, open, and diverse; as being loving and
welcoming to others."[51] In such cases, the national ideal is "not premised
on abstraction . . . , nor on whiteness, but on hybridity as a form of social-
ity, as the imperative to mix with others."[52] Within such a discourse, the
mixed-race woman becomes the fantasized image of the national subject,
"somebody who is hybrid, plural, and mobile."[53] Ahmed's analysis notes that
the multicultural nation loves difference by taking it in, and, thus, this love
for difference becomes a new form of "likeness" and consensus, a means to
reproduce the same image of the nation; an image of the national subjects as
tolerant and open because they love difference. Her claim that this "transformation of pluralism into consensus is telling. Others must agree to value difference: difference is now what we would have in common. In other words,
difference becomes an elevated or sublimated form of likeness."[54] From this
vantage, multicultural love can be seen to provide a new basis for a colonialist project of assimilating others into the nation's image.

In spite of Akiko's cross-identifications with minoritized Americans and
vernacular cultural forms, in her love of difference and her mixing with others she, as this passage reveals with its multileveled language of bodily incorporation, seems to be joyfully assimilated into an American national ideal,
one that revitalizes a nationalist and colonialist differentiation of inside and
outside and women's role in reproducing these national boundaries and exclusions through "love." While appearing to dismantle nationalist discourses
of homogeneity and purity, the multicultural nation's love of difference con-
sumes difference according to a slightly different incorporative logic, but
an incorporative logic, just the same. Embracing and mixing with others
becomes the new national imperative and the basis by which immigrants
and minority communities are assessed and in many cases pathologized for,
as Ahmed notes, "loving the same." In the novel, Joichi's investment in cultural purity and homogeneity is, in this way, a perverse counterpoint to the
women's multicultural love of difference. Wholly paradoxically, their love

of difference collapses those very differences as it operates according to an "idea of the world where we all love each other, a world of lovers, [which] is a humanist fantasy that informs much of the multicultural discourses of love" and their hope that "*if only we got closer we would be as one.*"[55]

In describing *My Year of Meats* and its multiculturalism, Monica Chiu, in "Postnational Globalization and (En)Gendered Meat Production in Ruth L. Ozeki's *My Year of Meats*," argues that "the invisible, national (read: multicultural) ideology that the novel creates—a type of overculture—reconstitutes the very localized, national framework that it initially attempts to subvert."[56] I agree that American nationalist logics of love and disgust, the incorporative logics of inside and outside they help realize, and women's role in reproducing them are recuperated in Jane's initial multicultural feminist project, even as they are recoded according to a multicultural, transnational, neoimperialist American love. While Jane rejects appeals to "authenticity and nostalgia, appeals to 'the real' [that] operate as a way of covering over many of the massive changes in terms of families, gender and sexual orders, local and global economies,"[57] she, nonetheless, attempts to recuperate and recontain micropractices of family, sex, eating, and intersubjectivity to otherwise familiarly nationalist and liberal humanist feminist ends. In this regard, Jane's project is quite similar to other contemporary transnational U.S. feminisms that remain remarkably unaware of how their efforts to "rescue" non-Western women from abusive, patriarchal, "traditional" cultures often provide a friendly face and alibi for American imperialism. Historically, transnational feminisms such as the global women's movement in the nineteenth century often worked hand in hand with American imperialism in what Amy Kaplan pointedly describes as its "civilizational" project of global housecleaning, its "manifest domesticity,"[58] a less than desirable connection to more recent transnational feminisms the novel may encourage us to see in Jane's initial transnational feminist networking. Jane fails to adequately question and depart from the incorporative logics of empire and nation embedded in a range of paratexts, which she thus, ends up unwittingly rerealizing through her interactions with Akiko.

While Jane's initial televisual project, reliant on transnational multicultural love and consumption, is deeply flawed for this reason, the *novel* also provides a distinctly different gloss on her efforts if one attends to its concluding comments on what gets left out of and lost in Jane's narrative as well as in her documentary exposing the beef industry's use of DES. These are, I'd suggest, losses and limits that are *not* overlooked by the novel. From this vantage, it is possible to see Jane's attempt to reproduce Akiko and her female Japanese audience members in her own American image as an aborted and incomplete project. In this reading, Jane's thwarted material effort to reproduce a multicultural, feminist America for and through her Japanese viewers might be understood to parallel her failed pregnancy, as a result of the injury she sustains at a slaughterhouse while attempting to film a revealing episode of *This American Wife!* Both events underscore key limits to Jane's initial efforts to deploy and to redescribe nationalist discourses and micropractices to alternate ends, though they may also recommend other ways to conceive these interrelations.

My Year of Meats remains preoccupied, even after the apparently successful release of Jane's independent documentary on the impact of DES and other toxic micropractices in the U.S. cattle farming and meat industries near the close of the novel, with what escapes and haunts official and unofficial narratives and the material life realized through the nation's micropractices. The "materiality of eating, sex, and bodies," Elspeth Probyn argues in *Carnal Appetites: Food Sex Identities*, can also "draw out alternate ways of thinking about an ethics of existence" and "allows us to rethink the ethics of bodies, . . . tracing out the connections between bodies that, in eating, open up and connect in different ways."[59] She stresses how "eating places different orders of things and ways of being alongside each other, inside and outside inextricably linked."[60] With this flip side to micropractices of eating, sex, and bodies in mind, it becomes clear that *My Year of Meats* attempts to register how the affective, intercorporeal relations nationalism encourages between differently racialized, gendered, classed, sexed, and cultured subjects and across species lines cannot be fully recuperated to serve nationalist ends, even apparently progressive, feminist, multicultural ones. Such micropractices resolidify and unsettle nationalism's affective economies and the interrelations they work to solidify. Nationalist and other attempts to categorize, classify, hierarchize, or otherwise render these forms of life distinct, stable, or fully meaningful are overshadowed by the interrelatedness and complexity of these lived spaces. It is in this sense that Jane's efforts to formulate, foster, and unambiguously embrace an explicit ethical, affective program through her documentary film at the end of the novel remain haunted and uncertain. Even after Jane triumphantly exposes the use of the animal growth hormone DES both in the production of American beef and in its former use as a means to prevent miscarriages in women (the latter of which turns out to have been the source of her own uterine cancer), she insists that "the truth is so much more complex. I am haunted by all the things—big things and little things, Splendid things and Squalid things—that threaten to slip through the cracks, untold, out of history."[61]

One of the things that slips through Jane's public exposé about beef is precisely her realization that, to use Akiko's words, "Life is bloody."[62] The novel's persistent attention to material, physical, and affective seepage and slippage is quite significant as it underscores the limitations to any use of affect, even that congealed on and through bodies, to secure social categories, let alone nationalism's insides and outsides. This marking of seepage and slippage underscores, as does the novel's comparative movement across a series of technical lists, categorizations, apparati, and materially realized paratexts, that these modes of interrelation are both realized and unsettled by the intercorporeal, intersubjective, affective, and symbolic intermingling of bodies and lifeworlds. One particularly unsettling and unrecuperated moment in Jane's narrative occurs after her filming of the Dunn & Sons feedlot, a factory farm producing American beef. She describes being watched by "slow and warm and solid cows," who "looked up as we passed, watching us with mournful, seeping eyes."[63] Jane and her cameraman, Suzuki, find an aborted calf fetus lying on the ground, its eyes full of maggots, and realize that it is the result of the administration of drugs to female cattle to prevent unwanted pregnancies.[64] A few days later, Jane dreams that she is giving birth, a stillborn that hits the ground with a thump: "It was wet, a misshapen tangle, but I could see a delicate hoof, a twisted tail, the oversize skull, still fetal blue, with a dead milky eye staring up at me, alive with maggots."[65] This scene anticipates Jane's actual experience giving birth to a stillborn baby in the hospital after a fateful visit to a nearby slaughterhouse in which she is knocked down by an oncoming carcass, all her senses stripped from her. Afterward, in the hospital, she describes how she "could not break through the jumble of chaotic fragments: the bleeding cattle and the bloody meat, the farmer's rage, the mother's stupor, and the child's disfigured and unnatural grace."[66] "Trapped by these images," she finds herself "trying to edit them, to put them in an order that made sense."[67] Several of these images, such as the outrage of Gale Dunn, the cattle farmer, when confronted about the use of DES and other drugs and the impact these animal hormones were having on his niece (her premature sexual development), or the mother Bunny Dunn's initial denial about these side effects eventually make their way into Jane's critical documentary on U.S. beef production practices. Nonetheless, the visceral, corporeal, cross-species identification in these passages is solidified by Jane's claim that she couldn't differentiate the blood of her stillborn child from the blood of the slaughtered cow on her stained clothes. These passages and their disturbing, graphic imagery "resonate to the exact degree to which" they are "in excess of any narrative or functional line," serving as a kind of "temporal sink, a hole in time as we conceive of it and narrativize it," as Brian Massumi describes the interference and unassimilability of affect.[68]

The passages remain largely irreconcilable with Jane's narrative or the novel's admittedly fabricated happy ending.

My Year of Meats's narratives remain haunted by affect they each, alone, cannot fully account for. These resonances, escaping Jane's multicultural feminist America and any socially mandated project of love and disgust, remain in the novel. The numerous cross-species, cross-class, cross-racial, and cross-cultural identifications in the novel retain a tangible, visceral micropolitical force, registering how affect unhinges, as well as congeals, distinctions between bodily insides and outsides and effectively traverses that which is perceived to be incommensurable. In this regard, the novel reveals how "actually existing, structured things live in and through what escapes them," which may be why emotional life is "more or less disorienting, and why it is classically described as being outside of oneself, at the very point at which one is most intimately and unshareably in contact with oneself and one's vitality."[69] In spite of its unassimilability, such affect, as engaged and registered in a range of micropractices, encourages and travels through complex, multilayered interrelations and linkages (not bonding) that traverse perceived differentials. In that way, such relays immanently open onto other ways of inhabiting the world and working through and against existing humanist categorizations of life and their allowed and disallowed interrelations. The material and affective intermingling between bodies and other forms of life suggests new ways of relating across difference that do not reproduce U.S. nationalism's incorporative logics and their introjection of others to their own ends, kinds of interrelation that are much more compelling and disorienting than Jane's explicit, packaged message of multicultural love.

Instead, *My Year of Meats* reveals the importance of micropractices of eating, sex, family, narrative, and other corporeal intimacies as a means of searching out linkages and disallowed modes of relating across and within established social categories, linkages that question established distances and proximities, unsettle easy oppositions of love and disgust, and reveal how ambiguous these delineations of forms of life may be, realizing their instability as well as their current and untapped force. Imagined as a site of embodied pleasure, vulnerability, and trauma, of intercorporeal and intersubjective intimacies that nationalisms' affective economies work hard to legislate, the meat communicates the embodied, visceral materiality of forms of life. It registers the bodily, affective force entering into and channeled through micropractices of eating, sex, reproduction, farming, and narrative, micropractices that nationalisms enlist to their own ends, but that transnational feminisms might also find ways to comparatively engage against U.S. nationalism's charged categorizations of life.

5 / Novel Diagnosis of Bioinformatic Circulation

> To resist a likely future in the present is to gamble that the present still provides substance for resistance, that it is populated by practices that remain vital even if none of them has escaped the generalized parasitism that implicates them all.
>
> —Isabelle Stengers, *Cosmopolitics I*[1]

As the preceding chapters illustrate, since the 1990s a strain of contemporary American novels is increasingly preoccupied with digital technics as they facilitate and alter interchanges between domestic national space and global networks, private and public space, and distinctly racialized, gendered, and sexed intersubjectivities. The novels featured in this book, to register and diagnose their own transformative interchanges with emergent economic, cultural, medial, and subjective transmissions, comparatively reconceive the novel and its relation to broader literary, media, and social systems. At a forum on the "Futures of the Novel," Nancy Armstrong stated that "we are experiencing a paradigm shift in science, politics, and literature" and, therefore, "in years to come, the novels that matter will, I believe, be those seen as having prepared us for an epistemic shift in how we imagine ourselves as human beings."[2] Referencing Kazuo Ishiguro's 2006 *Never Let Me Go* and David Mitchell's 2004 *Cloud Atlas*, which both address sciences of genetics and bioinformatics, she describes these and other contemporary novels' "move from the model of mankind as an aggregate of individuals to what it promotes as a more comprehensive model of man as a living being or species."[3] Such recent novelistic accounts reveal "an elaborate circulatory system connecting bodies, goods, and information in a single heterogeneous body with a generalized affect aimed at no greater good than to persist as it is."[4] While Armstrong does not elaborate in this short piece on the precise shifts catalyzing these emergent novelistic trajectories and these novels' concern with species-being and system-based circulations, variously understood, it seems clear that contemporary novels' concern with "an elaborate circulatory system connecting bodies, goods, and information" evidences an awareness of, if not direct engagement with, the shifts late capitalism and its bioinformatic networking processes and biomedicine introduce to the global geopolitical field. Armstrong here raises the crucial question: "What part does the novel play in this change, or does this change spell the end of the novel by rendering obsolete the terms in which novels have resolved the conflicts of modern life?. . . . What is the future *of* the novel once the household no longer shapes the future *in* novels?"[5]

Suggesting, as I have in previous chapters, that contemporary novels often evidence and diagnose these shifts in ways that are far from straightforward, in this chapter I will address this question in further detail, exploring one additional way that contemporary novels grappling with digital technics attempt to conceptually and critically respond, and to reimagine their relations to the biopolitical changes accompanying late capitalist networks, bioinformatics, and the materialities their digital technics help corealize. I will use the term "bioinformatics" in a broad sense in this chapter to describe a range of contemporary sciences and biotechnologies that are a product of distinct combinations of molecular biology and computer science. In spite of key differences between practices such as DNA computing or protein prediction, this bioinformatic constellation, as Eugene Thacker stresses in his careful analysis of "biomedia," begins with the primary assumption of a "fundamental equivalency between genetic 'codes' and computer 'codes,' or between the biological and the digital domains, such that they can be rendered interchangeable in terms of materials and functions."[6] The understandings and practices of life unfolded through these bioinformatic encounters with biological life have significantly transformed contemporary understandings of bodies, biological life, computation, and modes of material, technical, and economic circulation, a topic I will explore in more depth here. As Melinda Cooper argues in her thick analysis *Life as Surplus: Biotechnology and Capitalism in the Neoliberal Era*, the economic "project of U.S. neoliberalism" is "crucially concerned with the emergent possibilities of the life sciences and related disciplines,"[7] which serve as a material infrastructure and political economic imaginary for its operations.

Jeffrey Eugenides's 2002 novel, *Middlesex*, is organized around a multileveled thematic of global circulation and transmission that is explicitly, though complexly related to U.S. biopower and its relatively recent alliances with molecular genetics and other bioinformatic sciences.[8] *Middlesex* addresses key shifts in, and intensifications of, U.S. biopower over the last century and, importantly, measures them alongside earlier twentieth-century American nationalist strategies. Biopower, in the terms Michel Foucault first established in his early seminars, is "the set of mechanisms through which the basic biological features of the human species became the object of a political strategy, of a general strategy of power."[9] Biopower entails the management of people as "populations" and the orchestration of subjectivities to sustain the health and security of the "population" over and beyond individual people.[10] Twenty-first-century U.S. biopower, as subsequent theorists now stress, focuses on the spatial, discursive, biomedical, economic, and political management of populations so as to facilitate neoliberal capitalist circulation and its sustaining political forms, over and against other kinds and modes of circulation. Importantly, biopower is carried out both at the scale of populations (within and beyond the U.S. nation) and at the scale of subject formation through techniques that encourage subjectivities most conducive to these larger circulatory networks. This helps to explain the strange homologies between flexible logics of "just in time" production, which assemble products "on demand" by coordinating geographically distributed locations and the increasingly distributed, heterogeneous modes of subjectivity that are open to dis- and reassembly, components of this larger circulatory system. Such biopolitical coordinations actively circumscribe more and less "pertinent" individuals, in Foucault's terms, that is, individuals differentiated according to their service to these systems' objectives at the level of the "population."[11]

Middlesex's narrator, Cal, a third-generation Greek American retrospectively traces his family's genealogy, and, through it, retraces productive, shifting modes of American nationalism over the course of the twentieth and early twenty-first centuries. Recounting his grandparents' immigration to the United States, their family's subsequent acclimatization to Henry Ford's early twentieth-century Detroit, on through to the city and nation's midcentury racial strife, political scandals, and economic downturns, the novel recasts American nationalism as a dynamic, shifting process of *becoming American*. It is a process of becoming American in that the novel retraces the changing character of American national belonging and state power over time. It is also figured as a becoming American in that it involves the characters in a dynamic process of pursuing and navigating hegemonic national identities and practices of citizenship, which are informed by unofficial, underground, at times remarkably nonconscious material practices that subtend and catalyze shifting official discourses of American national identity and state power. As evidenced by his grandparents' immigration tale, twentieth- and early twenty-first-century modes of Americanness are always already predicated on global economic and cultural circulations of various sorts. The novel underscores these cross-cultural, economic circulations to suggest that practices of becoming American are inherently hybrid, a dynamic, ongoing, material and cultural *threading* across cultures, geographies, and time. Its vantage on becoming American runs directly counter to prior understandings of American nationalism and national identity premised on the absolute and homogenous cultural, racial, religious, and territorial space of the nation (outside time).

In this retrospective way, the novel queries the impact of neoliberal capitalist logics and practices of circulation on the domestic space of the nation, the space of its liberal humanist subjectivities, and, in turn, on the modern novel, which has been charged with delimiting and rerealizing those social spaces and fleshing out their privileged interiorities. It explores how late capitalist networks of circulation contravene and recalibrate modern territorial political forms, considering what happens, in particular, to the gendered, racialized, heterosexist modes of spatial differentiation and circulation twentieth-century nationalisms work so hard to secure. *Middlesex* situates itself at, and, I will argue, attempts to diagnose, an impending, emergent bifurcation in U.S. biopower and its late capitalist circulatory system at the turn of the century. It considers, in particular, what official and unofficial modes of national becoming might follow from the kinds of nonoppositional, deterritorializing, comparatively promiscuous interchanges between domestic and global, private and public, and feminine and masculine domains now encouraged by late capitalism.

Engaging with genetic transmission, sociobiology, and biomedicine in direct thematic, as well as more indirect formal and conceptual ways *Middlesex*'s family story about twentieth- and twenty-first-century American nationalisms pivots on the emergent sciences and technics of molecular genetics, sociobiology, and biomedicine. The appearance of these sciences and their practices of material transmission in the novel is far from incidental. The novel explores how bioinformatic sciences help to catalyze and justify neoliberal modes of transnational economic and geopolitical circulation and affiliated modes of becoming American—with a gendered, racialized, and sexed twenty-first-century difference. In multiple, if subtle, ways, the novel underscores the centrality of these emergent knowledges and technics of genetics, biomedicine, and bioinformatic networking to late capitalism's and the U.S. nation-state's neoliberal imaginaries. It remarks upon their "heroic" efforts to engage such practices to materially and discursively facilitate their flows and more literally manage their populations' mobilities, circulations, and, desires.

Middlesex reveals that emergent modes of twenty-first-century American becoming are predicated on and hard-pressed, as is the novel's protagonist, to evade the pull and influence of the U.S. nation-state's own globalizing, imperialist lust for becoming, its pursuit and production of ongoing, profitable differentiations in the name of a biomedically or bioinformatically administered "'freedom" indistinguishable in its discourses from futurity. Focusing in on this material and conceptual, genetic, and biomedical thread to the novel's historical and cultural queries, the chapter examines how *Middlesex* both diagnoses and obliquely recasts the material practices and knowledges emerging out of genetics and bioinformatics. The novel is well aware that these emergent, networked technics of bioinformatic transmission facilitate increasingly heterogeneous flows of people and goods and genetic material conducive to the U.S. nation-state's and neoliberalism's operations. The movement of the central protagonist and narrator Cal to post–Cold War Berlin to work as a cultural attaché for the U.S. State Department amid equally global, Nike-wearing cosmopolitans is, thus, no accidental end to the plot. Less obviously, perhaps, its engagement with genetic transmissions and technics implicated in late twentieth-century American nationalism works to unsettle readers' faith in neoliberalism's promise that contemporary genetics and biomedicine will deliver unprecedented freedoms to the population, a promise that frequently serves as an alibi and justification for U.S. biopower's political authoritarianism and brutal, thanatopolitical tendencies in the name of security.[12]

Middlesex unpacks neoliberal biopower's claims to preserve the security and health of the "population" by providing increased options of circulation to its privileged subjects. Cal's grandparents' and parents' nonconscious genetic transmission of a recessive, mutated gene leads to his unexpected inheritance of hermaphroditism or intersex, as these conditions are currently described. This intersex condition is what intrudes into and rescripts an otherwise familiar American immigrant tale of assimilation and eventual prosperity. It is, notably, an unacknowledged material microprocess and underlying genetic history that complicates the official family genealogy of becoming American and the nationalist discourses to which this genealogy adheres. Discovering hir condition just after puberty, Cal wrestles with a biomedical establishment that mandates surgery and gender conformity before deciding to embrace hir transgender subjectivity without any biomedical intervention.[13] Directly referencing *Herculine Barbin: Being the Recently Discovered Memoirs of a Nineteenth-Century French Hermaphrodite*, a text edited, introduced, and republished by Michel Foucault in 1978, *Middlesex* can be read as a creative, late twentieth-century rewriting of the former memoir. In this respect, the novel asks to be read as a comparative inquiry into contemporary U.S. biopower.[14] In an interview, Eugenides acknowledges that he drew on the former text, as well as explicitly citing it in the novel, yet wanted to provide, on the contrary, a story of a hermaphrodite with "the love story" he "expected to get from Herculine and didn't," which led to further research and an interest in the "medical and biological details . . . about intersex conditions."[15] These connections to this earlier memoir and to Foucault's work underscores the novel's thoroughgoing interest in biopower, past and present, and although the mention of a love story in this context might seem trite, I will suggest it is aligned with the novel's broader interest in developing a perspective on biopolitics that does not have death and/or death in life as its aim or end.

The juxtaposition of Cal's grandparents' and his own migration (across the absolute boundaries of the sex/gender system) foregrounds the gendered and racialized, biopolitical logics through which nationalisms and related geopolitical movements are understood and meaningfully realized. The novel's immigrant narrative reveals how geopolitical movements from East (present-day Turkey) to West (Detroit), understood as a movement from old world to new world, from the past toward futurity, or from tradition to modernity, are gendered and racialized within a modern colonial geopolitical imaginary. The gendering and racializing of geopolitical movement is not simply metaphorical because it is directly related to biopower in Foucault's sense of a mode of power that is directly involved in manipulating and managing life by working on bodies. Materially realized geopolitical imaginaries are key instruments in states' capacity to dictate the terms in which people live and die, as well as their modes of circulation. As discussed in chapter 3, such practices of spatially differentiating people tangibly co-realize subjectivities and intersubjective relations through this differential positioning.

While the novel is invested in Cal's intersex experience and the history of the intersex and transgender movements, more generally, it simultaneously marks the material and symbolic resonance of transgender with the neoliberal context, noting its relation to the similarly nonoppositional and deterritorialized circulations and subjectivities late capitalism's bioinformatic networks involve. Transgender, which is often understood as a crossing of formerly distinct, absolute territories of sex and/or gender, functions in the novel and in contemporary U.S. culture, more broadly, as a charged analogue to late capitalism's crossing of what are often believed to be the distinct, absolute national territories and gendered political imaginaries essential to earlier twentieth-century American and other modern nationalisms. Transgender is frequently figured in U.S. cultural texts as a symbol of flexibility, as a biomedically facilitated freedom from the constraints of sex and/or gender, and, thus, a symbol of futurity, as J. Jack Halberstam has noted.[16]

Directly linking the Stephanides family's transnational geographical movements and Cal's transgender to twentieth- and twenty-first-century geopolitical imaginaries and their binary, gendered, and racialized logics, *Middlesex* explores Cal's transgender subjectivity and intersex as a loaded site at which much broader and thoroughgoing biopolitical contests by and against biomedicine in the grips of global neoliberal circulatory networks can be understood to unfold. In a basic sense, the narrative is Cal's counternarrative, one that directly contests the initial biomedical accounts and diagnosis of his intersex condition. Yet in aligning the narrative trajectories of the Stephanides family's becoming American, their becoming modern, and Cal's eventual becoming masculine, *Middlesex* initially seems to renaturalize this modern geopolitical imaginary and its biopolitical imperatives. In this reading, Cal's trajectory of becoming masculine is the latest chapter in an American dream of limitless, white masculine self-invention, now facilitated by late capitalism's and molecular genetics and biomedicine's more flexible, less territorial transnational flows and flexible subjectivities. Instead, as I'll illustrate, *Middlesex* cites and problematizes this understanding of becoming American as a wholesale movement from tradition to modernity, from a feminized, ethnic "old world" of myth to a masculine, modern, white Protestant "new world" of science and parallel accounts of sexual liberation as a process of becoming modern and going West.[17] Bringing attention to the binary gendered and racialized oppositions on which the meaning of the former geopolitical movements rely, the novel intervenes in modern nationalism's absolute differentiation of a feminized domestic space outside time from a masculine and masculinist modernity and the resulting, privileged mobilities.

Recounting the twentieth- and early twenty-first-century history of the Stephanides family, *Middlesex* proceeds to trace contemporary genetics, sociobiology, and biomedicine in relation to the U.S. nation-state's long-standing biopolitical concern with the health of the "population" as a social body and its delimitation of modes of subjectivity appropriate to reproducing the former. More crucially, the novel engages with the materialist, evolutionary, "gene's-eye view" on circulation that contemporary sciences and practices of genetics and bioinformatics make available.[18] The novel recommends how such evolutionary processes might, instead, be recognized as they contravene neoliberal U.S. nationalism's biopower and its efforts to secure the "proper" circulation of its people and goods through its administration of technically facilitated, "flexible" techniques of rational self-mastery and population control, so clearly unfolding at the expense of others. The novel reveals how the highly circumscribed, questionable freedoms neoliberalism and official American nationalism and biomedicine offer are undone or, perhaps it is more appropriate to say, unfolded by the evolutionary time of material processes and the unpredictable agencies and trajectories they introduce.

Explicitly drawing on the evolutionary and materialist perspectives of molecular genetics and bioinformatic practices, *Middlesex* exploits these as a resource to reconceive social and historical change and the agencies through which these processes unfold. Its alternate, processual, materialist understanding of social and historical change occurring in evolutionary time suggests a way to pursue becoming, though insistently not in the mode of a becoming American through flexible forms of life (predicated on the immobility and putting to death of others) nor through affiliated modes of choice-based, consumer belonging. Its narrative engagements with material processes, microprocesses, and the evolutionary unfolding of the species, when read in relation to Elizabeth Grosz's feminist rethinking of Darwinian evolution, opens onto a slightly different mode of circulation, and an alternate understanding of the subject, the nation, or the novel's implication in these material transmissions. The novel reengages this evolutionary perspective molecular genetics offers, identifying its potential to open onto an alternate trajectory for thinking biopolitics that might provide ways to curb U.S. biopower's authoritarian and thanatopolitical efficacy and reach.

Reconceiving historical and cultural change in light of its materialist, evolutionary view on becoming, *Middlesex* reconsiders how historical change and the material force of evolutionary time enter into cultural understandings and practices of becoming American, affiliated subjectivities, and the co-incidental, "interior" space realized through the novel. It pays particular attention to the impact of unpredictable material and biological forces, such as sexual difference, on these materially realized spaces. It directly figures the potential of a nonoppositional biopolitical alternative through its intersex narrator, Cal, through a literal Middlesex—the family home and symbolic domestic space on Middlesex Boulevard—and through its own novelistic space-time and narrative technics, all of which are perceived to be thoroughly entangled with dynamic, unpredictable material processes of evolutionary time.

Drawing on a dynamic systems-theoretical understanding of bifurcation, as a systemic state-change involving the spatial, material, and temporal transformation of a system (not just a branching in time), I reconsider the novel's co-elaboration of national space, of "private" domestic space and subjectivity, and of the novel's space-time, arguing that all of these "interior" spaces are depicted as undergoing a bifurcation, depicted as a kind of "Middlesex," as analogous, co-implicated material spaces in the midst of becoming. Redescribing these spaces in terms of a Middlesex (the name of the family home as well as a reference to Cal's intersex and the novel's title), the novel suggests these national, familial, individual, and novelistic spaces are implicated in and responding to broader material, geopolitical, and economic flows rather than figuring a third space that is resolutely outside binary modern geopolitical oppositions or their current, bioinformatic recalibration. The novel examines all four spaces as charged points of interchange between modern U.S. nationalist spatiotemporal logics and emergent neoliberal transational flows. As material spaces in the midst of becoming, the novel suggests such dynamic sites of interchange are involved in a mutually transformative state change in the circulatory system of neoliberal capitalism and U.S. biopower, one that has significant implications for how we understand the gendered distinctions between public and private that these spaces have helped to realize.

Located at the crux between emerging domestic and global spaces, Cal's transgender subjectivity and his family's ongoing twentieth- and early twenty-first-century processes of becoming American seem designed to function in the novel as a retrospective, immanent diagnosis of historical and cultural change that is, therefore, also enactive or performative, poised to generate a viable alternative through its review of the past and present terrain. As Isabelle Stengers defines such kinds of *diagnosis*, drawing on Nietzsche, "It cannot be commentary, exteriority, but must risk assuming an inventive position that brings into existence, and makes perceptible, the passions and actions associated with the becomings it evokes."[19] Imagined in her terms, as a "speculative operation," the novel's diagnosis of twentieth- and late twenty-first-century biopower can be understood as one of the contemporary novel's tactics for opening onto unexpected "possibilities" through its concerted documentation of "probabilities" that would, otherwise, stand in the way of such changes.[20] Describing the domestic space of their family home on Middlesex Boulevard near the end of the novel, Cal describes it as a "beacon," "a place designed for a new type of human being, who would inhabit a new world," noting he "couldn't help feeling, of course, that the person was me, me and all the others like me."[21] At novel's close, Cal, the novel, and its readers remain poised on the doorstep of the house, Middlesex, with its door open to these familiar and unfamiliar, neoliberal circulations unsure of what is to come, unsure what direction the system, nation, and/or Cal will eventually take. Understood as a "speculative operation," the novel's diagnosis recommends a way of engaging with emergent modes of material transmission in an effort to creatively, differentially retrace recent bifurcations in social systems facilitated by the procedural, recursive logics of bioinformatics and neoliberal biopower.

Self-reflexively and retrospectively analyzing the novel's own role in global circulatory systems, past and present, *Middlesex* extends its novelistic diagnosis to the American novel's recent past and its potential literary future, reconsidering the contemporary novel in relation to these global, biopolitical flows and using its "speculative operations" to query the novel's current and potential occupation. This chapter will suggest the value of this novel's retrospective diagnostic mode, especially in the context of bioinformatic flows. *Middlesex* reconceives the novel as a co-implicated, pivotal site of interchange between national, familial, subjective, and late capitalist material *and* discursive flows. Its rethinking of the novel's occupation as a mode of diagnosis attempts to retrospectively retrace emergent modes of transmission and, thereby, to potentially influence neoliberal modes of circulation and publicity to open onto other trajectories. Similarly to other "media novels," as Daniel Punday describes them, *Middlesex* self-reflexively reconceives the novel's status as a point of interchange or threshold through which distinctions between public and private are realized and recommends, I will suggest, how contemporary novels might help teach us to comparatively register these shifting distinctions and the kinds of circulations they encourage or forestall.[22]

Smuggling Operations

In the opening section of the novel, Cal retraces his grandparents' journey from a war-torn Smyrna, circa 1922. They travel across the Atlantic, through the Ellis Island immigration center, to a reunion with their cousin Sourmelina in Detroit, where they decide to begin their lives as Americans. Unbeknownst to their fellow travelers, Eleutherios (Lefty) and Desdemona Stephanides were close kin before their supposed meeting and marriage en route to America. As brother and sister, the two directly parallel modern American nationalist discourses that, similarly, desire and attempt an incestuous reproduction of the same. The Stephanides, who have "a knack for self-transformation," according to Cal, spend their time on the ship "making up past histories for themselves" to legitimize their new life together as husband and wife.[23] Lefty was "aware that whatever happened now would become the truth, that whatever he seemed to be would become what he was—already an American, in other words," intent on a pure—because invented—origin.[24] While the grandparents succeed in their deceit, in their "made up" lives, at one level, grandson Cal underscores that such "genealogies tell you nothing," a knowledge he registers with a "dull pain" in his chest.[25] Lefty's and Desdemona's incestuous reproduction of the same results in their transmission of a genetic mutation on the fifth chromosome, which eventually, though somewhat circuitously, resurfaces and leads to Cal's intersex condition as a genetic male with male secondary sex characteristics and ambiguous genitalia due to his incapacity to process the male hormones, androgens (a condition formerly understood under the sign of hermaphroditism in mythology and science).

Hardly a reproduction of the same, at all, the Stephanides family's reinvention and the elaborate fictions they devise to support it are ultimately trumped by this materially transmitted genetic history and its circularity, its reiterative, evolutionary logic of repetition *and* difference. Cal explicitly differentiates the "patriarchal linearity" of genealogy and their "false histories," so thoroughly embraced by modern nationalisms, from a recursive, reiterative logic of evolutionary genetic change, noting the latter's similarities to the Greek belief that "to be happy you have to find variety in repetition; that to go forward you have to come back where you began."[26] The unacknowledged, unregistered, recessive genetic mutation, when it meets its match, reintroduces the unpredictable, divergent difference biological and cultural processes always involve; processes that modern American nationalism polices and frequently disavows.

The genetic mutation Lefty and Desdemona unknowingly "smuggle," en route to their new lives in America, is one of several cross-cultural smuggling operations that the novel describes, all illicit to the extent that they contravene, if not undermine, modern nationalist efforts to feign an absolute, homogenous cultural space outside time and, thus, to recapture an always already lost or fractured unity, purity, or univocity. Aware that he is "the descendent of a smuggling operation,"[27] Cal draws an explicit analogy between his grandparents' smuggling and the processes through which two missionaries snuck silkworm eggs and seeds out of a cultural protectionist China to grow the silkworms' favorite mulberry trees, after more than three thousand years of national secrecy. The latter cross-cultural smuggling practice allowed the Turkish Byzantium to become a center of sericulture, provided the elder Stephanides' family members' first livelihood as silkworm farmers, and even entered early American culture as Benjamin Franklin, champion of the silk industry, advocated planting mulberry trees to this end. Weaving this cross-cultural, material thread through its narrative, the novel underscores how silkworms, genetics, and other material evolutionary processes enter into and, acknowledged or not, recombine with individual, familial, cultural, national, and transnational practices to bolster and transform them in unexpected, ongoing, even nonconscious ways. Describing the last moments living in the childhood home on Middlesex Boulevard, Cal notes,

> As I picked those berries out my bedroom window, however, I had no idea that our mulberry tree had anything to do with the silk trade, or that my grandmother had had trees just like it behind her house in Turkey. That mulberry tree had stood outside my bedroom on Middlesex, never divulging its significance to me. But now things are different. Now all the mute objects of my life seem to tell my story, to stretch back in time, if I look closely enough."[28]

Registering the cross-cultural smuggling under way at multiple scales, the novel encourages a revaluation of processes of historical and cultural change understood to be in conversation with material and biological forces, as is silk weaving. It imagines these material forces in dynamic interrelation with social and cultural life, as forces furthering the repetition and heterogeneous difference on which material and biological, as well as social and cultural, life thrive. Attending to the acknowledged and unacknowledged, visible and invisible, intertwining agencies at work in such variously underground, resolutely nonconscious, unperceived practices, *Middlesex* conceives smuggling operations as a way to reconsider the interrelations between cultural discourses and material and biological processes. The novel reconceives these as multiplicit processes that work across and through what is more often thought of as the nature-culture divide to coproduce an unpredictable future.

Shortly after arriving in Detroit in 1922, Lefty Stephanides lands a job at the Ford Motor Company and begins to attend Henry Ford's English Language School. The school provides mandatory classes to the immigrant factory workers that conclude in a graduation ceremony requiring the workers to perform a play in which they don ethnic garb, jump into a melting pot, and then, after some stirring, reemerge dressed in modern black or blue, American suits.[29] Lefty and other workers also receive visits from plant inspectors who examine their homes to ensure they learn and follow "proper" notions of hygiene. Both scenes in the novel are historically accurate examples of American nationalist practices, here aimed at reproducing the same through assimilation to the white Protestant norm. Notably, such early twentieth-century American nationalisms are materially realized through a biopolitical policing and mandated self-regulation of the worker's and the social body. The novel also references American nationalist discourses of purity/impurity, normalcy/monstrosity, and masculinity/femininity as crucial to biopower's repertoire, its attempts to circumscribe the homogenous cultural space of the nation and force any challenges to the parameters it sets on American culture underground, if not outside its domain entirely.

Importantly, this productive power of official nationalist discourses and their biopolitical practices in the novel are frequently accompanied by less predictable or explicit cultural practices. Illicit smuggling operations—such as the bootlegging Lefty takes up with his cousin Sourmelina's Turkish-American husband, Jimmy Zizmo after Lefty is fired from the Ford plant due to his questionable family associations—reveal the under- and countercurrents following in the immediate wake of official discourses of American belonging, identity, and state power. These illicit practices are as much an act of ethnic and cultural, as they are economic, survival, enabling these recent immigrants to reshape the hegemonic culture's privileged discourses and practices to better suit their needs and to sidestep the dominant culture's self-serving, biopolitical imperatives. Similarly to the elder Stephanides' smuggling of a genetic mutation to the United States, the results of such smuggling operations, and the monstrous, cross-cultural, transformative burdens and gifts they bear are, initially, unclear.

Illustrating through these "smuggling operations" how twentieth-century American nationalisms and the identifications and affiliations they open onto can never be consolidated or secured, in spite of their determined efforts to evoke a homogenous, territorial place outside time or other pure origin, *Middlesex* reimagines American nationalisms and other cultural practices in dynamic interrelation to evolutionary material and biological processes. It launches a retrospective project of charting the interrelated, ongoing evolution of multiple, conflicting, and shifting modes of becoming American over the past century or so. As evidence of heterogeneous and changing modes of national belonging and experiences of national space-times and the subjectivities they facilitate, *Middlesex* features Greek and Turkish immigrant narratives, hegemonic American nationalist imaginaries such as the early twentieth-century "melting pot," black nationalist counterhistories emerging from the Nation of Islam, the queer time and space of Cal's lesbian aunt Sourmelina, and the Greek cultural beliefs his grandmother Desdemona refuses to relinquish (though she does eventually embrace American television). This conflictual and multifarious view of becoming American striates the homogenous space-times modern American nationalism attempts to secure, compromises its opposition of old world and new world, tradition and modernity, and underscores the persistent heterogeneity of American national space and modes of belonging at the level of people's lives and material practices as they regularly vie with official nationalist discourses and biopower.

Tracing official and unofficial processes of becoming American, the novel attempts to register material-based processes and cultural practices in evolutionary time as they inform and deform the supposedly absolute space of the nation and its privileged subjectivities. According to *Middlesex*, such processes might provide the basis for a biopolitics and affiliated modes of becoming American that are open to, impacted by, and responsive to dynamic, cross-cultural material and cultural practices. These alternate modes of becoming American operate along the lines of other smuggling operations in the novel, operations through which material and biological forces (such as a genetic mutation) enter into and transform cultural practices (such as a doctored family genealogy) and require cultural practices to, in turn, selectively engage certain material and biological forces to a mutually transformative, unpredictable end.

In this way, *Middlesex* engages Darwinian evolutionary theory and molecular genetic's dynamic, nonteleological, nonindividualistic understandings of biological change to counter modern American nationalism's understanding of biology and material processes as static territories, an understanding that also authorizes modern geopolitics and engenders a static, unchanging account of American national identity. The novel attempts, on this evolutionary basis, to generate an alternate, new materialist and feminist biopolitics designed to permanently destabilize modern nationalist efforts to locate cultural origins and practices or biology outside time, and, equally, to trouble more recent neoliberal efforts to instrumentally direct material processes toward late capitalism's immediate circulatory ends.

The novel's turn to Darwinian evolutionary theory and more recent theories of genetic transmission, read in the context of twentieth-century American nationalisms and their virulent social Darwinisms, may initially seem surprising. Throughout *Middlesex*'s retrospective, historically detailed retracing of twentieth-century and early twenty-first-century nationalisms, there are numerous, extensive references to evolution, to evolutionary psychology, to sociobiology, as well as to the social Darwinism informing the Immigration Act of 1917, which blocked "undesirables" who, according to Senator Henry Cabot Lodge, "threatened 'the very fabric of our race.'"[30] It is fair to say that the novel is well aware of Darwinian theory's previous engagements and evolutionary theory's loaded political history. *Middlesex* takes up these prior evolutionary perspectives, recombines them with molecular genetics and the distinct evolutionary perspective on genetic transmission it opens onto, yet it does so to contest the hegemonic biopolitical circulations they are more frequently used to support. Instead, it remarks on the ongoing material processes unfolding through evolutionary time at multiple scales to open onto a distinct, alternate mode of linking material processes and cultural life to a biopolitics.

The novel's reengagement of evolutionary, material history makes a bit more sense when considered in light of Elizabeth Grosz's groundbreaking rethinking of Darwinian evolutionary theory and the latter's conception of materially situated, yet dynamic, transformative time. In *Time Travels: Feminism, Nature, Power*, she argues that Darwin's understanding of evolution as an "asystematic systematicity coextensive with all life" remains invaluable to contemporary feminisms and cultural theory.[31] It provides a nuanced concept of life "as an opening up of matter to indeterminacy," as a process that serves as "a bridge, a point of connection and transition between the biological and the cultural."[32] The novel's, Grosz's, and other new materialist rereadings of evolutionary theory more attuned to the complexities of Darwinian theory are especially needed in light of contemporary sociobiology's and neoliberal bioinformatics' frequent, reductive engagements with genetics and evolutionary theory, which are prone to reduplicate social Darwinist understandings of an all-determining, teleological process of genetic transmission, of DNA, for instance, as an informational master-code that determines life.

"Ontologies of Change"

Grosz's feminist, new materialist rereading of Darwinian evolutionary theory, like *Middlesex*, is focused on "the question of becomings,"[33] though it does not extend these queries to a consideration of twenty-first-century American nationalisms or neoliberal space-times and their biopower, as the novel does. She stresses the significance of reconceptualizing historical, cultural, and biological change in ways that reject the oversimplistic, binary, gendered nature-culture divide and the masculinist instrumentalism it upholds. In this way, Grosz encourages subjectivities foreclosed by these binaries and their instrumental, anthropocentric, culturalist models of change, engendering a mode of feminist politics that, by engaging with Darwinian "ontologies of change," embraces these, among other, unpredictable, unintended outcomes.[34]

For Grosz, an attention to "becoming" is a means of reintroducing temporal dynamism into a pacified, bankrupt conception of nature via Darwin's understanding of materially based, dynamic processes of evolutionary time. Darwin's work, in her reading, "provides a dynamic and open-ended understanding of the intermingling of history and biology" and "a complex account of the movements of difference, bifurcation, and becoming that characterize all forms of life."[35] She pursues a more complex formulation of their interrelations, poignantly arguing that "the natural is *not* the inert, passive, unchanging element against which culture elaborates itself but the matter of the cultural, that which enables and actively facilitates cultural variation and change, indeed that which ensures that the cultural, including its subject agents, are never self-identical, that they differ from themselves and necessarily change over time."[36] Extending a Bergsonian understanding of the split between the virtual and the actual that divides time, Grosz describes how material and biological existence introduces subhuman or inhuman "microagencies" or "virtualities" and "potentialities" into "cultural, social, and historical forces" that enable them "to work with and actively transform that existence" while the cultural and social and historical forces introduce "virtualities and potentialities" into material and biological processes and productively transform them, in turn.[37] Elaborating on Grosz's theory in the novel's terms, one might argue that such processes involve smuggling operations with more than one kind of agency, unfolding at multiple scales.

Interested in this enabling, productive force of material and biological processes, Grosz's reading of Darwinian evolutionary theory gestures toward what might be gained via this understanding of biology and history in ongoing, dynamic, mutually transformative, nonrepresentational interrelation. As she illustrates, it has clear consequences for understandings of causality, agency, and, as I will address below, sexual difference. From this Darwinian vantage, evolutionary processes do not function on the order of linear, deterministic, or teleological change. Shaped by the particularity of their encounters and their ongoing, dynamic reciprocity, such co-productive interrelations between material and cultural processes are neither completely transparent nor fully recuperable or open to instrumentalization. Evolutionary processes are characterized by repetition *and* difference as a result of natural selection. Natural selection designates fitness to a particular, shifting environment (not fitness in the abstract, ahistorical notion in which "survival of the fittest" is often misunderstood). As a result, evolutionary processes can be understood as operating according to circular, recursive logics in which the future emerges out of the ongoing encounter of an existing system with a changing environment and vice versa. In the case of the recessive mutation that engenders Cal's intersex condition, which evidences a logic of "sporadic heredity"—a genetic trait that "goes underground for decades only to reappear when everyone has forgotten about it"—it is clear that even unactualized, past system-states can be actualized in the present, more than vexing linear notions of causality and historical change.[38]

In light of these ongoing, recursive, transformative, and, thus, unpredictable processes, agency has to be relocated on both sides of the former nature-culture divide. Agency comes to be understood as conscious, unconscious, and nonconscious material practices and forces at multiple, individual, cellular, subatomic, affective, human, and nonhuman scales, in addition to the agencies modern nationalist discourses align with individuals, families, civil society, the state, and capitalist economic circulation. Grosz stresses that "subjectivity, sexuality, intimate social relations" are, thereby, seen to be "structured not only by institutions and social networks, but also by impersonal or prepersonal, subhuman or inhuman forces, forces that may be construed as competing microagencies, rather than as a conflict between singular, unified, self-knowing subjects or well-defined social groups."[39] Individual and social forces, in other words, are no longer understood to operate from the top down as a unidirectional coding of an impassive natural world. Nor are biological and material processes understood as determining social and cultural life in the guise of a single, timeless source or origin. Instead, materially catalyzed or realized cultural and historical processes come to be seen as mutually transformative forces, literally working through each other in coimplicated, yet noninstrumental, nondeterministic relations.

Middlesex develops the consequences of a Darwinian rethinking of ongoing, dynamic, agential relations between processes of biological and historical change to modern U.S. nationalism and its biopolitical circumscription of subjectivities, in particular. The novel's central, first-person narrative, which describes Cal's ongoing process of self-transformation and self-realization, opens with what I'll describe as a "gene's-eye view," a term I borrow from contemporary sociobiologist Richard Dawkins's work, as will be explained below.[40] The novel's redeployment of a "gene's-eye view" contravenes what might otherwise be perceived as a typical American tale of self-invention. The narrator states:

> I was born twice: first as a baby girl, on a remarkably smogless Detroit day in January of 1960; and then again, as a teenage boy, in an emergency room near Petoskey, Michigan, in August of 1974. . . . My birth certificate lists my name as Calliope Helen Stephanides. My most recent driver's license (from the Federal Republic of Germany) records my first name simply as Cal. I'm a former field hockey goalie, long-standing member of the Save-the-Manatee Foundation, rare attendant of the Greek Orthodox liturgy, and, for most of my adult life, an employee of the U.S. State Department. Like Tiresias, I was first one thing and then the other. I've been ridiculed by classmates, guinea-pigged by doctors, palpated by specialists, and researched by the March of Dimes. A redheaded girl from Grosse Pointe fell in love with me, not knowing what I was. (Her brother liked me, too.) An army tank led me into battle once; a swimming pool turned me into myth; *I've left my body in order to occupy others—and all this happened before I turned sixteen.*
>
> But now, at the age of forty-one, I feel another birth coming on. After decades of neglect, I find myself thinking about departed great-aunts and -uncles, long-lost grandfathers, unknown fifth cousins, or, in the case of an inbred family like mine, all those things in one. And so before it's too late I want to get it down for good: *this roller-coaster*

ride of a single gene through time. Sing now, O Muse, of the recessive mutation on my fifth chromosome! Sing how it bloomed two and a half centuries ago on the slopes of Mount Olympus, while the goats bleated and the olives dropped. Sing how it passed down through nine generations, gathering invisibly within the polluted pool of the Stephanides family. And sing how Providence, in the guise of a massacre, sent the gene flying again; how it blew like a seed across the sea to America, where it drifted through our industrial rains until it fell to earth in the fertile soil of my mother's own mid-western womb.

Sorry if I get a little Homeric at times. That's genetic, too.[41]

The first two births represent the narrator's initial biological birth, when he was mistakenly identified as female and the subsequent discovery, after a road accident at the age of fourteen, that he was reaching maturity with male secondary sex characteristics and male and female genitalia. This realization eventually leads Cal to adopt the masculine gender but forgo sex-reassignment surgery, embracing his intersexuality and a transgender subjectivity that disregards the binary requirements a sex/gender system attempts to impose. Although Cal's transgender status, his decision to embrace his male and female as well as his masculine and feminine traits, can be interpreted as a *symbolic* leaving and taking up of other bodies, as a male-identified female in his youth or as a transgender male in adulthood, for instance, this "leaving and taking up of other bodies" also asks to be taken *literally* in the novel.

The focalization of the narrative, in this passage and in several others, adopts the perspective of an omniscient gene "leaving and taking up" other bodies. In this way, the narrative captures and conveys the temporal scale of the evolutionary microprocesses that inform Cal: this "roller-coaster ride of a single gene through time." These are temporal forces that, as mentioned above, compromise a nationalist project to reproduce the same that relies on the illusion of an absolute cultural space outside these material forces of evolutionary change. This perspective also recasts individualist understandings of subjectivity as an instrumental self-authorship or act of self-invention by acknowledging the multiple biological and environmental forces beyond Cal's knowledge and control that inform the Stephanides' "knack for self-transformation," the microagencies, as Grosz describes them, that are, the narrative concurs, knowable only in retrospect. Noting how Cal's Homeric excesses are "genetic, too," the novel suggests evolutionary forces function all the way up through expressive cultural forms, though in equally unpredictable, sporadic, indirect, nonteleological ways, quite contrary to the direct causal links sociobiologists establish between genes and social attributes (of aggression, etc.), for instance.

Directing its invocation of the muse to a heroic genetic mutation, this passage cites and *mocks* predominant twenty-first-century engagements with evolutionary theory by sociobiologists who tend to cast their abstract understanding of an informational genetic code as the immortals and to conceptualize their instructions in a language of destiny and fate inherited from Greek tragedy. The novel's *mock*-heroic tribute to this gene's DNA seems to respond directly to the claims of sociobiology and what prominent sociobiologist Richard Dawkins describes as his "gene's-eye view of Darwinism" in *The Selfish Gene*. Dawkins claims that "the genes are the immortals, or rather, they are defined as genetic entities that come close to deserving the title" in that "the gene does not grow senile. . . . It leaps from body to body down the generations, manipulating body after body in its own way and for its own ends, abandoning a succession of mortal bodies before they sink in senility and death."[42] While Dawkins's reference to immortals may appear incidental, his and other sociobiological accounts of genetically driven change have an understanding of causality troublingly similar to Greek mythology. In addition, the novel indicates how they are often fueled by similar desires for clear origins and ends.

It is a strategically different gene's-eye view that the novel develops in this and other passages. The omniscient gene-focalizer, describing the latest conception and subsequent rebirth, states:

The bedroom grows still. Inside my mother, a billion sperm swim upstream, males in the lead. They carry not only instructions about eye color, height, nose shape, enzyme production, microphage resistance, but a story, too. Against a black background they swim, a long white silken thread spinning itself out. The thread began on a day two hundred and fifty years ago, when the biology gods, for their own amusement, monkeyed with a gene on a baby's fifth chromosome. That baby passed the mutation onto her son, who passed it on to three of their children (my great-great-greats, etc.), until finally it ended up in the bodies of my grandparents. Hitching a ride, the gene descended a mountain and left a village behind. It got trapped in a burning city and escaped, speaking bad French. Crossing the ocean, it faked a romance, circled a ship's deck, and made love in a lifeboat. . . .

And then the gene moved on again, into new bodies. . . . It joined the Boy Scouts and painted its toenails red . . . always moving ahead, rushing along, only a few more curves left in the track now . . . *until the biology gods knew this was their time, this was what they'd been waiting for . . . the roller coaster was in free fall and there was no stopping it now . . . the gene is about to meet its twin.*[43]

Momentarily situating the gene in the role of the central protagonist and as the narrative's focalizer, this passage suggests that Cal, among other characters, is being "moved" by this gene, by subhuman, inhuman, evolutionary temporal forces, while it also, adeptly, critiques sociobiology's elevation of DNA sequences to the immortal status of "biology gods" and its wholesale conflation of cultural and biological levels. Contrary to Dawkins's and other sociobiologists' view of omniscient, immortal, "selfish genes" and the destiny they are believed to unproblematically encode, the principles of evolution and the self-admitted "themes" of Cal's life are *both* "chance and sex."[44] In Cal's words, "genetics, a crapshoot, entirely."[45]

Underscoring how biological determinist strains of sociobiology frequently leave out the dynamism and resulting chance of evolutionary processes here (and elsewhere), the novel's gene's-eye view reimagines the relations of continuity between biological and cultural processes, insisting that these relations are informed by the difference, variation, and mutation that define evolutionary time and its processes of becoming. In this sense, the passage's casting of DNA's double-helix as a roller-coaster ride reinforces its surprising twists and turns, as well as its resemblance to the wooden slats joining winding, parallel exterior tracks. In Cal's words, "What humans forget, cells remember. The body, that elephant."[46] This gene's-eye view on American self-invention contravenes social Darwinisms and more recent sociobiology that, continuing to rely on an opposition of nature and culture, attempt to reduce dynamic cultural processes to a static, deterministic, "normative (genetic or instinctually given) nature."[47] Nature, understood as the unchanging, passive origin or foundation for culture, is stripped of its dynamism, its difference, and its potential for bifurcation and change. As problematically, sociobiologists' fetishization of an abstract, informational genetic code disregards the heterogeneous material and environmental processes that regularly enter into genetic change. Quite notably, these are material and environmental processes that contemporary bioinformatics and biomedicine are increasingly adept at manipulating, not disregarding, as

Eugene Thacker convincingly illustrates in his book surveying recent bioinformatics and biotechnology, *Biomedia*.[48]

Biopolitics in Evolutionary Time

The significance of the novel's rethinking of material and cultural practices in relation to dynamic evolutionary time and its impact on how we understand emergent modes of U.S. biopower is clarified by close attention to Cal's struggle with hir intersex. Cal, as a third-generation Greek American born in Detroit, Michigan, in 1960 and raised as a girl, initially named Callie, recounts hir life story from Berlin in the 1990s, where he, now gendered masculine, is working as a cultural attaché for the American ambassador in the U.S. State Department. The clinical term, "intersex," describes "congenital conditions in which chromosomal, gonadal, or anatomical sex development is atypical," a term replacing previous terms such as hermaphroditism or sex reversal.[49] Cal has the second most common intersex condition, Androgen Insensitivity Syndrome (AIS), which renders a person with an XY karyotype unable to process the male hormones called androgens as a result of genetic defects on the X chromosome. This leads to male secondary sex characteristics and ambiguous genitalia (such as undescended testes) that often aren't fully apparent until a person fails to menstruate or encounters problems with fertility. As Katrina Karkazis stresses in her ethnography tracing understandings and practices of sex, gender, and sexuality emerging out of recent biomedical discourses of intersex and from intersex patients' and their family's experiences, intersexuality "does not represent a point of pure liminality between sexes," as the term and its gloss in the novel, as a middlesex, might, at first, seem to suggest.[50] The common understanding of intersex as a third sex reinforces a misleading understanding of biological sex as an absolute, unchanging territory or space outside time and often simply introduces a third term between the other two. Perhaps this is one of the reasons very few intersexuals opt to use this term. Nondimorphic sexual development, which is evident in as many as 1.7 percent of births according to Anne Fausto-Sterling, underscores the variability and "breadth of human physical variance" that biomedical and cultural discourses refuse to acknowledge as anything other than an unwelcome exception to the binary rule.[51] Importantly, intersexuality also calls into question a binary sex/gender system that assumes agreement between chromosomes, gonads, genitals, and secondary sex characteristics, as well as between gender and sexuality. It, thus, requires us to confront the material and cultural reality of sexual difference. In forcing awareness of the subtle differentiations dynamically comprising sexual difference, intersex raises the daunting specter of sexual difference itself, exactly that "sex which is not one," in Luce Irigaray's terms, that is, the sexual difference a patriarchal, binary sex/gender system refuses to acknowledge in its definition of the female only in opposition to the male, as lack, absence, or other.[52]

In the novel, Cal's intersexuality opens onto an alternative, what might best be described as a bifurcation of the binary sex/gender system in complex conversation with late capitalist biopolitics. Reintroducing sexual difference, intersexuality unsettles the patriarchal, heteronormative assumptions the sex/gender system reinforces. The concept of bifurcation, developed in systems-theoretical work on complex self-organizing systems, describes moments at which a system becomes unstable and opens onto multiple possibilities. Bifurcation points are "*where the system can 'choose' between or among more than one possible future.*"[53] Interestingly, Ilya Prigogine and Isabelle Stengers describe evolutionary processes in such terms, while also noting similar dynamics in "social phenomena, even with history" in that "such systems seem to 'hesitate' among various possible directions of evolution. . . . A small fluctuation may start an entirely new evolution that will drastically change the whole behavior of the macroscopic system."[54] Cal's ambiguous "middlesex" or "intersex," if read in terms of such processes of bifurcation, as an at once temporal and material, embodied subjectivity in the midst of becoming, comes to figure a dynamic point of interchange situated (spatially and temporally) between the present and future of sexual difference. It suggests we might reconceive sex, in this way, as an ongoing reelaboration on processes of sexual differentiation unfolding through dynamic, evolutionary time.

Living in Berlin, appropriately on the former, gendered, Cold War line between East and West, Cal claims "this once-divided city reminds me of myself. My struggle for unification, for *Einheit*."[55] He renders explicit the parallels between Cold War geopolitics and their binary, gendered, and racialized dualisms between East and West and his own biopolitical encounter with the imperative to align his sex and gender along analogous, oppositional, binary lines of male/female or masculine/feminine. Though Cal finds Berlin "hopeful," in contrast to his hometown Detroit, which remains "cut in half by racial hatred," Cal refuses this nationalist imperative to overcome difference.[56] When prestigious doctors decide to perform sex-reassignment

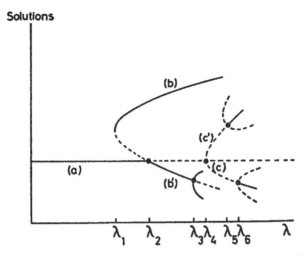

Solutions

Figure 17. Bifurcation diagram. Steady-state solutions are plotted against bifurcation parameter λ. For λ<λ₁ there is only one stationary state for each value of λ; this set of states forms the branch a. For λ=λ₁ two other sets of stationary states become possible (branches b and b′).

The states of b′ are unstable but become stable at λ=λ₂ while the states of branch a become unstable. For λ=λ₃ the branch b′ is unstable again, and two other stable branches appear.

For λ=λ₄ the unstable branch a attains a new bifurcation point where two new branches become possible, which will be unstable up to λ=λ₅ and λ=λ₆.

Fig. 5. "Bifurcation diagram" from *Order out of Chaos: Man's New Dialogue with Nature.* Courtesy of Isabelle Stengers.

surgery on hir at fourteen to realign hir sex with a young life gendered feminine, Callie flees. The biomedical establishment is explicitly aligned with the coercive force of U.S. biopower and its active production of gendered and heterosexist subjectivities and sexualities in that the doctors insist on surgical intervention without fully explaining his condition or the consequences of such surgery to either parents or child. Cal's subsequent exposure to other transgender and intersex subjects in San Francisco and to the intersex political movement leads him to refuse a modern nationalist desire for reunification.[57] After great deliberation and self-exploration, Cal gives up hir desire for an apparent univocity of sex, of sex and gender, or an appropriate (because keyed to both sex and gender) sexual orientation. He chooses to embrace hir multiplicit sex, to adopt the masculine gender (after having spent the first fourteen years of his life as a young girl), and to date women.

Refusing the modern nationalist imperative to overcome difference, which would require Cal to conform to the patriarchal norm of the binary sex/gender system by becoming a male and masculine subject or its other, a female and feminine subject through gender-reassignment surgery, Cal develops and embraces a transgender subjectivity. This decision serves, in the novel, to call into question a larger, materially realized geopolitical imaginary and its erasures. Transgender describes "a way of being a man or a woman, or a way of resisting categorization by those labels."[58] Since its first usage, transgender has come to operate as "a catchall term for all non-normative forms of gender expression and identity," encompassing a wide "range of gender-variant practices and identities."[59] Cal's intersexuality and his experimentation in finding a meaningful sex and gender identity align him with this loose use of the term, transgender, even though his experience and practices remain distinct from many of the other identities and practices transgender references (transsexuality and drag, for instance). While Cal's experiences are aligned with transgender practices, the novel's interest in intersex, specifically, underscores its interest in the transformative biological and cultural dimensions of sexual difference, as well as nonnormative, gender-variant practices and identities, more generally.

Through Cal's transgender subjectivity, *Middlesex* situates Cal's experience in direct relation to shifting neoliberal modes of U.S biopower and a transnational, late capitalist circulatory system. Juxtaposing Cal and his family's transnational migrations with his transgender migrations, the novel underscores their co-implication within twenty-first-century neoliberal logics of flexible, deterritorialized connectivity. The geopolitical movement across national lines, epitomized by late capitalism's neoliberal flows, is revealed to be closely intertwined with his biopolitical movement across what were formerly conceived, in analogous terms, as the absolute territories of sex and gender. Late twentieth- and early twenty-first-century practices of transgender embodiment and identification and contemporary neoliberal transnationalisms share, at least conceptually, in their disregard for modern nationalisms' link between absolute territories and the gendered and racialized, place-based identities that are supposed to find their ground in them. They share in the, at once, biopolitical and geopolitical promise of a deterritorialized flexibility in the linkages established between sex, gender, and sexuality, and in parallel, similarly flexible (because no longer territorially based) geopolitical modes of transnational American belonging. Just as there is, from the vantage of early twenty-first-century transgender movements, no single or necessary relation between biological sex and gender (as variously defined), there is, according to early twenty-first-century transnational late capitalist networks, no necessary or single relation between territorial place and national identity.

Read as a movement across "the boundaries between gender, sex, and sexuality and the boundary that structures each as a binary category,"[60] the transgendered subject's transgression of the "territories" of gender, sex, and sexuality is easily aligned with the mobile, abstract logics of late capitalist networks and their transnational flows. After all, these transnational networks are similarly involved in trespassing against the gendered logics of a nationalist imaginary. Transgender identities and practices make it quite clear that sex and gender are not absolute locations or places (and that one is not grounded in the body or the culture of the other) by moving across what were formerly believed to be mutually exclusive territories. In turn, neoliberalism and affiliated, transnational modes of becoming American make it clear that American nationalism no longer relies on a static, unchanging understanding of its relation to territorial place or on the stable identities assumed to follow from place.

Transgender beyond Flexibility

The novel cites this shift in the emerging neoliberal logics of twenty-first-century biopower and associated modes of becoming American. It is a shift that informs many recent cultural engagements with transgender. Asking why transgender is so prominent in postmodernism, in *In a Queer Time and Place: Transgender Bodies, Subcultural Lives*, J. Jack Halberstam argues that the "gender flexibility" informing transgender is "a site of both fascination and promise in the late twentieth century" that has to be read in relation to "other economies of flexibility in postmodernism."[61] "The transgender body has emerged as futurity itself, a kind of heroic fulfillment of postmodern promises of gender flexibility."[62] It is a fulfillment that shares key features with the much-vaunted ability of late capitalist networks (and their privileged information elite) to move across what were formerly conceived as absolute, unchanging, national territories. This cultural alignment, I'd add, serves to reinforce neoliberalism's insistence that its own and affiliated transgressions of modern national spaces are liberating, that they diminish the restrictions on these and other "free market" flows. In this respect it becomes clear how transgender might seem to support what Timothy Campbell describes as late capital's "hymns to neoliberal genetics," in which "the freedom to decide the qualities of a future human life through biotechnological processes is often located within this 'option of circulation,'" and, thus, endowed with fully liberatory dimensions.[63] Transgender can, in this way, become symbolically associated with "the widening network of circuits of exchange of genetic material" encouraged by neoliberal capitalist circulation.[64]

Two points seem key here. On the one hand, in spite of the disruptions late twentieth- and early twenty-first-century biopower introduce into modern nation-based, oppositional politics, these flexible, bioinformatic circulatory systems continue to rely on biopower's "integral link between micro- and macro-political levels" in that the "new techniques of self-regulation" encouraged through hegemonic symbols and practices of transgender are directly linked to "flexible" "forms of political rule and economic exploitation," as Thomas Lemke stresses.[65] Such ongoing biopolitical coordinations require careful consideration of this continued co-production of the modern nation-state and subjectivities. U.S. biopower and affiliated modes of becoming American no longer, uniquely, rely on the normalizing, static discourses of the modern-nation state and its homogenous, unchanging, territorial identities located outside time. Yet in producing newly flexible modalities of the human and newly sexed, gendered, and racialized subjectivities, biopower continues to link geopolitical "techniques of domination" and biopolitical "techniques of the self," realizing its neoliberal economic aims, in part, through this rendering of the social domain in its own, rational-economic terms.[66] What's central to neoliberalism and what Foucault identifies as its biopower, as Lemke underscores, is that "neoliberalism is not just a political-economic reality but above all a political project that endeavors to create a social reality that it suggests already exists."[67]

In this context, it is worth considering what kind of work transgender subjectivities are put to within late capitalist geopolitical imaginaries and terrain. In what instances are they effectively deployed as a symbol to sustain neoliberalism's purportedly limitless, flexible, deterritorialized economic "freedoms"? And, by extension, how can one lessen their alignment with affiliated, transnational understandings of becoming American as a series of flexible, choice-based identifications that function similarly to other highly privileged logics of consumer choice? In *Transnational America*, Inderpal Grewal stresses that "transnational connectivities," the networks of knowledge and power, cosmopolitan and "global," that have traversed and rearticulated national boundaries in the late twentieth and early twenty-first centuries, often reflect a neoliberal imaginary in which becoming American is based primarily on subjects' identification with America through commodity culture and a consumer-based understanding of democratic rights.[68]

How, in turn, do transgender and the biomedical technologies engaged in transgender's cross-identifying practices betray and complicate the futuristic, patriarchal ideal of instrumental control over one's embodiment and subjectivity, as a wealth of actual practices of transgender certainly do. Located within the context of neoliberal capitalism, hegemonic representations and understandings of transgender might initially appear to feed directly into a neoliberal notion of the subject as a rational actor, exercising consumer choice and a democratic right to freedom. It is a "freedom" that is extended, with the help of biomedicine, to previously untouched, personal realms of one's sex, gender, identity, and sexuality, promising to, at last, reveal "the truth of sex" through this economic rationality.[69] This does not mean transgender practices are in thrall to neoliberalism or that transgender subjects are dupes of American biopower, the kind of sweeping, overbroad arguments feminists initially used to critique early transsexual surgeries as gender-conformist. Instead, transgender evidences struggles that involve a reassertion of the instrumentalizing logics that neoliberalism works hard to naturalize and the active querying of such logics, as apparent in *Middlesex* and evident in transgender communities and practices, especially as they negotiate biomedicine.

In fact, transgender in *Middlesex* provides a timely means to *unsettle* neoliberalism's limitless, dynamic, flexible biopolitical and geopolitical imaginary by undermining its ability to fully rerealize its social aims through this intimate hinging of "techniques of the self" and political-economic "techniques of domination." The novel's weapon of resistance against neoliberalism's bioinformatics of goal-oriented differentiation is not fiction, nonnormative subjectivities, or myth per se, but its rereading of emergent genetic and bioinformatic sciences and their perspective on dynamic material processes of evolutionary time, reproduction, and species-being. *Middlesex* employs its intersex and transgender narrator and its distinct, retrospective view on biopolitics to counter this hegemonic neoliberal vision of the unlimited flexibility and transformability of American nationalism in the context of late capitalism and its technoscientific biopower.

Cal's decision to embrace his multiplicit sex, his male genetic traits, and his male secondary sex characteristics and to embrace a masculine-identified, transgender subjectivity is key to the novel's critical diagnosis of emergent neoliberal geopolitics and biopower. At one level, Cal appears to be a quintessential, privileged, Western, masculine, global subject, joining the Foreign Service because he has "never wanted to stay in one place."[70] In this he would conform to modes of transnational American circulation and state power that are increasingly mobile and deterritorialized. His mobility and flexibility as a transnational and transgender American working for the U.S. State Department in Berlin, in this reading, relies on a circulatory system and flexible modes of cross-cultural and cross-racial genetic transmission, reinforcing biopower's claims to manipulate natural and cultural processes, without apparent limit or territorial boundaries, in the name of a patriarchal futurity. Though the idea is less thoroughly developed than Cal's intersex, the novel suggests that Cal may be of mixed racial descent, as one of his grandparents, Jimmy Zizmo, migrates to the United States from Turkey, is darker skinned, and plays some part in the emergence of the Nation of Islam in Detroit, though there is no clear identification of his racial or ethnic status other than the suggestion that it calls into question racial binaries between white and nonwhite. Cal's cross-racial movement might, equally, appear to align him with the widening scope of genetic transmissions neoliberalism encourages.

Bioinformatic Circulations and Becoming in Evolutionary Time

Instead, Cal's intersexuality, and his family's processes of becoming American *recast* U.S. biopower's modes of crossing sexed and gendered and racialized national territories in thrall to neoliberalism's transnational flows. They open onto an alternate understanding of migration or moving across (i.e., *trans*) that puts a transformative, material, and evolutionary time back into play, revealing its consequence to the domestic space of the nation, the home, and to a bourgeois subjectivity modeled on the former private, "interior" spaces. The Stephanides' family home, fondly called "Middlesex" in reference to its location on Middlesex Boulevard in the suburb of Grosse Pointe, Michigan, encapsulates Cal's and his family's processes of becoming American. These becomings divert the dominant linear, developmental discourses American nationalism, neoliberalism, and even some feminisms rely on. According to developmental narratives, national becoming is cast as a straightforward, progressive movement from tradition to modernity, from a feminine, "ethnic" East to a masculine, white West, from economic dependence to economic self-determination, or from oppression to sexual freedom.

The family's economic trajectory, leading up to the momentous purchase of the first family home, already contravenes the typical progressive, developmental account of American economic and class mobility. Cal's family moves to the suburbs after the family restaurant is burned down during protests against racial and economic oppression in Detroit's inner-city neighborhoods in the summer of 1967. Thus, the Stephanides' upward mobility is an unexpected consequence of this racial strife and the insurance dividends that follow from the fires, not simply hard work and gumption, as the story usually goes. In fact, grandfather Lefty has gambled away his life's earnings. In addition, it is only because Cal's father, Milton, is able to purchase their home with cash, that these Greek Americans are able to evade the elaborate "point system" realtors used to disqualify home-buyers who were not white or Protestant enough, in their view, to live in the more affluent, suburban neighborhoods.

Equally vexed and paradoxical from this developmental point of view on familial, national, and individual space-time is the family home, Middlesex. The home as domestic space, in recent American history, symbolizes and helps rerealize a privileged private, bourgeois, subjective interiority, the private, feminine space of the family, and, by extension, the American nation (cultivated in the former through appropriate feminine sentiment). It is typically opposed to the masculine, public space of the market and political spheres and their more worldly, transnational flows. Built in 1909, by a lesser-known Prairie School architect, the Stephanides' home, Middlesex, was designed with transparent glass walls "to harmonize with the natural surroundings."[71] Cal notes, its architecture

was an attempt to rediscover pure origins. At the time, I didn't know about all that. But as I pushed through the door into the skylit guest house I was aware of the disparities. The boxlike room, stripped of all embellishment or parlor fussiness, a room that wished to be timeless or ahistorical, and there, in the middle of it, my deeply historical, timeworn grandmother. Everything about Middlesex spoke of forgetting and everything about Desdemona made plain the inescapability of remembering.[72]

As a symbol and material realization of national space, Middlesex evidences modern nationalism's failed attempts at self-invention, its unsuccessful attempts to delimit a space outside time and, thus, ground a "pure," "timeless or ahistorical" origin.

The novel suggests that processes of becoming American, like those the architecture of Middlesex encapsulates, are, instead, both "futuristic and outdated at the same time," both innovative and repetitive, at once, like all processes of evolution.[73] What are more often presumed to be feminine and masculine, traditional and modern, domestic and global, private and public tendencies are, instead, recursively co-implicated and intertwined in this picture of the glass-walled, "meditative, pastel yellow cube" of a house.[74]

In the case of *Middlesex*, the domestic space of the family home is a space evidencing a (feminine) anachronism and (masculine) futurity intertwined in one mutually entangled, open-ended process that casts these familiar, gendered spatiotemporal oppositions into doubt. The physical structure of the house has been designed as a wide-open, glass-walled space, reinforcing the relative permeability of its interior, private space and exterior, public environment. Imagined as an ongoing site of recursive, reiterative interchange between a feminine past of the old world and a masculine future of the new world, the house is explicitly poised between a materially realized and resonant past and an imminent, yet unactualized, unknown future. In other words, like Cal, the Stephanides' house is imagined on the edge of a bifurcation in historical and evolutionary time. It is a material space in the midst of becoming, that is, an interchange or "middlesex," in the novel's terms.

The house's modern architecture attempts to realize a new-world, futuristic vision of a nonbinary, nonteleological future, yet as mentioned above, it necessarily fails at the wholesale reinvention it attempts. Apparently attempting to intervene in just such progressive, developmental, gendered national space-times, the architect designed Middlesex without stairs, closets, or doors. The architect believed that stairs "represented a teleological view of the universe, of one thing leading to another, whereas now everyone knew that one thing didn't lead to another," and the "concept of the door, of this thing that swung one way or another was outmoded" because binary.[75] Closets and their absolute separation of inside and outside, private and public were also another thing of the past, much to the family's dismay. These masculine, new-world, American architectural dreams, though, remain inhabited by the feminine, old-world Greek American woes of Cal's ill-fated grandmother, Desdemona. In this way, the house on Middlesex Boulevard, like Cal, confounds the spatial logics of inside and outside, private and public, feminine and masculine, past and future, domestic and global, as well as the architect's efforts to engineer an American reinvention from scratch. The house is involved in and transformed by a "smuggling operation," like Cal and so many of the cultural practices in the novel. Grandmother Desdemona's continued, nonassimilationist, old-world presence in the house symbolically points attention toward the futility of attempts, either past or present, to close any national, domestic, familial, or individual space off from its material and cultural history, from the forces and impact of material processes of evolutionary time. Her presence equally confounds efforts to engineer or control the future directions of these material spaces in the midst of becoming, as did the architect and as hegemonic American national discourses, neoliberalism, and biosciences continue to attempt to do in their relentless pursuit of a patriarchal, "new world" futurity.

Reconceiving these co-implicated national, domestic, and subjective spaces as material spaces in the midst of a recursive, evolutionary becoming, as analogous to Cal's intersex, the novel attempts to figure a moment of bifurcation in the global circulatory systems of neoliberal capital, U.S. biopower, and American nationalism. It registers the impact of twenty-first-century, transnational, neoliberal flows on the U.S. nation-state's binary gendered and racialized subjectivities, and the materially realized spatiotemporal imaginaries on which they rely. The house, as a domestic, "private" space is, like the American nation, increasingly permeated by global flows of biotechnology and other neoliberal circulations. In situating the late twentieth-century nation and its subject formation in the unpredictable, materialist, bioinformatic, and evolutionary time of becoming, *Middlesex* disrupts modern nationalism's absolute, homogenous, feminine domestic space outside time. Less obviously, perhaps, its understanding of becoming also unsettles neoliberal U.S. biopower's technoscientific attempts to completely master and instrumentalize biological and material processes. The novel's evolutionary and materialist perspective on interrelated processes of nation and subject formation comes to the fore in Cal's final description of the seventy-year old house:

> Though we had ruined it with our colonial furniture, it was still the beacon it was intended to be, a place with few interior walls, divested of the formalities of bourgeois life, a place designed for a new type of human being, who would inhabit a new world. I couldn't help feeling, of course, that that person was me, me and all the others like me.[76]

Cal and the house are, as this passage underscores, both "beacons," poised between the past and future, attempting to embrace the nonbinary force of sexual difference and of evolutionary time, whether through practices of transgender in Cal's case, or, in the architect's case, through glass walls and by refusing the binary opening and closing of doors and closets or the teleological linearity of stairs, yet the full consequences of these efforts remain unclear. Cal and the domestic space each, in their own way, embrace complex, ongoing, material heterogeneities that betray modern American nationalism's insistence on the one and the same of white, Protestant, heterosexist patriarchy. Through these similarly co-implicated subjective and domestic spaces of becoming, or middlesexes, the novel develops its biopolitical engagement with the material forces of evolutionary time to recommend a mode of becoming that recognizes recent neoliberal capitalist shifts and their bioinformatic modes of material transmission, but remains equally cognizant of the more complex material histories and evolutionary forces that subtend and reenter these emergent modes of circulation, greatly diminishing their apparent agency.

The novel's retrospective, diagnostic retracing of such processes of becoming serves as a "speculative operation," which is a mode of diagnosis, as Stengers notes in another context, able to open onto unexpected "possibilities" through this concerted documentation of "probabilities" that would, otherwise, stand in the way of such ongoing change.[77] Retrospectively retracing individual, cultural, historical, national, transnational, and evolutionary becomings, *Middlesex* recommends one way to register the intrusion of sexual difference, evolutionary time, and other material microagencies into cultural practices. It stages a reencounter with becomings that might open onto alternate modes of inhabiting late capitalist circulatory systems, that is, possibilities.

Novel Diagnosis

The novel, *Middlesex*, is itself relevant here. It is envisioned in comparable terms as a "middlesex" or materially realized space in the midst of becoming something other. Titled so that the novel shares the name of the family domicile and also references Cal's emergent intersex subjectivity, *Middlesex* underscores the genre and its print-based narrative technics' historical implication in the biopolitical co-realization of national, familial, and subjective spaces. It acknowledges, in this way, its status as a biopolitical interchange key to consolidating the imagined communities (of readers) and the imaginaries that help realize these "private" spaces. *Middlesex* extends its retrospective and comparative retracing of modes of circulation and material transmission to self-reflexively and comparatively diagnose the novel's past and its potential future roles in relation to late capitalist, bioinformatic circulatory systems. In this way, the novel retrospectively marks the genre's own becom-

ings, its ongoing material and cultural transformation through such circulations and system relations, revealing novelistic operations are not confined
to objects or absolute, private spaces (if they ever were) and insisting they are
more adeptly understood as materially realized points of *interchange* between
readers, subjectivities, nations, economic and political networks, other media, and material lifeworlds (including the gene and silkworms that feature
so prominently in this novel).

In *Writing at the Limit: The Novel in the New Media Ecology*, Punday
stresses that contemporary novels "circulate as technical artifacts" in ways
that are "inherent to how we use them, and how they negotiate between
public and private" spaces, a circulation that the "media novels" he describes,
like *Middlesex*, self-reflexively query by featuring multiple media and inquiring into their distinct modes of circulation.[78] In *Middlesex* these self-
reflexive queries retrospectively reimagine the novel's past and present novelistic and narrative technics in relation to emergent bioinformatic technics
and their preferred modes of circulation. This novel diagnosis serves as a
means of exploring the novel's actual and potential modes of circulation,
material transmissions, and the becomings they might open onto at this
early twentieth-first century point of bifurcation in U.S. nationalism and
emergent bioinformatic networks of transnational circulation. The novel experimentally reconceives its own print-based technics of material transmission, its cross-cultural threading and the modes of circulation these print
technics open onto as a means to differentiate and reassess shifting modes
of circulation and publicness accompanying bioinformatic networks and
U.S. biopower. In this way, it reveals the contemporary novel's potential
role not only as "a material site where cultural and technical changes can
be studied,"[79] as Punday suggests about "media novels," but as a mode of
experimentally, comparatively retracing past and present modes of material
transmission, circulation, and the modalities of relation the latter enable or
forestall to open onto other possibilities through such comparative, novelistic diagnoses.

Importantly, *Middlesex* extends its materialist perspective on historical
and cultural change in evolutionary time to its thinking about transformations in the novel and other narrative modes as they increasingly engage with
and circulate through digital media. It self-reflexively retraces and reconceives its own artifactual, circulatory status by aligning its technics of writing with material practices such as silk-spinning by silkworms, with genetic
transmissions and collaborations between sperm and egg, and other trans-
missive, circulatory modes of "threading" across divergent spaces. Cal's (as

well as his gene's) narrative circles recursively between past and present, as do the reiterative logics of evolutionary time, only finding a meaningful pattern through such retrospective inquiry. Through this alternate understanding and practice of writing and self-narration, the novel underscores how material forces unfolding in evolutionary time precede and exceed their instrumentalization by cultural processes such as writing or biomedicine. Such material processes are, in this view, only partially and momentarily captured by privileged technics of human self-authorship and instrumental mastery.

The novel's materialist, evolutionary perspective on cultural practices is also registered at the level of the genre of the novel and its narrative, not just its writing practices. Most obviously, *Middlesex* demonstrates the ongoing evolution of the genre by reconceiving its novelistic tactics in response to genetics, bioinformatic modes of circulation, and the evolutionary perspectives they open onto. As Franco Moretti brilliantly argues in his work on "literary evolution" and continues to illustrate through computational methods of "distant reading," the novel has undergone significant transformation over the past centuries.

Middlesex illustrates how the genre of the novel, even as it reimagines itself, continues to transmit its material history and nonconscious social and cultural knowledges and spatiotemporal logics embedded within and often, unwittingly, transmitted through these generic conventions and narrative forms. Situating itself at a point of bifurcation between the novel's recent past and impending future, this novel includes modes of epic (Calliope is, after all, the muse of epic poetry), Greek mythology, the bildungsroman, drama, autobiography, and biomedical narrative within its novelistic frame. This retrospective bricolage of narrative and novelistic technics illustrates its evolutionary view that transformations in the genre of the novel, like other materially realized cultural processes, are similarly "punctual," not progressive, "imperfect," "bifurcating," and more of a matter of "bricolage" than engineering.[80] Novels, like other cultural practices in *Middlesex*, are implicated in smuggling operations, carrying along their conscious and nonconscious material histories even when they are most intent on their "novel" status. This helps to explain why this contemporary novel's concerns remain so closely intertwined with epic poetry and mythology, yet also why the most futuristic of sciences, biomedicine, is still citing Greek mythology and relying on its temporal logics to conceive bioinformatic change.

Elaborating on the subject, nation's, and novel's implication in past and present material transmissions, *Middlesex* recommends and practices a novelistic mode of diagnosis to reckon with bioinformatic circulations. It engages the genre in a mode of retrospectively, comparatively retracing the biopolitical systems relations in which it participates and, in this way, circumscribing their privileged modes of circulation in light of its own material technics. Retrospectively compiling and reviewing these discrepant modes of circulation, even those residually embedded in narrative forms and genres, the novel's immanent, diagnostic mode provides a compelling means to reconceive circulatory options both within and beyond neoliberal biopower's domain. Through its evolutionary, materialist perspective, it encourages a reconception of the contemporary novel as a dynamic point of interchange between emergent subjectivities and bioinformatic circulatory systems. Because the ways that novels "circulate as artifacts" are "inherent to how we use them, and how they negotiate between public and private space," as Punday suggests, these novelistic becomings are well worth retracing as we attempt to come to terms with agency and cultural and historical change occurring in and through late capitalist networks, among other material transmissions.

The novel's recommended practice of diagnosis is not without its risks, the most obvious of which is the risk of falling back into and unwittingly reinforcing the discourses and practices it is describing such as the social Darwinist, sociobiological, and neoliberal discourses the novel retraces. The continued prevalence and intensification of U.S. biopower, though, equally requires that we seek out means to redescribe and circumscribe the materialisms that, otherwise, will continue to circumscribe us further within the modus operandi of late capital. While pursuing circulatory options is itself a ruse of neoliberal biopower extended to select subjects to secure its networks and modes of circulation, it is equally detrimental to accept biopower's present delimitation of modes of circulation and to assume it is impossible to influence these or our own modes of circulation, however tactically and unequally.

Contemporary novels' comparative methods, such as the retrospective diagnosis *Middlesex* undertakes, encourage readers to learn to read the differential modes of becoming and the kinds of material transmissions and modes of circulating they enable and foreclose. Such a novel mode of diagnosis might provide means to read digital technics and the circulatory systems they facilitate, comparatively registering how different media, modes of subjectivity, and writing might enter into these interchanges. It might enable us to reconceive processes of material and cultural change in dynamic, nonidentical relation to material and biological forces and to begin to see bioinformatic sciences' evolutionary, processual perspectives as a resource for rethinking social and historical change and more critically entering into present struggles over the nature of becoming.

Coda

Unfolding Technics

We live with and through the negotiability of the human on a daily basis, continually confronting the instability of this category and the biological, political, visceral experiences the human works to circumscribe. This variability requires our continual reconsideration of the politics, ethics, culture, and parameters of modes and forms of life, from cochlear implants for deafness, identity theft, reproductive technologies, ravens' facial recognition of humans, Botox, manufactured meatless food, artificial DNA, or life-expectancy by zip code, just to mention those I have encountered over the past day or two. If the practices prompting us to query the boundaries of life were not now so commonplace, they might be (more comfortably) relinquished to the news of the weird. Instead, such constant incursions and excursions across boundaries believed to secure the irrevocably human, nonhuman and their lifeworlds are increasingly everyday. These movements—at once conceptual, technical, and material—are no less unsettling in their ubiquity.

And yet, remarkably, the question of what to do with or about the continually recalibrated plasticity of the human, its relations to the nonhuman, and their shared lifeworlds remains elusive. Answers are elusive, in part, because these are questions provoked by technics at multiple sites and scales ranging from DNA, to writing technologies, to subjectivities, to foodways, to global information networks, and geopolitics. Relatedly, yet even more importantly, the emerging technics that preoccupy this book involve complex relations between material, social, cultural, and technological life that insistently confound the usual ways of approaching and, however momentarily, resolving such questions, not just the scope and scale at which we grasp and retrace such processes. As the book illustrates through its literary queries into U.S. digital cultures, these emergent technics require new ways of approaching and grappling with these questions.

Tactics of the Human reveals how the comparative methods through which these literary texts creatively engage with early digital cultures might enable and equip us to reapproach some of the unsettling questions raised by technics, to think about them in a different way, and even begin to more reflexively acclimate ourselves to their processual systems thinking. As invested as it is in the specific contributions of these literary texts to emerging posthumanist perspectives on the human, the book is equally determined to elucidate their methods and the resulting reconceptualizations of technics they open onto. Together, they point toward compelling ways to differentially register the boundary formation of the human. As should be quite clear by the end of chapter 5, the book does not offer a unified, programmatic answer to the question of how to live with the negotiability of the human so apparent in contemporary digital cultures. In fact, I reveal why posthumanism, alone, is not an adequate answer to these quandaries. Since we are already living with variously posthumanist practices and perspectives on the changeable, plastic boundaries of the human, simply invoking the posthuman and calling into question the absolute, unchanging boundaries of the human that previous print cultures and strains of humanism took for granted is clearly inadequate. As the analysis of Eugenides's *Middlesex* reveals through this diagnosis of increasingly flexible modes of American nationalism and neoliberal capitalism, it is politically naive or, at the least, very shortsighted to embrace posthuman becomings *tout court* if the negotiability of the human already entails economic renegotiations that play directly into neoliberal capitalism's least sustainable, most suspect tendencies.[1] Assuming posthumanisms provide a clear antidote is also, as the book illustrates, to overlook the unexpected similarities and continuities between emergent perspectives on the human and their liberal humanist, print companions.

As importantly, posthumanisms' nonsubstantialist accounts of the human are not necessarily accompanied by a revaluation of nonhuman animals, modes of life, or the human beings categorized alongside them as the "meat" or medium for reproducing and sustaining national life. The renegotiation of the human can work in the other direction, a reminder that recognizing the plasticity of species distinctions is the beginning, not the end of cultural, ethical, and political inquiries into technics, as *My Year of Meats* makes clear.[2] For these reasons, I have avoided using the term posthumanist as a primary distinction in the book in favor of comparing a range of post-humanisms as they reconceive and reorient twentieth-century humanisms in quite different ways. Those differences and the complexity they betray is at the core of our difficulties in assessing emergent technics and the perspective on the human and her systems relations they actually or potentially unfold.

Cognizant of the posthumanist perspectives on the human digital cultures are opening onto, these literary texts recommend a way to comparatively examine technics and, by rerouting these material, discursive, and technological processes poetically, to elaborate on the systems relations distinct technics afford and on their political consequence to twentieth- and twenty-first century digital cultures. Their comparative modes of inquiry into systems relations—the technological, social, cultural, and material practices through which differential boundaries of the human and nonhuman are established, stabilized, and destabilized—provide a crucial methodology to query the social, cultural, and political orientations these technological apparati further. By playing out and upon emerging technics as they enter into and transform key, previously print-based social processes in the United States, they encourage us, through such speculative modes of observation and inquiry, to gain a material, conceptual, and socially attuned grasp on the multilayered, mutually transformative, distributed processes through which contemporary social spaces, intersubjective modalities of relation, and embodied subjectivities emerge. In the face of such complexity, their microcosmic fictional systems generate the momentary traction that can facilitate more adept diagnosis and tactical reelaboration of distinct systems relations toward alternate futures.

Through their experimental technics, which move between print and digital media and modes, they register and trace ongoing processes of human boundary formation at multiple sites and scales. *Patchwork Girl* pursues digital hypertext writing technologies to comparatively register their impact on processes of gendered and racialized subject formation.[3] Reconceiving the relations of nonidentity that suture subjectivities to their shifting technological, discursive, and material lifeworlds in terms of hypertextual links that both differentiate and join discrepant bodies in specific relations, this early digital fiction recommends how we might more actively develop upon the nonoppositional modalities of relation such technics seem to afford. And in *Almanac of the Dead*, the novel's spatiotemporal remapping of the symbolic and material practices that jointly realize and resolidify social spaces such as the nation-state or transnational global capitalist networks reveals how tactical media practices and, similarly place-based, spatiotemporal narratives can serve as reorientation devices that change experiences and understandings of social spaces. From this vantage, space-making processes come to be understood as generative material practices that realize culturally specific orientations, yet must also reckon with preceding and competing orientations as well as with the nonhuman and material multipotentiality of lifeworlds. At the micropolitical scale, *My Year of Meats* traces shifting practices of food production, reproduction, cuisine, sexuality, and other material and symbolic transmissions to reveal their importance to U.S. nationalism and, in particular, to the affective economies through which the nation reproduces and prohibits distinct modes of life and their intermingling. Or, reapproaching U.S. nationalism from the evolutionary, spatial, and temporal perspective of a gene, *Middlesex* encourages us to explore the dense interrelations between cultural and biological processes, suggesting we reconceive these interdynamics as smuggling operations to fully credit the competing microagencies with which any formation of biopower is required to contend.

If there is a single axiom to be drawn from the book's inquiries it is that taking U.S. digital cultures on their own terms is never a good idea. Taking hegemonic U.S. digital cultures on their own terms, as we've learned over the past fifteen years, consigns us to the socially and cognitively fatal grip of their combined novelty (emergent forms of neoliberal global capitalism, social media consumerism, high-stakes futures trading, a state of surveillance, etc.) and familiar legacies (enforced poverty, environmental devastation, ultra-stratification along combined lines of class, gender, race, and nation, among other legacies). These literary texts purposefully opt to think the technicity of contemporary U.S. digital cultures beyond their present, privileged terms, sustaining self-descriptions, and imagined actualities in several, interrelated ways. Their multidimensional, multiagential approach to technics as systems relations changes the way we perceive technics as they co-realize subjects, national and transnational social formations, and the micropractices supporting various modes of life.

As a result, this literary fiction clarifies defining dimensions of technicity as it participates in the boundary formation of the human in U.S. digital cultures. It reveals the spatially, materially, and culturally embedded historicity of technological systems and their ongoing, dynamic reciprocity. While enhancing our understanding of how technological and media systems work in various social fields, this approach also enables one to directly confront the ongoing relays between print and digital technics, which remain central to processes of subjectivity, social formation, U.S. nationalism, and transnational critical geographies. Such a comparative, cross-media view attends to the social practices and cultural relations print and digital cultures still jointly facilitate more than fifteen years since political theory predicted the end of the nation-state in the wake of digital information economies, and proponents of the "digital revolution" claimed the latter information networks were soon to resolve the conflicts and class warfare endemic to industrial capitalism. In addition to explaining the uneven character of transitions and points of interchange between print and digital cultures and media, this attention to technics as they unfold in distinct social fields brings forth the, at once, social, cultural, and material processes through which technics are co-realized. This clarifies both how and why material lifeworlds and social relations are so subtly, unevenly, unpredictably transformed. It also undercuts the digital's continued, self-described newness and self-originating claims, which support celebratory and fatalistic accounts of these emerging, supposedly unique technics, which are, thereby, presumed to change everything.

Instead, these literary texts open lines of inquiry into the multipotentiality and determination, as well as the historicity, of technics. They register the socially embedded and embedding processes in which technics participate without ever being fully determined or delimited (either materially or temporally) by their contexts. Attending to technics as they enter into U.S. processes of social and subject formation at distinct, yet co-articulated, scenes of writing and materially realized spatial formations, and through the identificatory and biopolitical practices of U.S. nationalisms and transnationalisms, the book underscores the somewhat different trajectories similar technological infrastructures and processes take at these different sites. Narrowing in on the multipotentiality and, thus, inherent multistability of these interrelations, while also evidencing their sedimentation and force once in play in the social field, these texts' comparative methods and their systems thinking enables reflection, diagnosis, and potential reorientations of the gendered, racialized, and subaltern intersubjectivities, social spaces, micropractices of the nation, and textual practices distinct technics co-realize.

As the book intends to illustrate, these texts' methodologies encourage an understanding of technics as *tactics of the human* through which late twentieth- and early twenty-first-century American social systems unfold, stabilize across time, and are reimagined, for better and for worse. Developed over the course of the book, this view on technics reconceives subject-technology relations as co-productive reorientations of evolutionary, material, and historical processes that always precede and exceed existing interrelations (i.e., they remain both sedimenting and open to recalibration). Contrary to previous understandings of subject-technology relations as relations of user and tool, through this posthumanist, systems-theoretical reformulation, agency is reconceived as a force released through these distributed interrelations and subsequently attributed to distinct human, nonhuman, material, and technological agents. It suggests how we might reformulate both human-centric and technology-centric views of agency in social systems in this way.

Redescribing technics as *tactics of the human*, the book finds traction in American social and cultural life through such creative, circumspect engagements with, and a retrospective retracing of, these transformative interrelations. It reveals how literary texts and the comparative media practices they develop to work through emerging technics can help register the impact of shifting relations on the human and nonhuman and their lifeworlds. Their diagnoses provide new ways to tactically reengage the topographies of late capitalism and, in doing so, to shed light on the spatiotemporal orientations and material practices sustaining digital cultures and their circulatory systems. Drawing on network topographies influencing geopolitical space well before the World Wide Web rendered the idea of an information network commonplace, *Almanac of the Dead*, for instance, questioned capitalist economic networks' clear disregard for existing place-based social formations and challenged their much-celebrated supra-territoriality.[4] The novel not only provides a prescient vision of transnational, informational "network societies," it recommends how tactical literary and digital practices can help redescribe and reorient networking and other material practices through which social knowledges are embedded and unsettled, encouraging other agencies and kinds of lived space. Close attention to the spatiotemporal, place-based or locative, and tactical dimensions to narrative practices in increasingly pervasive computational environments has only increased since Silko's novel identified the literary's potential, in this way, to change the way we see and move through computationally networked, social spaces. Through this and other tactical methods, these literary texts help elucidate the variability, contingency, and force with which specific technics unfold in U.S. digital cultures. They recommend how we might develop adequate abilities to retrace, diagnose, and differentiate between distinct posthumanist practices, materialities, and spatiotemporal becomings rather than taking technics in digital cultures at face value, as an unquestioned and stable given. They encourage recognition that not all becomings, systems, or networking processes are the same, for instance, and increase awareness of their unique material and epistemological limits, enabling otherwise unperceived alternatives, other ways to "realize these possibilities," to borrow *Almanac of the Dead*'s terminology.

This understanding of technics as *tactics of the human* that work discrepantly for and against highly differentiated social formations at multiple sites, in turn, prompts a reconception of the *literary*'s possible modes of address and its relations to digital cultures, questioning the terms in which we're encouraged to greet and inhabit these emerging social and cultural formations and the technicity of the human they rerealize. In the introduction, I broached the question of how literary texts participate in and are relevant to contemporary digital cultures and the bioinformatic scientific, technological, and cultural practices that sustain them. I want to return to that question to unpack the full significance of these texts' reapproach to digital cultures, their concerted, critical, yet notably non-oppositional reengagement of the privileged concepts, practices, and traits of digital cultures (and the twentieth-century advances in physical, biological, and informational systems sciences they draw upon) to socially, culturally, and politically attuned literary ends.

Taking up key components and concepts of digital cultures to identify, unfold, or exploit their untapped uses or dimensions, these late twentieth- and early twenty-first-century literary fictions engage these sciences and the new processes of materialization and symbolization they introduce as poetic, conceptual, social, cultural, and political *resources*, as well as increasingly familiar actualities. They turn the defining processes, media, and conceits of digital cultures to alternate, expressive ends to reobserve such practices through a slightly different register. For example, they incorporate comparative literary moves between print and digital media into their textual signifying practices and fictions as a means to explore these key points of interchange between print and digital cultures and their social systems. In this regard, these literary texts anticipate the "expressive processing" Noah Wardrip-Fruin has identified in digital fiction and other expressive practices that unfold more directly through computational media. In particular they share the dual aims he attributes to creative engagements with computational media, which are to, at once, realize the creative affordances of digital media practices to help create a fictional world and in doing so, to use these experiments to reflect back on these same computation-based processes and their social and cultural meaning and impact. As he argues in relation to expressive processing in digital fictions, computer games, and software studies, "Coming to understand fictional worlds as systems—and exploring their potential through play—is also a powerful means of coming to understand our evolving society, in which (often hidden) software models structure much of how we live now."[5] Without overlooking key differences in their media-specific print as opposed to computationally based methods of understanding "fictional worlds as systems," and in their modes of fictional play with these systems processes (with the exception of *Patchwork Girl*), it is nevertheless worth noting the underlying similarities in some of their digital literary approaches and aims.

In elaborating on these texts' experimental technics, their creative reengagements with emergent digital practices and social systems, I want to join in their wager that we can, in this intently differential way, come to understand how digital cultures work and find new resources for social, cultural, and political life well suited to these emerging contexts. Exploring technics across the supposed print/digital divide, these literary texts clearly refuse the positioning of literary print cultures outside or in opposition to U.S. digital cultures. More importantly, their comparative media practices proceed to register through their expressive processes, and to reflect on, digital cultures' inclination and capacities to re- and dematerialize defining elements of our biological, economic, cultural, and social lives. They begin to come to terms with the fact that in contemporary late capitalism "the world of things has become a world of signs—a universe that both brings into being and is brought into being by symbolic codes."[6] Writer Steve Tomasula suggests that "perhaps it is for this reason alone that that most symbolic of all codes, the literary text, can foreshadow a future world while the contemporary world suggests the future of poetics."[7] He remarks on the reciprocal interplay between literary text and extraliterary world that now involves the literary's anticipation of the significantly symbolic operations of the real world of finance capital and futures trading while the real world of things seems on the verge of outmaneuvering the poetic in the creativity, dynamism, and affective power of its symbolic, world-building maneuvers. At the core of these influential relays between the literary and its environments is this broader intertwining and interplay between symbolic and material processes today that confounds previous, oppositional understandings of the symbolic and material (and the cultural and economic spheres with which they are respectively aligned).

In this context, comparative media practices, involved in a similar transposition of symbolic practices from one medium to another, or a transposition that engages the material preconditions of digital or print media to divergent symbolic, expressive ends, can be understood as a poetic method or micropractice designed to comparatively register and cast into differential relief precisely the kinds of de- and rematerializing processes that define late capitalist economic and cultural topographies and their privileged epistemologies. One begins to understand, in light of these literary texts, how the very operations of such comparative media practices register and critically respond to the "unprecedented things" "now being done with and to matter, nature, life, production and reproduction," which theorists now actively query under the sign of "new materialisms."[8]

Rather than representing digital cultures and their emergent technics from the outside, as it were, these literary texts take up key concepts and practices from digital cultures and explore them through a literary register, momentarily reoperationalizing these kinds of systems relations to literary and poetic ends. It is no accident that they actively pursue the breakdown and recalibration of Cartesian dualisms between material and symbolic, outside and inside, spatial and temporal, feminine and masculine, body and mind, living and nonliving, vital and mechanical—reformulations that are catalyzed by the processes of materialization and symbolization currently transforming experiences and understandings of everyday life.

Through these literary relays, they examine the productivity and constraints of the literary in the context of digital cultures and, in turn, use the literary to differentially inquire into the productivity and constraints materially realized, computation-based system processes introduce to subjectivities and social systems in the United States. It is through this recursive, redoubling movement of reapproaching digital processes, media, and methodologies through a literary print apparatus and reconceiving the literary in terms of digital processes, media, and systems relations that these texts' comparative media practices reckon with and shed light on the distinct "ontogenetic processes" accompanying digital technics, which increasingly, in Thrift's insightful terms, render "the logic of the system, as it becomes both necessary and general," "the logic of the world," receding "from human perception, becoming a part of the landscape which the body 'naturally' adjusts to and which it regards as a normal part of its movement."[9] Adapting the dynamic recursivity of system formation and, in particular, of digital technics and computational processes, these literary texts poetically embody and, thus, elaborate on the charged interrelations between symbolic and material practices that so trouble prior assumptions about writing, cognition, gender and sex, narrative, cultural practices, space, economic circulation, agency, and politics today.

Their literary explorations of the points of interchange between textual, biological, discursive, technological, social, nonhuman, and physical systems processes diagnose new understandings of materiality and processes of materialization accompanying digital technics, physics, bioinformatic and computer sciences that have only intensified since 2002. Through these methods, they underscore the literary's contributions to contemporary conversations surrounding the new materialisms. As the book has worked to illustrate, recent work in science studies, critical geographies, feminism and gender studies, philosophy, and political economy grapples with the altered status, efficacy, and impact of the material that has accompanied twentieth-century developments in particle physics, molecular biology, and complexity and systems theory. Whether they align themselves with new materialisms or not, these fields are all involved in thinking through emergent conceptualizations, elaborations, and practices of materiality informing contemporary technics at multiple, interrelated scales. The unpredictable dynamics to contemporary material life (at genetic, environmental, subjective, communicational, national, and geopolitical levels) "requires a well-informed understanding of new scientific and technological developments" and their "material implications and context," as Frost and Coole stress in their introduction to the collection on *New Materialisms*.[10] Furthermore, as philosopher and literary critic Pheng Cheah notes in his essay in the collection titled "Non-dialectical Materialism," "what we consider as concrete political forms, institutions, practices, and activities, and the discourses that irrigate them such as rational choice theory, positivism, empiricism, and dialectical materialism are underwritten by ontologies of matter and life."[11] He stresses that as these ontologies of matter and life are increasingly called into question by twenty-first-century physical, biological, and system sciences and the technicities they open onto, so are the political and social concepts and practices, assumptions about the human and her agencies that prior frameworks for approaching matter and life have sustained.

These literary texts certainly grapple with the altered status, efficacy, and impact of the material that has accompanied twentieth-century developments in particle physics, molecular biology, and complexity and systems theory. They take an awareness of contemporary genetics, sociobiology, and intersex (*Middlesex*), or of theories of embodied cognition emerging from cognitive science (*Patchwork Girl*), or U.S. beef production, factory farming, and synthetic hormones and reproductive biotechnology (*My Year of Meats*), or of the productive power of capitalism to create social space and administer biopower through its material practices (*Almanac of the Dead*), or of rhetorics of web-based hypertext ("Click") as the catalyst for their nuanced reconceptualization of processes of materialization in light of such knowledges and practices. As importantly, they pursue the potential consequence of these emergent materialisms to the U.S. social field, to the political, cultural, and economic terms through which we map, navigate, and redescribe contemporary social life at multiple sites and scales. These fictions provide us with concepts drawn from these sciences and practices and, therefore, well attuned to the topographies of late capitalism and its computation-based technics. These concepts are then speculatively followed through to their expected or potential social, cultural, and political ends and, in this process, tactically reconceived and reoriented in light of a careful observation of this thick environment.

As a result, these literary texts reveal how such emergent knowledges and processes of materialization, and the complex interrelations they delineate between human cultures, social systems, and material lifeworlds provide quite essential conceptual and practical resources for literary, cultural, political, and social theories, as they, quite literally, work through contemporary U.S. digital cultures. In this way, these texts unleash the literary's potential as a mode of diagnosis. It is a diagnostic mode that, as Isabelle Stengers stresses after Nietzsche, is grounded in a reflection on the present material, empirical realities, yet precisely because of that momentary entrenchment is capable of opening open onto speculative, prospective futures through its grounded, reiterative, creative diagnostic inquiries.[12] Importantly, such diagnoses serve as immanent, nonoppositional, experimental modes of registering the present, empirical realities and finding openings through which these trajectories might otherwise unfold or bifurcate.

Borrowing and adapting key concepts and processes from systems thinking in cybernetics and information theory, biological and social systems theory, and the emerging technics already, notably, well under way in early digital cultures, the book joins these literary texts in creatively exploring the multipotentiality and necessity of these new modes of thinking through and, quite literally, grappling with materially realized technics and the systems relations they dynamically and forcefully engender. The book draws upon these late twentieth- and early twenty-first-century literary methods to devise new materialist tactics for engaging the technical apparati and processes under way in contemporary technoscience, neoliberal economic networks, and their U.S. digital cultures, tactics that are, thus, closely attuned to the latter's blind spots and unpursued potential.

Additionally, in looking back to these early literary engagements with digital cultures, which clearly begin to "understand fictional worlds as systems" (though not necessarily using computational media), I want to underscore an important trajectory linking these literary practices and more recent comparative literary and media practices. These texts evidence the literary's capacity to inquire about, and differentially enter into, our understandings and practices of technics, and, in this way, to attend to these dynamic interchanges between textual practices, intersubjectivities, lived space, social systems, and their economic circulations. In the book's view, there is much to be learned about print and digital technics, the technicity of the human, and contemporary late capitalist social systems from these literary and expressive texts (among others), if read with these relays and aims in mind. The book's trajectory, thus, also points forward to more recent digital literary and expressive practices as a robust site for inquiries into not only the notoriously complex interplay of language and code in computation-based literary and expressive practices, but, equally, into the computational processes and wider digital cultures and "code/spaces" that these texts both engage *and* diagnose.[13] In the introduction to their recent collection *New Narratives: Stories and Storytelling in the Digital Age*, Ruth Page and Bronwen Thomas describe a "fresh phase of digital narratology" that "concerns itself less with stylistic or textual characteristics than with the environments and social and cultural formations that produce and consume them, as well as the cultural uses to which narrative practices may be put."[14] Other recent work on digital narrative, electronic literatures, and expressive computational practices is similarly interested in exploring, more directly and thoroughly, the complex interrelations between these literary and expressive practices and the wider social, medial, technological, cultural, and political systems through which they emerge and gain meaning. In his recent work on "the novel in the new media ecology," Daniel Punday illustrates how "the formal innovations of the contemporary novel" are "an embrace of the novel's place within systems of dissemination and circulation."[15] In a recent review, he suggests that such efforts to think through the "causal, material links between literary works and their institutional and commercial context" and to understand the consequence of the latter for contemporary literary and cultural practices—a concern with "the networks within which writing is located"—are a "condition of this post-postmodern moment," more broadly.[16] Recent critical and creative work addressing the digital and literary's complex co-imbrication are similarly interested to elaborate on the *literary's* system relations, its dynamic, transformative relays to social, medial, material, and intersubjective processes. They join these earlier literary engagements with digital cultures in illustrating the value of reapproaching literary texts in relation to these systems processes, social and cultural formations, and shifting material and technological infrastructures.

As suggested in the introduction of the book, how we understand the place and operations of the literary directly impacts, and translates into, its ability to facilitate our understanding and negotiation of digital cultures. The literary's repositioning and reimagined occupations in relation to these emergent relays productively and creatively subtends our own approaches and lines and modes of inquiry and engagement within digital cultures. Reconceiving these literary texts and subsequent literary engagements with digital cultures and their computation-based systems processes as a resource in a broader toolkit for creatively retracing complex systems and the processes through which they emerge, transform, and are undone, this book suggests how such comparative work across the lines of the literary and digital is an invaluable response to the literary's growing immanence to digital cultures. The literary now emerges from computers and circulates through digital technologies, and, increasingly, it will elaborate its poetics in greater degrees of direct interaction with computational methods and technologies, as do digitally based electronic literatures, interactive narratives, generative texts, Twitterature and other "bot" poetics, locative narratives, and a range of cross-platform, cross-genre literary hybrids. Further, as late capitalist economic practices become remarkably adept at manipulating symbolic and cultural operations through computation to their profit-driven material ends, it is even more pressing to differentiate between distinct literary, cultural, and economic practices and their privileged modes of realizing symbolic operations within material lifeworlds.

Reading these early literary encounters with U.S. digital cultures as one possible prehistory to an emergent digital literary may help us to appreciate and read the increasing prevalence of comparative media practices and other literary hybrids of the present for the diagnostic, speculative, and experimental work that they do at several levels through their negotiations with technics and media systems. The book's project, demonstrating how literary poetics can take up, modulate, and cast comparative light on the actualized and unactualized potential of emerging technics to forestall, engender, and reorient shifting modes of the human and her social life, intends to remark on the persistence, relevance, and purpose to their comparative media practices, which reengage tactics of the human we cannot live without and, thus, one way or another, we learn to live with.

Notes

Introduction

1. These texts were published between 1991 and 2002, at the moment in which the implementation of the World Wide Web (1991), combined with an explosion in personal computer usage in the United States, consolidated a global information network accessed by a critical mass both in the United States and more globally. Digital information and scientific practices, many of which significantly predate this moment, made their presence known to a broader U.S. audience during these years. My reference to a "digital revolution" acknowledges this transitional moment and the transformative influence of digital media in American culture throughout the 1990s at the same time that it aims to explode the dominant readings of this moment in U.S. history as evidencing a wholesale (i.e., revolutionary) shift from an industrial to a postindustrial, informational economy. Theorists such as Daniel Bell initially conceptualized shifting economic practices emerging in the 1970s as a revolutionary resolution to the class conflicts of industrial capitalism, and many others shared his view that the postindustrial, informational economy was soon to largely supersede industrial capitalism. Daniel Bell, *The Coming of Post-Industrial Society* (New York: Basic, 1973).

2. Influential studies on electronic literatures and other expressive computational practices that have been essential to developing this more comprehensive view of the digital literary include Janet H. Murray, *Hamlet on the Holodeck: The Future of Narrative in Cyberspace* (Cambridge: MIT Press, 1997); Jay David Bolter, *Writing Space: Computers, Hypertext, and the Remediation of Print*, 2nd ed. (Mahwah, NJ: Lawrence Erlbaum Associates, 2001); Loss Pequeño Glazier, *Digital Poetics: The Making of E-Poetries* (Tuscaloosa: University of Alabama Press, 2001); Marie-Laure Ryan, ed. *Narrative across Media: The Languages of Storytelling* (Lincoln: University of Nebraska Press, 2004) and *Avatars of Story* (Minneapolis: University of Minnesota Press, 2006); Adalaide Morris and Thomas Swiss, eds., *New Media Poetics: Contexts, Technotexts, and Theories* (Cambridge: MIT Press, 2006); N. Katherine Hayles,

Electronic Literature: New Horizons for the Literary (Notre Dame, IN: University of Notre Dame Press, 2008); and Hayles, *My Mother Was a Computer: Digital Subjects and Literary Texts* (Chicago: University of Chicago Press, 2005); and Pat Harrigan and Noah Wardrip-Fruin, eds., *First Person: New Media as Story, Performance, and Game* (Cambridge: MIT Press, 2004); Harrigan and Wardrip-Fruin, eds., *Second Person: Role-Playing and Story in Games and Playable Media* (Cambridge: MIT Press, 2007); Harrigan and Wardrip-Fruin, eds., *Third Person: Authoring and Exploring Vast Narratives* (Cambridge: MIT Press, 2009; Noah Wardrip-Fruin, *Expressive Processing: Digital Fiction, Computer Games, and Software Studies* (Cambridge: MIT Press, 2009); and Ruth Page and Bronwen Thomas, eds., *New Narratives: Stories and Storytelling in the Digital Age* (Lincoln: University of Nebraska Press, 2011).

3. I approach posthumanisms as a series of critical perspectives on shifting understandings of the human rather than as a wholesale supercession of liberal humanism. This allows for an examination of practices of the human that both unsettle *and* realign prior domains of humanistic knowledge, experience, and political action. The book pursues multiple understandings of the human and her shifting relations to technicity, examining several quite different ways of theorizing and inhabiting posthumanisms in the contemporary U.S. social field. It recommends and takes on the task of analyzing competing understandings and modalities of the human circulating in American culture today. I will return to this question of where these various posthumanisms seem to lead in the coda.

4. James Patrick Kelly and John Kessel, *Rewired: The Post-Cyberpunk Anthology* (San Francisco: Tachyon Publications, 2007), xi.

5. Cisco Systems, "Class Trip," television advertisement, July 15, 2010.

6. Murray, *Hamlet on the Holodeck*, 71.

7. Their collection surveys a broader set of discussions of technicity that attempt to address the inadequacy of humanism's understanding of technologies in terms of a prosthesis, supplement, or tool. This larger field of inquiry draws upon Jacques Derrida's inquiries into the material supplement constitutive to the human and his *différance* and Bernard Stiegler's thinking through the specifically historical and material processes involved in the technological basis of human memory, exploring technicity at various material, conceptual, historical, discursive, and evolutionary levels. In this book, I develop on this line of inquiry as it is taken up by biological and social systems theory, feminist science studies, and in light of these literary texts' experiments with the subject-technology relations I redescribe in this context as technics. See Arthur Bradley and Louis Armand, *Technicity* (Prague: Litteraria Pragensia, 2006), 3.

8. Ibid., 9.

9. Here I draw on Jameson's elaboration on this term to describe the post–World War II economic and cultural context emerging in the 1950s, sharing his desire to acknowledge continuities between industrial and late capitalism, as opposed to theories of a postindustrial break with prior logics of capital. Fredric Jameson, *Postmodernism, or, The Cultural Logic of Late Capitalism* (Durham, NC: Duke University Press, 1997), xxi.

10. Mary Wollstonecraft Shelley, *Frankenstein: The 1818 Text, Contexts, Nineteenth-Century Responses, Modern Criticism*, 2nd ed., ed. Paul J. Hunter (New York: W. W. Norton & Company, 2012).

11. David E. Wellbery, "Foreword: Post-Hermeneutic Criticism," in Friedrich A. Kittler's *Discourse Networks: 1800/1900*, trans. Michael Metteer with Chris Cullens (Stanford, CA: Stanford University Press, 1990), xii.

12. Shelley Jackson, *Patchwork Girl by Mary/Shelley and Herself* (Watertown, MA: Eastgate Systems, 1995).

13. Bolter, *Writing Space*.

14. John Johnston, *Information Multiplicity: American Fiction in the Age of Media Saturation* (Baltimore: John Hopkins University Press, 1998), 12.

15. I intend to illustrate how these literary texts anticipate and inform what have recently been termed "new materialisms," "critical materialisms," and "renewed materialisms" (Coole and Frost), which include "material feminisms" (Alaimo and Hekman) as a primary, motivating force. Developing out of feminism, science studies, phenomenological theory, postcolonial theory, gender studies and queer theory, and critical geographies, "new materialisms," at their most basic level, are engaged in rethinking liberal humanisms' oppositions between nature and culture, feminine and masculine, passive and active, matter and meaning, nonhuman and human, nonwhite and white, space and time, as jointly impacted by contemporary technoscientific and economic practices and/or by prior knowledges and practices of materialization. I'm using "new materialisms" as an umbrella term for these inquiries, though in my understanding of this term "new" designates a new series of openings from the vantage of the present into long-standing explorations and concerns with material knowledges and practices. The "new" is, for this reason, often considered as an ironic or interrogative descriptor here, though all of these inquiries into material processes are, to some degree, motivated by contemporary scientific and technological processes and knowledges as they pose the question of what is or isn't new about our understandings and practices. The field of new materialisms is intently plural, describing several distinct approaches to rethinking and responding to instrumental, oppositional understandings of the material and the cultural, which also differ according to their chosen, though overlapping, fields of inquiry (environmental ethics, animal studies, philosophy of technology, gender studies, queer theory, biology, physics, philosophy, subaltern studies, etc.). For an introduction to these concepts and the cultural and historical contexts prompting these inquiries see Diana Coole and Samantha Frost, eds., *New Materialisms: Ontology, Agency, and Politics* (Durham, NC: Duke University Press, 2010), and Stacy Alaimo and Susan Hekman, *Material Feminism* (Bloomington: Indiana University Press, 2008). In *New Materialism: Interviews & Cartographies* (Ann Arbor: Open Humanities Press, MPublishing, University of Michigan Library, 2012), Rick Dolphijn and Iris van der Tuin provide an informative review of Manuel DeLanda and Rosi Braidotti's early contributions to this field of inquiry and an overview of its key lines of thinking.

16. Here I'm referencing Isabelle Stengers's concept of a "speculative operation," which she uses to describe a mode of diagnosis that serves to document "probabili-

ties" in order to provide openings for unstated, unseen "possibilities." The relevance of this concept to contemporary novels' modes of diagnosis is developed in greater depth in chapter 5. Isabelle Stengers, *Cosmopolitics*, trans. Robert Bononno, vol. 1 (Minneapolis: University of Minnesota Press, 2010), 12.

17. My use of this term draws on Laura U. Marks's work, in which she applies the term "minor science" to her discussion of experimental film, video, and digital art. See Marks, *Touch: Sensuous Theory and Multisensory Media* (Minneapolis: University of Minnesota Press, 2002), xiv. The term originates with Gilles Deleuze and Félix Guattari, "Treatise on Nomadology—the War Machine," in *A Thousand Plateaus: Capitalism and Schizophrenia*, trans. Brian Massumi (Minneapolis: University of Minnesota Press, 1987), 361–74.

18. John Barth, "Click," *Atlantic Monthly* (December 1997): 81–96.

19. Leslie Marmon Silko, *Almanac of the Dead* (New York: Penguin, 1991).

20. Ruth L. Ozeki, *My Year of Meats* (New York: Penguin, 1998).

21. Jeffrey Eugenides, *Middlesex* (New York: Farrar, Straus and Giroux, 2002).

22. Karen Barad, *Meeting the Universe Halfway: Quantum Physics and the Entanglement of Matter and Meaning* (Durham, NC: Duke University Press, 2007), 3.

23. Lisa Nakamura, *Cybertypes: Race, Ethnicity, and Identity on the Internet* (New York: Routledge, 2002).

24. See Norbert Wiener, *The Human Use of Human Beings: Cybernetics and Society* (1954; Cambridge, MA: Da Capo Press, 1988), for instance.

25. Donna Haraway, "A Cyborg Manifesto: Science, Technology, and Socialist Feminism in the Late 20th Century," in *Simians, Cyborgs, and Women: The Reinvention of Nature* (New York: Routledge, 1991), 150.

26. Thomas Pynchon, *Gravity's Rainbow* (New York: Penguin, 1995), 412.

27. Claire Colebrook, *Deleuze and the Meaning of Life* (London: Continuum, 2010), 38–39.

28. Ibid., 39.

29. Cary Wolfe, *Critical Environments: Postmodern Theory and the Pragmatics of the "Outside"* (Minneapolis: University of Minnesota Press, 1998), 57,8.

30. Steve Joshua Heims, *Constructing a Social Science for Postwar America: The Cybernetics Group, 1946–1953* (Cambridge: MIT Press, 1993), 23.

31. Heinz von Foerster, *Observing Systems*, 2nd ed. (Seaside, CA: Intersystems, 1985), 285.

32. Humberto Maturana and Francisco Varela, *The Tree of Knowledge: The Biological Roots of Human Understanding*, trans. Robert Paolucci, rev. ed. (Boston: Shambhala Press, 1998), 11.

33. Dirk Baecker, "Why Systems?," *Theory, Culture, & Society* 18.1 (2001): 61, doi:10.1177/02632760101800105.

34. Niklas Luhmann's *Social Systems* provides the most thoroughgoing and foundational of his several works on social systems and predominant modern subsystems. See Luhmann, *Social Systems*, trans. John Bednarz Jr. with Dirk Baecker and Foreword by Eva M. Knodt (Stanford, CA: Stanford University Press, 1995).

35. Don Ihde, *Ironic Technics* ([Copenhagen]: Automatic Press, 2008), 14, 13. Notably, Ihde's concept of multi-stability overlaps in significant ways with Gilbert

Simondon's characterizations of the "metastability" of technicity, which is equally concerned to think through both the durability and instability of these sustained relations to technologies. For Simondon, "metastability refers to the provisional equilibrium established when a system rich in potential differences resolves inherent incompatibilities by restructuring itself topologically and temporally," as Adrian Mackenzie unpacks and extends the significance of this companion term in his remarkable work on the technicity of clocktime in *Transductions: Bodies and Machines at Speed* (London: Continuum, 2002), 103.

36. This work provides an important, influential trajectory of engagements with materiality that have emerged since early cyberfeminists began to explore technologies as material practices and examined their impact on material spaces, subjectivities, gender, race, and sexuality. The project of this book is not so much to define a single mode of new materialism or systems thinking as it is to examine the different scales and sites at which rethinking key assumptions about matter and material processes categorically changes the terms in which such processes (writing, subject formation, material space-making, nationalism, late capitalist networks, gendering and racialization) are understood. One of the book's overarching assumptions is, that reacknowledging materiality in cultural understandings and practices, alone, is inadequate to the task of responding to contemporary late capitalist, biotechnological, and neoliberal practices and the struggles over "life" they introduce. The question of how various new materialisms reenter these conversations, what understandings of the human in dynamic, situated relation to nonhuman animals and material and technical worlds they generate, and what political and cultural work these perspectives and practices open onto is key.

37. N. Katherine Hayles, *How We Became Posthuman: Virtual Bodies in Cybernetics, Literature, and Informatics* (Chicago: University of Chicago Press, 1999) and *My Mother Was a Computer*; Doreen Massey, *For Space* (London: Sage, 2005); Barad, *Meeting the Universe*; Judith Butler, *Undoing Gender* (New York: Routledge, 2004); Elizabeth Grosz, *Time Travels: Feminism, Nature, Power* (Durham, NC: Duke University Press, 2005), and Sara Ahmed, *Queer Phenomenology: Orientations, Objects, Others* (Durham, NC: Duke University Press, 2006).

38. Maturana and Varela, *The Tree of Knowledge*, 75.

39. Ahmed, "Orientations Matter," in Coole and Frost, *New Materialisms*, 234.

40. Joseph Tabbi, *Cognitive Fictions* (Minneapolis: University of Minnesota Press, 2002).

41. Bruce Clarke, *Posthuman Metamorphosis: Narrative and Systems* (New York: Fordham University Press, 2008).

42. Ibid., 7, 60.

43. Ibid., 63.

44. Michel de Certeau, *The Practice of Everyday Life*, trans. Steven Rendall (Berkeley: University of California Press, 1984), xix.

45. Ibid., xi.

46. Timothy C. Campbell, *Improper Life: Technology and Biopolitics from Heidegger to Agamben* (Minneapolis: University of Minnesota Press, 2011).

47. Hayles, *Electronic Literature*.

48. Campbell, *Improper Life*, 119.

49. Friedrich W. Bloch, "Digital Poetics or On the Evolution of Experimental Media Poetry," in *Media Poetry: An International Anthology*, ed. Eduardo Kac (Chicago: Intellect, 2007), 241, 233.

Chapter 1

1. Bernard Stiegler, *Technics and Time, 1: The Fault of Epimetheus*, trans. Richard Beardsworth and George Collins (Stanford, CA: Stanford University Press, 1998), 12.

2. Vivian Sobchack, *Carnal Thoughts: Embodiment and Moving Image Culture* (Berkeley: University of California Press, 2004), 133.

3. Rather than exhausting current conceptualizations of technicity, my emphasis on historical, material, social, and cultural dimensions to technicity in this book intends to complement other approaches, such as those centering on technicity's relation to human evolution and an ontogenetic enframing of life. Technicity is variably defined as "a philosophical concept or idea, a historical or material process, an anthropological tool or prosthesis, an ontological condition, a mode of discourse, a way of thinking," and "even the basic state of life itself" (Bradley and Armand, *Technicity*, 9). Approaching technicity through recent shifts from print to digital media brings to the fore the question of how these human technology interrelations change over time and, thus, differentiates as well as connects specific cultural experiences and engagements with technicity from technicity *tout court*.

4. Admittedly, these socially embedded and embedding dimensions to technics are a well-known secret, yet remain a significant theoretical blind spot in humanist theories of technology with the notable exception of Don Ihde's long-standing phenomenological and now postphenomenological grappling with human-technology-embodiment relations and more recent work in feminist science studies and comparative media studies. See *Technology and the Lifeworld: From Garden to Earth* (Bloomington: Indiana University Press, 1990) and, more recently, *Ironic Technics* (2008) and *Embodied Technics* ([Copenhagen]: Automatic Press, 2010). His work contributes, in important ways, to the alternative approach to technics this book will pursue.

5. George P. Landow, *Hypertext 2.0: The Convergence of Contemporary Critical Theory and Technology*, 2nd ed. (Baltimore: Johns Hopkins University Press, 1997); Bolter, *Writing Space*; Richard A. Lanham, *The Electronic Word: Democracy, Technology, and the Arts* (Chicago: University of Chicago Press, 1994).

6. Stiegler, *Technics and Time, 1*, 21.

7. Barth, "Click."

8. Theodor Nelson, *Literary Machines* (Sausalito, CA: Mindful Press, 1988).

9. All references to digital hypertext in this chapter intend to emphasize the unique affordances digital media contribute to hypertext fiction and writing practices, not to exclude print hypertexts such as those Katherine Hayles and others insightfully analyze. N. Katherine Hayles, *Writing Machines* (Cambridge: MIT Press, 2002), 26.

10. Jacques Derrida, *Archive Fever: A Freudian Impression*, trans. Eric Prenowitz (Chicago: University of Chicago Press, 1998); Jacques Derrida, *Of Grammatology*, trans. Gayatri Chakravorty Spivak, corrected ed. (Baltimore: Johns Hopkins University Press, 1997).

11. Lanham, *The Electronic Word*, xi.

12. Landow, *Hypertext 2.0*, 91.

13. Although hypertext author and theorist Michael Joyce is often grouped with fellow early hypertext theorists Landow, Lanham, and Bolter, his work provides an important exception to the latter work due to its more exacting engagement with the material differences between hypertext and print writing technologies. Joyce's close attention to the technological materiality of hypertext is a valuable by-product of his theoretical stance, which takes seriously the transformative effects that perceptual and experiential differences (occurring at the level of the technology) have on practices of reading, writing, of thinking, and, ultimately, on subjectivity. See Michael Joyce, *Of Two Minds: Hypertext Pedagogy and Poetics* (Ann Arbor: University of Michigan Press, 1996) and *Othermindedness: The Emergence of Network Culture* (Ann Arbor: University of Michigan Press, 2001). In "Reveal Codes: Hypertext and Performance," Rita Raley highlights and engages this aspect of Joyce's work when she pinpoints his "emphasis on the uniterable, untranslatable '*experience* of this new textuality'" as a crucial component of the transformative experience of hypertext that she goes on to theorize as "the performance of hypertext: the connection and interaction between the user-operator and the machinic-operator, both language processors, but of a different order." See Rita Raley, "Reveal Codes: Hypertext and Performance," *Postmodern Culture* 12.1 (2001): 3.

14. Espen J. Aarseth, *Cybertext: Perspectives on Ergodic Literature* (Baltimore: Johns Hopkins University Press, 1997); Sue-Ellen Case, *The Domain-Matrix: Performing Lesbian at the End of Print Culture* (Bloomington: Indiana University Press, 1996); Lev Manovich, *The Language of New Media*, 2nd ed. (Cambridge: MIT Press, 2001); Jenny Sundén, *Material Virtualities: Approaching Online Textual Embodiment* (New York: Peter Lang, 2003); Hayles, *Writing Machines*.

15. Matthew G. Kirschenbaum, *Mechanisms: New Media and the Forensic Imagination* (Cambridge: MIT Press, 2008), 17.

16. Ibid., xiv.

17. Ibid., 11, 12.

18. Ibid., 13.

19. Jay David Bolter and Richard Grusin, *Remediation: Understanding New Media*, 3rd ed. (Cambridge: MIT Press, 2000), 5.

20. Ibid., 53.

21. Ibid., 48.

22. Ibid., 53.

23. Ryan shares my reservations about Bolter and Grusin's reading of remediation exclusively as an attempt by media to "achieve the real" or feign transparency. See Marie-Laure Ryan, *Narrative across Media*, 31–32.

24. Notably, not all forms of remediation fall into this category of a comparative technics.

25. Ihde, *Ironic Technics*, 13–14.

26. *This Old House*, Time, Inc., WXXI, Rochester, accessed March 15, 2011.

27. Ihde, *Ironic Technics*, 14.

28. Case, *The Domain-Matrix*, 11, 28.

29. Bolter and Grusin, *Remediation*, 231.

30. The subtitle of Barth's *Lost in the Funhouse, Fiction for Print, Tape, Live Voice*, also situates its musings on the self-referentiality of language in relation to what was, at the time, an emergent technology of communication: the tape recorder. See John Barth, *Lost in the Funhouse: Fiction for Print, Tape, Live Voice* (New York: Doubleday, 1988); and John Barth, *Coming Soon!!! A Narrative* (Boston: Houghton Mifflin Company, 2001).

31. Daniel Punday, *Five Strands of Fictionality: The Institutional Construction of Contemporary American Fiction* (Columbus: Ohio State University Press, 2010), 39.

32. Ibid., 40.

33. Barth, "The Literature of Exhaustion," qtd. in Punday, *Five Strands of Fictionality*, 171.

34. Barth, "Click," 81.

35. Ibid., 82.

36. Landow, *Hypertext 2.0*, 181.

37. Barth, *Coming Soon!!!* 19.

38. See Hans Ulrich Gumbrecht's "A Farewell to Interpretation" in the groundbreaking collection, *Materialities of Communication*, ed. Hans Ulrich Gumbrecht and K. Ludwig Pfeiffer, trans. William Whobrey (Stanford, CA: Stanford University Press, 1994) for an anatomy of the hermeneutic tradition's tendency to view the physical medium (human body, signifier, textual apparati, or means of production) as nonconsequential, secondary instruments for the all-important abstract, transcendent meaning. The collection draws from deconstruction, discourse theory, media studies, and systems theory to counter this tradition through an attention to processes of "meaning-constitution," which "literally obliges us to take into account those 'nonspiritual' phenomena that used to be excluded from the thematic field of the humanities." Gumbrecht, "A Farewell to Interpretation," 399.

39. Mark B. N. Hansen, *Embodying Technesis: Technology beyond Writing* (Ann Arbor: University of Michigan Press, 2003), 4, 18.

40. Ibid., 8.

41. Ibid., 6.

42. Sobchack, *Carnal Thoughts*, 110.

43. Ibid., 120.

44. Ibid.

45. Ibid.

46. Ibid., 109.

47. Ibid., 122.

48. Barth, "Click," 94.

49. Ibid., 96.

50. Ibid., 92, 91, 92, 95.

51. Ibid., 96.

52. Judith Roof, *Come as You Are: Sexuality and Narrative* (New York: Columbia University Press, 1996), 63.

53. Ibid., 60.

54. Teresa de Lauretis, *Technologies of Gender: Essays on Theory, Film, and Fiction* (Bloomington: Indiana University Press, 1987), 43.

55. Ibid., 44.

56. Ibid.

57. Barth, "Click," 88.

58. Lanham, *The Electronic Word*, 5–6.

59. Barth, "Click," 82.

60. Ibid., 95.

61. Ibid., 81.

62. C. B. Macpherson, *The Political Theory of Possessive Individualism: Hobbes to Locke* (Don Mills, Ontario: Oxford University Press, 1962).

63. Barth, "Click," 96.

64. Steven Johnson, *Interface Culture: How New Technology Transforms the Way We Create and Communicate* (San Francisco: Harper Collins, 1997), 24.

65. Golan Levin, "Art That Looks Back at You," TED Conference, California, 2009.

66. Ryan, *Narrative across Media*, 18, 34.

67. Ibid., 18, 19.

68. Ibid., 337, 329–30.

69. Barth, "Click," 82, 83.

70. Ibid., 84, 81.

71. This fountain pen also functions to self-referentially implicate John Barth, the author, in this fiction, perhaps, as he continues to write with a 43-year-old Parker 51 fountain pen he purchased in England. This reinforces my suggestion here that the story is concerned with the potential destabilization of this print scene of writing.

72. Ibid., 83–84.

73. Ibid., 86.

74. Campbell, *Improper Life*, 4.

75. Ibid., 5.

76. Ibid.

77. Ibid., 2.

78. Ihde, *Technology and the Lifeworld*, 75.

79. Judith Roof, "Is There Sex after Gender? Ungendering / *The Unnameable*," *Journal of the Midwest Modern Language Association* 35 (Spring 2002): 50–67, 50.

80. Ibid., 54.

81. Ibid., 56.

82. Sobchack, *Carnal Thoughts*, 109.

83. Ibid., 132.

84. Ibid., 130.

85. Ibid., 133.

86. See André Leroi-Gourhan, *Gesture and Speech*, trans. Anna Bostock Berger (Cambridge: MIT Press, 1993).

87. Byron Hawk, David M. Rieder, and Ollie Oviedo, eds., *Small Tech: The Culture of Digital Tools* (Minneapolis: University of Minnesota Press, 2008), xiv.

Chapter 2

1. Jackson, *Patchwork Girl*.

2. Shelley, *Frankenstein*.

3. Gilbert Simondon, *Du mode d'existence des objets techniques* (Paris: Aubier, 2001).

4. Leroi-Gourhan, *Gesture and Speech*.

5. Stiegler, *Technics and Time, 1: The Fault of Epimetheus*; Bernard Stiegler, *Technics and Time, 2: Disorientation*, trans. Stephen Barker (Stanford, CA: Stanford University Press, 2009).

6. Hayles, *How We Became Posthuman*; Hayles, *My Mother Was a Computer*.

7. Haraway, *Simians, Cyborgs, and Women*.

8. Sadie Plant, *Zeros + Ones: Digital Women + the New Technoculture* (New York: Doubleday, 1997).

9. Barad, *Meeting the Universe*.

10. I recommend pursuing emerging posthumanist perspectives as a means to reapproach the human and develop modes of inquiry into the ongoing production of boundaries that differentiate subjectivities' and social systems' insides and outsides beyond humanism's instrumental frame. For this very reason, posthumanist theory is a starting point, not a wholesale alternative or answer, and, therefore, I use the term sparingly in future chapters. Exploring what I describe as distinct, enactive, subject-technology relations or technics as "tactics of the human," through which specific human/nonhuman boundaries emerge and are realized, I will examine a range of recent posthumanist perspectives to differentiate them and clarify some of the critical questions and stakes raised by specific posthumanisms. I will return to the question of posthumanisms in the book's coda.

11. Cary Wolfe, *What Is Posthumanism?* (Minneapolis: University of Minnesota Press, 2010), xv, i.

12. The term "enactive," which is used in biological systems theory and subsequent cognitive science and philosophy to describe forms of embodied action through which an organism and an environment mutually and dynamically "bring forth a world," in Maturana and Varela's words, is the basis from which I explore this and closely related nonrepresentational understandings of human subject formation emerging from feminist and queer theories of performativity. See Varela, Thompson, and Rosch, *The Embodied Mind: Cognitive Science and Human Experience* (Cambridge: MIT Press, 1996), for an influential, early introduction to theories of embodied cognition, and Andy Clark's *Being There: Putting Brain, Body and World Together Again* (Cambridge: MIT Press, 2001) for an engaging exploration of how these theories change cognitive science.

13. Karen Barad, "Posthumanist Performativity: Toward an Understanding of How Matter Comes to Matter," in Alaimo and Hekman, *Material Feminisms*, 139.

14. Butler, *Undoing Gender*, 11.

15. Ibid., 185.

16. Ibid., 186.

17. Luhmann, *Social Systems*.

18. While the connection between biological and social systems theory and new materialist work in feminist science studies and philosophy may initially seem an unwarranted pairing, these distinct disciplinary and intellectual trajectories, in fact, share an engagement with systems frameworks emerging from cybernetics and information theory, systems-thinking that subsequently developed into the late capitalist informational economies and the bioinformatic technologies that confront us today. These distinct strains of posthumanist theory share an interest in using dynamic systems models to reimagine social and cultural processes, and both pursue the problematic questions resulting scientific and economic practices pose to liberal humanism's absolute, hierarchical distinctions between nature and culture. Notably, their reencounter with the agency of material worlds is prompted by larger shifts that traverse disciplines and generate widespread inquiries into the material, technical, and discursive processes through which the human emerges and evolves (inquiries that inform theories of "embodied cognition" in cognitive science and postphenomenological theories of new media, to name a few). New materialisms are an unruly outgrowth of Donna Haraway's and other cyberfeminist and feminist science studies' work on these questions and broader efforts to critically engage scientific and technological discourses and practices to counter disempowering gendered and racialized knowledges of the human and to enhance our understanding of intersecting material and cultural worlds. See Coole and Frost, *New Materialisms* and Alaimo and Hekman, *Material Feminisms* for an introduction to these inquiries.

19. Bruce Clarke and Mark B. N. Hansen, eds., *Emergence and Embodiment: New Essays on Second-Order Systems Theory* (Durham, NC: Duke University Press, 2009), 2.

20. Ibid., 1–2.

21. Hansen follows Francisco Varela's lead in theorizing multiple "forms of closure" at "different levels of cognitive operation (117), some of which operate as "system-environment hybrids" that "realize their autonomy . . . *through a constitutive relation with alterity*" that is not operationally closed or autopoietic in a strict sense (115). His approach usefully pursues the "provisional" and "heterogeneous" dimensions to systems closure at distinct levels and the resulting "*heteropoiesis*" of some system operations, illustrating the need to significantly extend and rethink Luhmann's systems-theoretical framework (114, 124). Mark B. N. Hansen, "System-Environment Hybrids," in Clarke and Hansen, *Emergence and Embodiment*.

22. Colebrook, *Deleuze*.

23. Catherine Waldby, "The Instruments of Life: Frankenstein and Cybercul-

ture," in *Prefiguring Cyberculture: An Intellectual History*, ed. D. Tofts, A. Jonson, and A. Cavallaro (Cambridge: MIT Press, 2002), 35, 32.

24. Nigel Thrift, "Remembering the Technological Unconscious by Foregrounding Knowledges of Position," in *Knowing Capitalism* (London: Sage, 2005), 212.

25. von Foerster, *Observing Systems*.

26. Heims, *Constructing a Social Science*, 23.

27. Ibid.

28. Ibid.

29. von Foerster, *Observing Systems*, 258.

30. For a thoroughgoing analysis of Luhmann's systems theory in relation to Jacques Derrida's deconstruction, see Cary Wolfe's "Meaning and Event; or, Systems Theory and 'The Reconstruction of Deconstruction,'" in *What is Posthumanism?* 3–29. In this chapter, Wolfe extends his prior reading of Luhmann's posthumanist tendencies in *Critical Environments*, exploring points of overlap and divergence between Luhmann and Derrida. William Rasch provides similarly insightful, approachable readings of Luhmann's key theoretical contributions in *Niklas Luhmann's Modernity: The Paradoxes of Differentiation* (Stanford, CA: Stanford University Press, 2000).

31. Luhmann, *Social Systems*, xx.

32. Maturana and Varela, *The Tree of Knowledge*, 27.

33. Baecker, "Why Systems?," 61. Here Baecker is applying an earlier insight of von Foerster to Luhmann's work.

34. Ibid., 63–64.

35. Ibid., 64.

36. Luhmann, *Social Systems*, 249.

37. Ibid., 251.

38. Niklas Luhmann, "The Cognitive Program of Constructivism and the Reality that Remains Unknown," in *Theories of Distinction: Redescribing the Descriptions of Modernity*, ed. William Rasch (Stanford, CA: Stanford University Press, 2002), 133.

39. Maturana and Varela, *The Tree of Knowledge*, 75.

40. Luhmann, *Social Systems*, 19, 17.

41. Ibid., 245.

42. Ibid., 35. As Luhmann states this point in "The Cognitive Program": "If a knowing system has no entry to its external world, it can be denied that such an external world exists. But we can just as well—and more believably—claim that the external world is as it is. Neither claim can be proved; there is no way of deciding between them. " 132–33.

43. Rasch characterizes Luhmann's constructivism as a "two-front war" against realism and idealism that oscillates "between positions, now defending the presupposition of reality with a rhetorical flair that evokes Cartesian certainty in the sea of modern doubt, now defending, with an ironic gesture or two, the 'political' nature of the whole enterprise of describing the nature of reality, both physical and social." See Rasch, *Niklas Luhmann's Modernity*, 82–83. This insight does not diminish Luhmann's problematic repriviledging of meaning and bracketing of matter, though it clarifies his aims.

44. Luhmann, *Social Systems*, 83.

45. Ibid., 63.

46. Ibid., 166.

47. Hans Ulrich Gumbrecht, "Form without Matter vs. Form as Event," *MLN* 111.3 (1996): 581.

48. Luhmann, *Social Systems*, 63.

49. Gunther Teubner, "Economics of Gift—Positivity of Justice: The Mutual Paranoia of Jacques Derrida and Niklas Luhmann," in *Theory, Culture, and Society* 18.1 (2001): 40, accessed December 12, 2012: doi: 10.1177/02632760122051625.

50. Ibid., 41.

51. N. Katherine Hayles, "Theory of a Different Order: A Conversation with Katherine Hayles and Niklas Luhmann," interview with Niklas Luhmann; William Rasch; Eva Knodt; Cary Wolfe, *Cultural Critique* 31 (Autumn 1995): 34; Hayles, *My Mother Was a Computer*, 30.

52. Luhmann, *Social Systems*, 249.

53. References to *Patchwork Girl* will follow the conventions for citing digital hypertext fiction, listing the section title followed by the subsection title (if applicable), and by the specific lexia title. Jackson, *Patchwork Girl* (story / M/S / birth).

54. L. Frank Baum, *The Patchwork Girl of Oz* (Chicago: Reilly and Lee, 1913); Hélène Cixous, *Coming to Writing and Other Essays*, trans. Sarah Cornell, Deborah Jenson, Ann Liddle, and Susan Sellers (Cambridge: Harvard University Press, 1991); and Deleuze and Guattari, *A Thousand Plateaus*.

55. Jackson, *Patchwork Girl* (crazy quilt / research).

56. "graveyard," with links between its text boxes structured to circle between a headstone and the boxes that represent each of the body parts lying prone beneath this marker, reassembles the patchwork girl out of the body parts of various women, a few men, and a cow. The text describes the defining characteristics the patchwork girl has inherited from the previous owners of her disparate parts. "journal" features Mary Shelley's account of her amorous, yet tumultuous relations with the patchwork girl she created and then reencounters, unexpectedly, during a morning walk. "body of text" self-reflexively considers the process of constructing *Patchwork Girl* as a work of digital hypertext, using multiple, recursive links that compromise linear narrative development and resist the single point of narrative departure or origin that might be considered as her textual birth.

57. Jackson, *Patchwork Girl* (body of Text / all written). George Landow reads this lexia in these terms, explaining that "Jackson is showing us the way we always thus stitch together narrative, notions of gender, and the identities of ourselves and others." See "Twenty Minutes into the Future, or How Are We Moving Beyond the Book?," in *The Future of the Book*. ed. Geoffrey Nunberg (Berkeley: University of California Press, 1996), 231.

58. Jackson, *Patchwork Girl* (body of text / bodies).

59. Barad, *Meeting the Universe*, 148.

60. Ibid., 337.

61. Ibid., 206.

62. Ibid., 25.

63. Ibid. (body of text / bodies too).

64. Ibid. (journal / scars / cut).

65. Ibid.

66. Ibid. (body of text / it thinks).

67. My use of the term "entanglement" draws on Donna Haraway's concept and also travels through Karen Barad's recent use of the term to describe the distinct technological and epistemological engagements through which we engage natural and cultural worlds in the matter and meaning of the human. Barad, *Meeting the Universe*, 74.

68. Barad, *Meeting the Universe*, 139.

69. Plant, *Zeros + Ones*, 77; Irigaray, *This Sex Which Is Not One*, qtd. in Plant, 107.

70. Plant, *Zeros + Ones*, 67, 66.

71. Digital hypertext author and theorist Stephanie Strickland insightfully characterizes readings of hypertext fiction as "emergent" in that they involve an ongoing, temporally variable product of both reader and work. The work that emerges "depends on interactions between internal rules and completely unpredictable gradients in the external environment at that time. The pathway to the present thus makes all the difference." See Stephanie Strickland, "Dali Clocks: Time Dimensions of Hypermedia," *Electronic Book Review*, January 1, 2001, accessed April 30, 2014.

72. Jackson, *Patchwork Girl* (graveyard / graveyard).

73. The interactivity involved in reading *Patchwork Girl* is, therefore, distinct from more recent approaches to generative electronic writing in important ways. Marie-Laure Ryan, "The Interactive Onion: Layers of User Participation in Digital Narrative Texts," in Page and Thomas, *New Narratives*, 35–62.

74. Shelley Jackson, "Stitch Bitch: The Patchwork Girl," lecture presented at the Transformations of the Book Conference, Massachusetts Institute of Technology, Cambridge, MA, October 24, 1998, accessed online April 30, 2014.

75. Alice Bell, "Ontological Boundaries and Methodological Leaps: The Importance of Possible Worlds Theory for Hypertext Fiction (and Beyond)," in Page and Thomas, *New Narratives*, 68, 67.

76. Ibid., 67.

77. Ibid., 77.

78. Hayles, "Flickering Connectivities in Shelley Jackson's *Patchwork Girl*," in *My Mother Was a Computer*, 163, 161.

79. Ibid., 154, 159, 161.

80. Ibid., 31.

81. Ibid.

82. Plant, *Zeros + Ones*, 77.

83. Jackson, "Stitch Bitch."

84. Ibid.

85. Plant, *Zeros + Ones*, 244.

86. Ibid., 59.

87. Jackson, *Patchwork Girl* (story / seagoing / guises).

88. Chancy is later revealed to be a woman who disguises her sex in order to pursue a seagoing career. Ibid.

89. Ibid. (story / seagoing / femininity).

90. Ibid.

91. Ibid. (story / re-thinking / what shape).

92. Ibid.

93. Ibid. (story / M/S / I AM).

94. Ibid. (journal / she stood).

95. Emily Apter, "Postcolonial Cyberpunk: Dirty Nationalism in the Era of Terminal Identities," in *Continental Drift: From National Characters to Virtual Subjects* (Chicago: University of Chicago Press, 1999), 216.

96. Jackson, *Patchwork Girl* (story / M/S / I AM).

97. Ibid. (story / falling apart / craft).

98. Ibid. (body of text / dotted line).

99. Roof, *Come as You Are*, 82, xxx.

100. Jackson, *Patchwork Girl* (story / falling apart / I made myself over / Elsie triumphant).

101. Ibid. (story / falling apart / diaspora).

102. Roof, *Come as You Are*, 45.

103. Jackson, *Patchwork Girl* (journal / scars / cut).

104. Ibid. (journal / female trouble).

105. Ibid. (story / severance / us).

106. Certeau, *Practice of Everyday Life*, xiv, xix.

107. Ibid., xix.

108. Ibid., xiv.

109. In suggesting that digital technics open onto a range of distinct ways of operating or doing things, I recommend situating Jackson's *Patchwork Girl* and its experimental technics in relation to more recent "tactical media" practices that extend Michel de Certeau's understanding of tactics to address emergent digital media practices, though they use this term in a more specialized sense that does not fully encompass what I'm arguing here about technicity as a tactical relation. Growing out of the Dutch cultural group Next 5 Minutes' (N5M) events in Amsterdam in 1993, 1996, and 1999, the specific term "tactical media" "refers to a critical usage and theorization of media practices that draw on all forms of old and new, both lucid and sophisticated media, for achieving a variety of specific noncommercial goals and pushing all kinds of potentially subversive political issues" (qtd. in Critical Art Ensemble, *Digital Resistance: Explorations in Tactical Media* [Brooklyn: Autonomedia, 2001], 5). The next chapter will pursue these connections, among other distinct types of tactical engagements with digital and print media.

110. "Flexible accumulation" is David Harvey's term to describe the distinct, new labor practices, markets, products, and practices of consumption and geographical mobility emerging since 1973, which directly contravene previous modes of production and consumption modeled on the assembly line and mass consumption. One of the most ubiquitous examples is "just-in-time production." David Harvey, *The Condition of Postmodernity: An Enquiry into the Origins of Cultural Change* (Malden, MA: Blackwell, 1990), 124.

Chapter 3

1. Manuel Castells, *The Information Age: Economy, Society, and Culture*, vol. 1, *The Rise of the Network Society*, 2nd ed. (Malden, MA: Blackwell, 2000), 14.

2. John Perry Barlow, "A Declaration of the Independence of Cyberspace," February 8, 1996, Electronic Frontier Foundation, http://w2.eff.org/Censorship/Internet_censorship_bills/barlow_0296.declaration.

3. Sherry Turkle, *Life on the Screen: Identity in the Age of the Internet* (New York: Simon and Schuster, 1995).

4. Adam Greenfield, *Everyware: The Dawning Age of Ubiquitous Computing* (Berkeley, CA: New Riders, 2006).

5. Rob Kitchin and Martin Dodge, *Code/Space: Software and Everyday Life* (Cambridge: MIT Press, 2011), 16.

6. Thrift, "Remembering the Technological Unconscious," 212–26.

7. I borrow this term from China Miéville's speculative fiction *The City and the City* (New York: Ballantine Books, 2010). In the novel, two cultures have learned to inhabit the same geographic territory by learning to "unsee" members of the other population and respecting unstated social practices, not at all dissimilar from the dimensions to social space we habitually learn to unsee.

8. Silko, *Almanac of the Dead*.

9. Following Michel Foucault, I use this term to designate a political and economic shift from governing individuals through discipline to one of proactively governing the life of "populations" by taking control of managing health, hygiene, diet, fertility, and sexuality and, thus, making life itself a central site for the exercise of power. I will forgo an extensive review of the literature in biopolitics and biopower in order to focus in on the contributions the novel makes to these conversations. In chapter 5, I explicitly address these competing views on contemporary U.S. biopower and biopolitics.

10. Alexander R. Galloway and Eugene Thacker, *The Exploit: A Theory of Networks* (Minneapolis: University of Minnesota Press, 2007).

11. The three-worlds system, a mapping of global space that became standard following the 1955 Bandung conference, divides the world in terms of the first, second, and third worlds. In practice this has often reinforced a temporal differentiation of the spaces of the world, locating much of the planet in a social space anterior to modernity.

12. Looking at both residual and emergent capitalist spatial practices, at once, clarifies how these shifts might facilitate critical rearticulations of hegemonic discourses and socio-spatial formations from the perspective of people in subaltern positions, what Walter D. Mignolo describes as a "border thinking."

13. My conceptualization of reorientation both draws upon and extends Sara Ahmed's postcolonial and queer engagement with a phenomenological concept of "orientation" and her conceptualization of feminist and other practices of disorientation. I extend the concept in order to address late capitalist technics and to address how the literary and other media practices tactically engage such spatial practices

to distinct ends. See Ahmed, *Queer Phenomenology* and "Orientations Matter," in Coole and Frost, *New Materialisms*, 234–57.

14. Ahmed, "Orientations Matter," 234.

15. Ahmed, *Queer Phenomenology*, 13.

16. Massey, *For Space*, 95.

17. In choosing to use the terms "material space" and "social space," I intend to complicate and rethink the opposition between place and space on which so many theories of postmodern space have relied and to suggest ways that we might resist the assumptions reinforced by the opposition of (material) place from (social) space.

18. Rita Raley, *Tactical Media* (Minneapolis: University of Minnesota Press, 2009).

19. Ranajit Guha, *Elementary Aspects of Peasant Insurgency in Colonial India* (Durham: Duke University Press, 1999), 333.

20. Neil Brenner, "Global, Fragmented, Hierarchical: Henri Lefebvre's Geographies of Globalization," in *Public Culture* 10.1 (1997): 141. See also Henri Lefebvre, *The Production of Space*, trans. Donald Nicholson-Smith (Oxford: Blackwell, 1991).

21. Lefebvre, *The Production of Space*, 109–10.

22. Critical materialisms, such as those pursued by Open Marxism, the Regulation School, and other scholars of late provide important exceptions to this general rule and pursue lines of inquiry, in many ways, compatible with the new materialisms emerging from critical geographies, feminist, and subaltern studies.

23. Harvey, *The Condition of Postmodernity*.

24. Doreen Massey, "Power-geometry and a Progressive Sense of Place," in *Mapping the Futures: Local Cultures, Global Change*, ed. Jon Bird, Barry Curtis, Tim Putnam, George Robertson, and Lisa Tickner (New York: Routledge, 1993), 60.

25. Ibid., 61.

26. Castells, *Rise of Network Society*, 453.

27. Massey, "Power-geometry," 61.

28. Jon May and Nigel Thrift, eds., *TimeSpace: Geographies of Temporality* (New York: Routledge, 2001), 3.

29. Ibid., 3–5.

30. Soja, *Postmodern Geographies*, 58.

31. In this chapter, as elsewhere in the book, I intend to bring together distinct materialisms, drawing on them (without conflating them) to reapproach predominant liberal humanist and posthumanist understandings of how technics enter into lived spaces at multiple scales. The various social, epistemological, and disciplinary backgrounds and emphases of these materialisms are, in my view, key to their abilities to unpack the operations of digital technics and emergent social practices. As mentioned in the introduction, the book is interested in assessing and employing these proposed, expanded materialisms to understand shifting digital technics.

32. Silko, *Almanac of the Dead*, 632, 707.

33. Gordon Brotherston, *Book of the Fourth World: Reading the Native Americas through Their Literature* (Cambridge: Cambridge University Press, 1992).

34. Tom Foster, "Cyber-Aztecs and Cholo-Punks: Guillermo Gómez-Peña's Five Worlds Theory," *PMLA* 117.1 (2002): 46.

35. Doreen Massey, *Space, Place, and Gender* (Cambridge: Polity Press, 1994), 5.

36. Henry Jenkins acknowledges several important print and place-based precedents for what he describes as spatial or environmental storytelling in game design. See Jenkins, "Game Design as Narrative Architecture," in Harrigan and Wardrip-Fruin, *First Person*, 122–23.

37. Silko, *Almanac of the Dead*, 428.

38. Mary Pat Brady, *Extinct Lands, Temporal Geographies: Chicana Literature and the Urgency of Space* (Durham, NC: Duke University Press, 2002), 13.

39. Nigel Thrift, "Movement-Space: The Changing Domain of Thinking Resulting from the Development of New Kinds of Spatial Awareness," in *Non-representational Theory: Space, Politics, Affect* (New York: Routledge, 2008), 92.

40. Castells, *Rise of Network Society*, 14.

41. Ibid., 1.

42. Ibid., 442, 453.

43. Ibid., 443.

44. Manuel Castells, *The Informational City: Information Technology, Economic Restructuring, and the Urban-Regional Process* (Cambridge, MA: Blackwell, 1989), 349.

45. Castells, *Rise of Network Society*, 102.

46. Ibid., 102, 106.

47. Ibid., 442, 443.

48. Massey, *For Space*, 63, 84.

49. Castells, *Rise of Network Society*, 132.

50. Ibid., 134–35.

51. Ibid.

52. Ibid., 134.

53. Ibid., 101, 131. On this point, theorists such as Nick Dyer-Witheford, among others, argue that labor movements likely played a significant role in prompting these global capitalist restructurings, which are designed to circumvent organized labor through more flexible and widely distributed modes and means of access to workers around the globe. See Nick Dyer-Witheford, *Cyber-Marx: Cycles and Circuits of Struggle in High-Technology Capitalism* (Urbana: University of Illinois Press, 1999).

54. Manuel Castells, *Communication Power* (New York: Oxford University Press, 2009).

55. Silko, *Almanac of the Dead*, 292.

56. Ibid., 292.

57. Ibid., 329.

58. Ibid., 15.

59. Ibid., 261.

60. Enrique Dussel, "Beyond Eurocentrism: The World System and the Limits of Modernity," in *The Cultures of Globalization*, ed. Fredric Jameson and Masao Miyoshi (Durham, NC: Duke University Press, 1998), 5.

61. Ibid., 4.

62. Silko, *Almanac of the Dead*, 155.

63. Ibid., 257.

64. Coole and Frost, *New Materialisms*, 7.

65. Silko, *Almanac of the Dead*, 224.

66. Ibid., 224.

67. Ibid., 201.

68. Ibid., 167.

69. Ibid., 336.

70. Ibid., 151.

71. Ibid., 155.

72. Ibid., 154, 156.

73. Ibid., 155–56.

74. Ibid., 156.

75. Ihde, *Ironic Technics*.

76. Silko, *Almanac of the Dead*, 159.

77. Through the Yupik woman's "plane-crashing spell," which explicitly draws on Native American cultural knowledges in which one's ancestors are a living, material force, the novel also links these specifically Native American understandings of living material forces to other subaltern knowledges that acknowledge the importance of material spaces and nonhuman agencies on social formations. Massey's concept of the "emergent powers" of the spatial, in its own way, attempts to describe this nonhuman force of materiality. See Massey, *Space, Place, and Gender*, 268.

78. Ahmed, *Queer Phenomenology*, 12.

79. Ibid.

80. Ibid., 14.

81. Ibid., 9.

82. Ahmed, "Orientations Matter," 254.

83. Ibid.

84. Eva Cherniavsky, "Eskimo Television and the Critique of Whiteness (Studies)," in *Incorporations: Race, Nation, and the Body Politics of Capital* (Minneapolis: University of Minnesota Press, 2006), 70.

85. Title 22 of the U.S. Code, Section 2656f(d), Central Intelligence Agency website, https://www.cia.gov/news-information/cia-the-war-on-terrorism/terrorism-faqs.html.

86. Ranajit Guha, preface to *Selected Subaltern Studies*, ed. Ranajit Guha and Gayatri Spivak (New York: Oxford University Press, 1988), 35.

87. Graham Meikle, *Future Active: Media Activism and the Internet* (New York: Routledge, 2002), 119.

88. Guha, *Elementary Aspects*, 333.

89. John Beverley, *Subalternity and Representation: Arguments in Cultural Theory* (Durham, NC: Duke University Press, 1999), 26.

90. Ibid., 135.

91. Gayatri Chakravorty Spivak, "Can the Subaltern Speak?, "in *Marxism and*

the Interpretation of Culture, ed. Cary Nelson and Lawrence Grossberg (Urbana: University of Illinois, 1988).

92. Beverley, *Subalternity and Representation*, 142.

93. Silko, *Almanac of the Dead*, 707.

94. Ibid., 683.

95. Eva Cherniavsky, "Subaltern Studies in a U.S. Frame," *Boundary 2* 23.2 (1996): 86.

96. Dussel, "Beyond Eurocentrism," 19–21.

97. Dyer-Witheford, *Cyber-Marx*, 145.

98. Ibid.

99. Ibid., 145–46.

100. Castells, qtd in Meikle, *Future Active*, 145.

101. Dyer-Witheford, *Cyber-Marx*, 158.

102. Leslie Marmon Silko, "An Expression of Profound Gratitude to the Maya Zapatistas, January 1, 1994," in *Yellow Woman and A Beauty of the Spirit: Essays on Native American Life Today* (New York: Simon and Schuster, 1996), 152–54.

103. Raley, *Tactical Media*, 5, 1. Also, for an introduction to Critical Art Ensemble's initial approach to tactical media practices, see *Digital Resistance: Explorations in Tactical Media.*

104. Next Five Minutes (N5M), qtd. in Raley, *Tactical Media*, 6–7.

105. Raley, *Tactical Media*, 6.

106. Silko, *Almanac of the Dead*, 316, 311.

107. Ibid., 515.

108. The novel's transformative politics of networks has been *misread* as envisioning and asserting a reactionary, place-based, ethnic identity, one that relies on a nationalist understanding of identity grounded in place rather than offering a politics of networks that, as I've argued, both responds to *and* renegotiates global capitalist spatial logics. This misreading completely elides the novel's unwillingness to ground social relations, as nationalisms do, by reference to an unchanging space or origin *outside* time. In his most recent book, *The Shape of the Signifier*, Walter Benn Michaels, for example, reads Silko's novel as offering a "more or less straightforward ethnonationalism." Michaels's characterization of *Almanac of the Dead* as "ethnonationalist" evidences a wholesale refusal to engage with the novel's reconceptualization of the relation between the social and the spatial, which *Almanac of the Dead* stages, quite explicitly, in terms of *epistemological*, not ethnic difference. See Walter Benn Michaels, *The Shape of the Signifier: American Writing from 1967 to the End of History* (Princeton, NJ: Princeton University Press, 2004), 24.

109. Giorgio Agamben, *Homo Sacer: Sovereign Power and Bare Life*, trans. Daniel Heller-Roazen (Stanford, CA: Stanford University Press, 1998).

110. Silko, *Almanac of the Dead*, 252; emphasis added. The materiality of the almanac is integral, not incidental, to its meaning and to the sustenance it provides, though it delimits possibilities for an ongoing process of meaning-production rather than determining that meaning. This point is quite clear when the young slave fugitives journeying north with the almanac survive by eating pages of the almanac that

are made out of pressed horses' stomachs. They draw sustenance from the material form of the almanac, yet the possibility or necessity of eating the pages is most likely one not foreseen by the former keepers of the almanac.

111. Ibid., 134.

112. Ibid., 570.

113. Ibid., 569.

114. Ibid., 142.

115. Ibid., 138.

116. Ibid., 143–44.

117. Ibid., 569.

118. Ibid., 137.

119. Ibid., 14.

120. Involving and crediting the spatial dimensions of the text, equally, with the production of meaning, the almanac refuses to privilege the narrative's temporal development at the expense of its material, spatial form. *Almanac of the Dead* thereby marks the imbrication of hegemonic understandings of narrative in a Cartesian spatiotemporal distinction that abstracts the narrative's temporal progression, read as its "meaning," from its medium, its spatial instantiation. The subordination of the spatial aspects of texts to the narrative's figurative meaning was the basis of a wholesale discrediting of the glyphs, colors, and pictographs that were central to the Azteca codices' meaning. This discrediting of Azteca expressive forms was, furthermore, part and parcel of a broader subjugation of non-European cultures to the narratives as well as the narrative forms of European history.

121. Silko, *Almanac of the Dead*, 129.

122. Massey, *For Space*, 9.

123. Silko, *Almanac of the Dead*, 233.

124. Anna Lowenhaupt Tsing, *Friction: An Ethnography of Global Connection* (Princeton, NJ: Princeton University Press, 2005), 4, 5.

125. Teri Rueb, "Shifting Subjects in Locative Media," in Hawk, Rieder, and Oviedo, *Small Tech*, 130, 129.

126. Ibid., 130.

Chapter 4

1. Lauren Berlant, *The Queen of America Goes to Washington City: Essays on Sex and Citizenship* (Durham, NC: Duke University Press, 1997), 5.

2. Jeffrey T. Nealon, *Post-Postmodernism or, The Cultural Logic of Just-in-Time Capitalism* (Stanford, CA: Stanford University Press, 2012).

3. Ozeki, *My Year of Meats*.

4. Ibid., 8.

5. Emily Cheng, "Meat and the Millennium: Transnational Politics of Race and Gender in Ruth Ozeki's *My Year of Meats*," *Journal of Asian American Studies* 12.2 (June 2009): 191–220, 237.

6. For a detailed account of the history of DES in the United States and an

analysis of *My Year of Meats* through this specific biotechnological lens, see Julie Sze's article "Boundaries and Border Wars: DES, Technology, and Environmental Justice," *American Quarterly* 58.3 (September 2006): 791–814, 985.

7. Françoise Lionnet and Shu-mei Shih, "Introduction: Thinking through the Minor, Transnationally," in *Minor Transnationalism*, ed. Lionnet and Shih (Durham, NC: Duke University Press, 2005).

8. Thrift, "Movement-Space," 89.

9. Ibid., 89, 91.

10. Ibid., 91–92.

11. Ozeki, *My Year of Meats*, 8.

12. Marshall McLuhan, *Understanding Media: The Extensions of Man* (New York: New American Library, Times Mirror, 1964).

13. Sara Ahmed, *The Cultural Politics of Emotion* (New York: Routledge, 2004), 10.

14. Ibid.

15. Lisa Lowe, "Decolonization, Displacement, Disidentification: Asian American 'Novels' and the Question of History," in *Cultural Institutions of the Novel*, ed. Deidre Lynch and William B. Warner (Durham, NC: Duke University Press, 1996), 100.

16. Ibid., 111.

17. David Palumbo-Liu, "Rational and Irrational Choices: Form, Affect, and Ethics," in Lionnet and Shih, *Minor Transnationalism*.

18. Lionnet and Shih, "Introduction: Thinking through the Minor, Transnationally," 7.

19. Ibid., 8.

20. Ibid., 21.

21. Ozeki, *My Year of Meats*, 8.

22. Ibid., 9.

23. Ibid.

24. Ibid.

25. Ibid.

26. Aihwa Ong, "Latitudes of Citizenship: Membership, Meaning, and Multiculturalism, in *People out of Place: Globalization, Human Rights, and the Citizenship Gap*, ed. Alison Brysk and Gershon Shafir (New York: Routledge, 2004), 55.

27. Lowe, "The International within the National: American Studies and Asian American Critique," in *The Futures of American Studies*, ed. Donald Pease and Robyn Wiegman (Durham, NC: Duke University Press, 2002), 81.

28. Ibid., 77, 81.

29. Ibid., 81.

30. Ozeki, *My Year of Meats*, 9, 15.

31. Sei Shōnagon, *The Pillow Book*, trans. and ed. Ivan Morris (New York: Columbia University Press, 1991).

32. Ozeki, *My Year of Meats*, 8.

33. Ruth Ozeki, "A Conversation with Ruth Ozeki," in *My Year of Meats*, 6.

34. Susan McHugh, "The Fictions and Futures of Farm Animals: Semi-Living to 'Animalacra' Pig Tales," in *Animal Stories: Narrating across Species Lines* (Minneapolis: University of Minnesota Press, 2011), 175.

35. Ozeki, *My Year of Meats*, 365–66.

36. Ibid.

37. Ibid.

38. Carol Adams, *The Sexual Politics of Meat: A Feminist-Vegetarian Critical Theory* (New York: Continuum, 2010).

39. Thrift, "Movement-Space," 91.

40. Ozeki, *My Year of Meats*, 89.

41. Ibid., 11.

42. Lionnet and Shih, "Introduction," 9.

43. Ozeki, *My Year of Meats*, 42.

44. Ibid., 15.

45. Ibid., 177.

46. Ibid.

47. Ibid., 231.

48. Ibid., 318.

49. Ibid., 337.

50. Ibid., 339.

51. Ahmed, *Cultural Politics of Feeling*, 133.

52. Ibid., 134.

53. Ibid., 136.

54. Ibid., 138.

55. Ibid., 139.

56. Monica Chiu, "Postnational Globalization and (En)Gendered Meat Production in Ruth L. Ozeki's *My Year of Meats*, *LIT* 12 (2001): 101.

57. Elspeth Probyn, *Carnal Appetites: Food Sex Identities* (New York, Routledge, 2000), 8.

58. Amy Kaplan, "Manifest Domesticity," in Pease and Wiegman, *Futures of American Studies*, 111.

59. Probyn, *Carnal Appetites*, 3.

60. Ibid., 32.

61. Ozeki, *My Year of Meats*, 360.

62. Ibid., 251.

63. Ibid., 267.

64. Ibid.

65. Ibid., 277.

66. Ibid., 296.

67. Ibid.

68. Brian Massumi, *Parables for the Virtual: Movement, Affect, Sensation* (Durham, NC: Duke University Press, 2002), 26.

69. Ibid., 35.

Chapter 5

1. Stengers, *Cosmopolitics I*, 10.
2. Nancy Armstrong, "Futures *in* and *of* the Novel," *Novel: A Forum on Fiction* 44.1 (Spring 2011), 8.
3. Ibid., 10.
4. Ibid.
5. Ibid., 8.
6. Eugene Thacker, *Biomedia* (Minneapolis: University of Minnesota Press, 2004), 5.
7. Melinda Cooper, *Life as Surplus: Biotechnology and Capitalism in the Neoliberal Era* (Seattle: University of Washington Press, 2008), 3.
8. Eugenides, *Middlesex*.
9. Michel Foucault, *Security, Territory, Population: Lectures at the Collège de France, 1978–1979*, trans. Graham Burchell ((New York: Picador, 2009), 1.
10. Michel Foucault, *The Birth of Biopolitics: Lectures at the Collège de France, 1978–1979*, trans. Graham Burchell (New York: Palgrave, 2008).
11. Foucault, *Security, Territory, Population*, 42.
12. Although the novel was published during the aftermath of the 9/11 attacks, its perspective on biopower precedes a growing awareness, in light of the treatment of prisoners at the Guantánamo Bay detention center and at other undisclosed locations outside the territory and juridical domain of the United States, of what philosophers such as Giorgio Agamben and Roberto Esposito now regularly describe as the thanatopolitical tendencies of biopower, facilitated by computation-based technics, to actively push or put people to a kind of death in life, subjecting them to a "state of exemption." See Giorgio Agamben's recent *What Is an Apparatus? and Other Essays*, trans. David Kishik and Stefan Pedatella (Stanford, CA: Stanford University Press, 2009); Roberto Esposito's *Immunitas: The Protection and Negation of Life* (Cambridge: Polity Press, 2011), and Achille Mbembe, "Necropolitics," trans. Libby Meintjes, *Public Culture* 15.1 (2003): 11–40. Notably, there are limits to their emphasis on these thanatopolitical tendencies of biopower, which only underscores, in my view, why it is important to continue to develop these and more multifaceted perspectives on the complex relations involved in technicity.
13. The question of what personal pronouns to use to describe Cal/lie reflects the challenges intersex and transgender pose to gendered conventions of language as they open onto larger questions of sex and gendered subjectivities. There are a series of emerging pronouns such as "ze" and "hir" for transgender subjects wishing to avoid the gender binary upheld by he and she, yet it is also common practice to respect the wishes of a transgender subject. As the adult Cal self-identifies as a transgender male, I use the masculine pronoun throughout the essay to reflect that choice, except where it may confuse readers, as in this initial reference.
14. Herculine Barbin, *Herculine Barbin: Being the Recently Discovered Memoirs of a Nineteenth-Century French Hermaphrodite*, trans. Richard McDougall, introduction by Michel Foucault (New York: Pantheon Books, 1980).

15. James Schiff, "A Conversation with Jeffrey Eugenides," *Missouri Review* 29.3 (2006): 108-9, accessed October 20, 2008, Project Muse, doi:10.1353/mis.2007.0007.

16. J. Jack Halberstam, *In a Queer Time and Place: Transgender Bodies, Subcultural Lives* (New York: New York University Press, 2005).

17. The novel explicitly cites Horace Greeley's statement in an 1865 editorial, "Go West, young man, go West and grow up with the country," which participates in nineteenth-century American discourses of manifest destiny. The first part of the phrase introduces a chapter describing Cal's flight to San Francisco and introduction to an intersex and transgender community. In this, the novel explicitly plays off of the 1979 song by the Village People, "Go West," which characterizes San Francisco as the promised land for the gay liberation movement and came to be aligned with sexual freedom, more generally, in these communities. The song was also covered in 1993 by the Pet Shop Boys. Notably, in Cal's case, "going West" also entails a becoming male-identified, as ze first dons a suit while hitchhiking from Detroit to San Francisco.

18. This phrase is drawn from Richard Dawkins, *The Selfish Gene* (Oxford: Oxford University Press, 1976), 35.

19. Stengers, *Cosmopolitics I*, 12.

20. Ibid.

21. Eugenides, *Middlesex*, 529.

22. Daniel Punday, *Writing at the Limit: The Novel in the New Media Ecology* (Lincoln: University of Nebraska Press, 2012).

23. Eugenides, *Middlesex*, 312, 67.

24. Ibid., 67.

25. Ibid., 72.

26. Ibid., 68–69, 72.

27. Ibid., 71.

28. Ibid., 396–97.

29. Like a wealth of other seemingly implausible dimensions to the novel's twentieth-century American history, the reference to Henry Ford's English Language School and, in particular, to a "melting pot" play in which graduating workers emerge from a black cauldron onstage is confirmed by the historical record. As described on the University of Michigan's web archive "Auto Life": "Established in 1914, the Ford English School taught the company's immigrant workers more than just how to speak English. It taught them about American culture and history and instilled the importance of such virtues as thriftiness, cleanliness, good manners, and timeliness." The web archive includes pictures of the school's graduating class emerging from the "Melting Pot," a symbol of their having put aside their ethnic identity and become good Americans, on July 4, 1917." See "Automobile in American Life and Society," University of Michigan–Dearborn and Benson Ford Research Center website, accessed December 12, 2012. The play is likely an adaptation of Israel Zangwill's play, *The Melting Pot*, which was first staged in 1908 and popularized this conceit through its Russian-Jewish immigrant family's narrative of assimilation.

30. Eugenides, *Middlesex*, 73.

31. Grosz, *Time Travels*, 27.

32. Ibid., 41, 37.

33. Ibid., 2.

34. Ibid., 8.

35. Ibid., 17.

36. Ibid., 47.

37. Ibid., 6, 14.

38. Eugenides, *Middlesex*, 71.

39. Grosz, *Time Travels*, 6.

40. Dawkins, *The Selfish Gene*, 35.

41. Eugenides, *Middlesex*, 3–4; emphasis added.

42. Dawkins, *The Selfish Gene*, 35.

43. Eugenides, *Middlesex*, 210–11; emphasis added.

44. Ibid., 216.

45. Ibid., 119.

46. Ibid., 99.

47. Grosz, *Time Travels*, 43.

48. Thacker, *Biomedia*.

49. Katrina Karkazis, *Fixing Sex: Intersex, Medical Authority, and Lived Experience* (Durham, NC: Duke University Press, 2008), 4.

50. Ibid., 9.

51. Anne Fausto-Sterling, *Sexing the Body: Gender Politics and the Construction of Sexuality* (New York: Basic Books, 2000), 51; Karkazis, *Fixing Sex*, 9.

52. Luce Irigaray, *This Sex Which Is Not One*, trans. Catherine Porter with Carolyn Burke (Ithaca, NY: Cornell University Press, 1993).

53. Ilya Prigogine and Isabelle Stengers, *Order Out of Chaos: Man's New Dialogue with Nature* (New York: Bantam Books, 1984), 169–70; emphasis added.

54. Ibid., 14.

55. Eugenides, *Middlesex*, 106.

56. Ibid.

57. The Intersex Society of America is the result of a movement founded by Cheryl Case in San Francisco in the early 1990s to end pediatric genital reconfiguration surgeries on babies, like herself, born with ambiguous genitalia. Such surgeries, as the novel suggests in Cal's case, are often conducted without the parents' or young child's full understanding of this specific intersex condition and without awareness of the potential consequences of the surgeries, such as diminished sexual response. Whether or not one is in favor of sex-reassignment surgery in these kinds of intersex cases, an issue that raises distinct and difficult questions depending on the specific intersex condition and other particulars of each person's situation, the lack of full disclosure and education on the part of biomedical practitioners is quite disturbing.

58. Susan Stryker, *Transgender History* (Berkeley, CA: Seal Press, 2008), 137.

59. Ibid., 123, 19.

60. Jay Prosser, *Second Skins: The Body Narratives of Transsexuality* (New York: Columbia University Press, 1998), 21–22.

61. Halberstam, *Queer Time and Place*, 18.

62. Ibid.

63. Campbell, *Improper Life*, 124.

64. Ibid.

65. Thomas Lemke, "'The Birth of Biopolitics': Michel Foucault's Lecture at the Collège de France on Neo-liberal Governmentality," *Economy and Society* 30.2 (May 2001): 203.

66. Ibid.

67. Ibid.

68. Iderpal Grewal, *Transnational America: Feminisms, Diasporas, Neoliberalisms* (Durham, NC: Duke University Press, 2005), 38.

69. Here I'm referencing this primary, rationalizing aim of the sciences of sexuality since the eighteenth century when, as Michel Foucault argues, medicine and law began to demand that "hermaphrodites have a sex—a single, a true sex" rather than valuing "the reality of the body and the intensity of its pleasures." See Michel Foucault, introduction to *Herculine Barbin: Being the Recently Discovered Memoirs of a Nineteenth-Century French Hermaphrodite*, trans. Richard McDougal (New York: Pantheon Books, 1980), vii.

70. Eugenides, *Middlesex*, 106.

71. Ibid., 258.

72. Ibid., 273.

73. Ibid., 258.

74. Ibid., 260. Interestingly, Julia Ward Howe, the poet who wrote the lyrics to "The Battle Hymn of the Republic," also wrote a novel about a hermaphrodite in the 1840s, though it has only recently been published. Howe, influenced by Margaret Fuller's comments on George Sand in *Woman in the Nineteenth Century*, noted that "To the literary merit of [Sand's] work was added the interest of a mysterious personality, which rebelled against the limits of sex, and, not content to be either man or woman, touched with a new and strange protest the imagination of the time." See Gary Williams, "Speaking with the Voices of Others: Julia Ward Howe's Laurence," introduction to *The Hermaphrodite*, by Julia Ward Howe, ed. Gary Williams (Lincoln: University of Nebraska Press, 2004), xxxii. It is worth considering how this reflects on the long-standing, tenuous character of gendered biopolitical divisions between masculine and feminine or public and private in American national life even at the height of early America's instantiation of the gendered "two spheres" spatial division between private and public. Within the latter context, simply being a female author was to "transgress the limits of sex" and, thus, sheds light on the tenuousness of these binary logics in past as well as present practices of American nationalism.

75. Eugenides, *Middlesex*, 258.

76. Ibid., 529.

77. Stengers, *Cosmopolitics I*, 12.

78. Punday, *Writing at the Limit*, 229.

79. Ibid., 210.

80. Franco Moretti, "On Literary Evolution," in *Signs Taken for Wonders: Essays in the Sociology of Literary Forms*, trans. Susan Fischer, David Forgacs, and David Miller (New York: Verso Books, 1997), 262–78.

Coda

1. Eugenides, *Middlesex.*
2. Ozeki, *My Year of Meats.*
3. Jackson, *Patchwork Girl.*
4. Silko, *Almanac of the Dead.*
5. Wardrip-Fruin, *Expressive Processing*, 19.
6. Steve Tomasula, "Three Axioms for Projecting a Line (or why it will continue to be hard to write a title sans slashes or parentheses)," *Review of Contemporary Fiction* 16.1 (Spring 1996): 100, Proquest Research Library #02719290. 05.09.12.
7. Ibid.
8. Coole and Frost, *New Materialisms*, 4.
9. Thrift, "Movement-Space," 92.
10. Coole and Frost, *New Materialisms*, 24.
11. Pheng Cheah, "Non-Dialectical Materialism," in Coole and Frost, *New Materialisms*, 89.
12. Stengers, *Cosmopolitics I.*
13. Kitchin and Dodge, *Code/Space.*
14. Page and Thomas, *New Narratives*, 3, 6.
15. Punday, *Writing at the Limit*, 205.
16. Daniel Punday, "Looking for Writing after Postmodernism," *Electronic Book Review* (ebr). 2012.06.28, http://www.electronicbookreview.com/thread/fictionspresent/canonized.

Bibliography

Aarseth, Espen J. *Cybertext: Perspectives on Ergodic Literature*. Baltimore: Johns Hopkins University Press, 1997.

Adams, Carol. *The Sexual Politics of Meat: A Feminist-Vegetarian Critical Theory*. New York: Continuum, 2010.

Agamben, Giorgio. *Homo Sacer: Sovereign Power and Bare Life*. Trans. Daniel Heller-Roazen. Stanford, CA: Stanford University Press, 1998.

Agamben, Giorgio. *What Is an Apparatus? and Other Essays*. Trans. David Kishik and Stefan Pedatella. Stanford, CA: Stanford University Press, 2009.

Ahmed, Sara. *The Cultural Politics of Emotion*. New York: Routledge, 2004.

Ahmed, Sara. "Orientations Matter." In *New Materialisms*, ed. Diana Coole and Samantha Frost. Durham, NC, 2010. 234–57.

Ahmed, Sara. *Queer Phenomenology: Orientations, Objects, Others*. Durham, NC: Duke University Press, 2006.

Alaimo, Stacy, and Susan Hekman. *Material Feminisms*. Bloomington: Indiana University Press, 2008.

Apter, Emily. "Postcolonial Cyberpunk: Dirty Nationalism in the Era of Terminal Identities." In *Continental Drift: From National Characters to Virtual Subjects*. Chicago: University of Chicago Press, 1999. 213–24.

Armstrong, Nancy. "Futures *in* and *of* the Novel." *Novel: A Forum on Fiction* 44.1 (Spring 2011): 8–10.

"Automobile in American Life and Society." University of Michigan-Dearborn and Benson Ford Research Center website. http://www.autolife.umd.umich.edu/. Accessed December 12, 2011.

Baecker, Dirk. "Why Systems?" *Theory, Culture, & Society* 18.1 (2001): 59–74. doi: 10.1177/02632760101800 1005.

Barad, Karen. *Meeting the Universe Halfway: Quantum Physics and the Entanglement of Matter and Meaning*. Durham, NC: Duke University Press, 2007.

Barad, Karen. "Posthumanist Performativity: Toward an Understanding of How

Matter Comes to Matter." In *Material Feminisms*, ed. Stacy Alaimo and Susan Hekman. Bloomington: University of Indiana Press, 2008. 120–54.

Barbin, Herculine. *Herculine Barbin: Being the Recently Discovered Memoirs of a Nineteenth-Century French Hermaphrodite*. Introduced by Michel Foucault. Trans. Richard McDougall. New York: Pantheon Books, 1980.

Barlow, John Perry. "A Declaration of the Independence of Cyberspace." February 8, 1996. *Electronic Frontier Foundation*, http://w2.eff.org/Censorship/Internet_censorship_bills/barlow_0296.declaration.

Barth, John. "Click." *Atlantic Monthly* (December 1997): 81–96.

Barth, John. *Coming Soon!!! A Narrative*. Boston: Houghton Mifflin, 2001.

Barth, John. *Lost in the Funhouse: Fiction for Print, Tape, Live Voice*. New York: Doubleday, 1988.

Baum, Frank L. *The Patchwork Girl of Oz*. Chicago: Reilly and Lee, 1913.

Bell, Alice. "Ontological Boundaries and Methodological Leaps: The Importance of Possible Worlds Theory for Hypertext Fiction (and Beyond)." In *New Narratives: Stories and Storytelling in the Digital Age*, ed. Ruth Page and Bronwen Thomas. Lincoln: University of Nebraska Press, 2011. 63–82.

Bell, Daniel. *The Coming of Post-Industrial Society*. New York: Basic, 1973.

Berlant, Lauren. *The Queen of America Goes to Washington City: Essays on Sex and Citizenship*. Durham, NC: Duke University Press, 1997.

Beverley, John. *Subalternity and Representation: Arguments in Cultural Theory*. Durham, NC: Duke University Press, 1999.

Block, Friedrich W. "Digital Poetics or On the Evolution of Experimental Media Poetry." In *Media Poetry: An International Anthology*, ed. Eduardo Kac. Chicago: Intellect, 2007. 229–43.

Bolter, Jay David. *Writing Space: Computers, Hypertext, and the Remediation of Print*. 2nd ed. Mahwah, NJ: Lawrence Erlbaum Associates, 2001.

Bolter, Jay David, and Richard Grusin. *Remediation: Understanding New Media*. 3rd ed. Cambridge: MIT Press, 2000.

Bradley, Arthur, and Louis Armand. *Technicity*. Prague: Litteraria Pragensia, 2006.

Brady, Mary Pat. *Extinct Lands, Temporal Geographies: Chicana Literature and the Urgency of Space*. Durham, NC: Duke University Press, 2002.

Brenner, Neil. "Global, Fragmented, Hierarchical: Henri Lefebvre's Geographies of Globalization." *Public Culture* 10.1 (1997): 135–67.

Brotherston, Gordon. *Book of the Fourth World: Reading the Native Americas through Their Literature*. Cambridge: Cambridge University Press, 1992.

Butler, Judith. *Undoing Gender*. New York: Routledge, 2004.

Campbell, Timothy C. *Improper Life: Technology and Biopolitics from Heidegger to Agamben*. Minneapolis: University of Minnesota Press, 2011.

Case, Sue-Ellen. *The Domain-Matrix: Performing Lesbian at the End of Print Culture*. Bloomington: Indiana University Press, 1996.

Castells, Manuel. *Communication Power*. New York: Oxford University Press, 2009.

Castells, Manuel. *The Informational City: Information Technology, Economic Restructuring, and the Urban-Regional Process*. Cambridge, MA: Blackwell, 1989.

Castells, Manuel. *The Information Age: Economy, Society, and Culture.* Vol. 1: *The Rise of the Network Society.* 2nd ed. Malden, MA: Blackwell, 2000.

Certeau, Michel de. *The Practice of Everyday Life.* Trans. Steven Rendall. Berkeley: University of California Press, 1984.

Cheah, Pheng. "Non-Dialectical Materialism." In *New Materialisms: Ontology, Agency, and Politics*, ed. Diana Coole and Samantha Frost. Durham, NC: Duke University Press, 2010. 70–91.

Cheng, Emily. "Meat and the Millennium: Transnational Politics of Race and Gender in Ruth Ozeki's *My Year of Meats.*" *Journal of Asian American Studies* 12.2 (June 2009): 191–220, 237.

Cherniavsky, Eva. "Eskimo Television and the Critique of Whiteness (Studies)." In *Incorporations: Race, Nation, and the Body Politics of Capital.* Minneapolis: University of Minnesota Press, 2006. 49–70.

Cherniavsky, Eva. "Subaltern Studies in a U.S. Frame." *Boundary 2* 23.2 (1996): 85–110.

Chiu, Monica. "Postnational Globalization and (En)Gendered Meat Production in Ruth L. Ozeki's *My Year of Meats. LIT* 12 (2001): 99–128.

Cisco Systems. "Class Trip." Advertisement. July 15, 2010.

Cixous, Hélène. *Coming to Writing and Other Essays.* Trans. Sarah Cornell, Deborah Jenson, Ann Liddle, and Susan Sellers. Cambridge: Harvard University Press, 1991.

Clark, Andy. *Being There: Putting Brain, Body and World Together Again.* Cambridge: MIT Press, 2001.

Clarke, Bruce. *Posthuman Metamorphosis: Narrative and Systems.* New York: Fordham University Press, 2008.

Clarke, Bruce, and Mark B. N. Hansen. *Emergence and Embodiment: New Essays on Second-Order Systems Theory.* Durham, NC: Duke University Press, 2009.

Colebrook, Claire. *Deleuze and The Meaning of Life.* London: Continuum, 2010.

Coole, Diana, and Samantha Frost, eds. *New Materialisms: Ontology, Agency, and Politics.* Durham, NC: Duke University Press, 2010.

Cooper, Melinda. *Life as Surplus: Biotechnology and Capitalism in the Neoliberal Era.* Seattle: University of Washington Press, 2008.

Critical Art Ensemble. *Digital Resistance: Explorations in Tactical Media.* Brooklyn: Autonomedia, 2001.

Dawkins, Richard. *The Selfish Gene.* Oxford: Oxford University Press, 1976.

de Lauretis, Teresa. *Technologies of Gender: Essays on Theory, Film, and Fiction.* Bloomington: Indiana University Press, 1987.

Deleuze, Gilles, and Félix Guattari. *A Thousand Plateaus: Capitalism and Schizophrenia.* Trans. Brian Massumi. Minneapolis: University of Minnesota Press, 1987.

Derrida, Jacques. *Archive Fever: A Freudian Impression.* Trans. Eric Prenowitz. Chicago: University of Chicago Press, 1998.

Derrida, Jacques. *Of Grammatology.* Trans. Gayatri Chakravorty Spivak. Corrected ed. Baltimore: Johns Hopkins University Press, 1997.

Dolphijn, Rick, and Iris van der Tuin. *New Materialism: Interviews & Cartographies.*

Ann Arbor: Open Humanities Press, MPublishing, University of Michigan Library, 2012.

Dussel, Enrique. "Beyond Eurocentrism: The World System and the Limits of Modernity." In *The Cultures of Globalization*, ed. Fredric Jameson and Masao Miyoshi. Durham, NC: Duke University Press, 1998. 3–31.

Dyer-Witheford, Nick. *Cyber-Marx: Cycles and Circuits of Struggle in High-Technology Capitalism*. Urbana: University of Illinois Press, 1999.

Esposito, Roberto. *Immunitas: The Protection and Negation of Life*. Cambridge: Polity Press, 2011.

Eugenides, Jeffrey. *Middlesex*. New York: Farrar, Straus and Giroux, 2002.

Fausto-Sterling, Anne. *Sexing the Body: Gender Politics and the Construction of Sexuality*. New York: Basic Books, 2000.

Foster, Tom. "Cyber-Aztecs and Cholo-Punks: Guillermo Gómez-Peña's Five Worlds Theory." *PMLA* 117.1 (2002): 43–67.

Foucault, Michel. *The Birth of Biopolitics: Lectures at the Collège de France, 1978–1979*. Trans. Graham Burchell. New York: Palgrave, 2008.

Foucault, Michel. *Security, Territory, Population: Lectures at the Collège de France, 1978–1979*. Trans. Graham Burchell. New York: Picador, 2009.

Galloway, Alexander R., and Eugene Thacker. *The Exploit: A Theory of Networks*. Minneapolis: University of Minnesota Press, 2007.

Glazier, Loss Pequeño. *Digital Poetics: The Making of E-Poetries*. Tuscaloosa: University of Alabama Press, 2001.

Greenfield, Adam. *Everyware: The Dawning Age of Ubiquitous Computing*. Berkeley, CA: New Riders, 2006.

Grewal, Inderpal. *Transnational America: Feminisms, Diasporas, Neoliberalisms*. Durham, NC: Duke University Press, 2005.

Grosz, Elizabeth. *Time Travels: Feminism, Nature, Power*. Durham, NC: Duke University Press, 2005.

Guha, Ranajit. *Elementary Aspects of Peasant Insurgency in Colonial India*. Durham: Duke University Press, 1999.

Guha, Ranajit. Preface. *Selected Subaltern Studies*. Ed. R. Guha and Gayatri Spivak. New York: Oxford University Press, 1988.

Gumbrecht, Hans Ulrich. "Form without Matter vs. Form as Event." *MLN* 111.3 (1996): 578–92.

Gumbrecht, Hans Ulrich, and K. Ludwig Pfeiffer. *Materialities of Communication*. Trans. William Whobrey. Stanford, CA: Stanford University Press, 1994.

Halberstam, J. Jack. *In a Queer Time and Place: Transgender Bodies, Subcultural Lives*. New York: New York University Press, 2005.

Hansen, Mark B. N. *Embodying Technesis: Technology beyond Writing*. Ann Arbor: University of Michigan Press, 2003.

Hansen, Mark B. N. "System-Environment Hybrids." In *Emergence and Embodiment: New Essays on Second-Order Systems Theory*, ed. Bruce Clarke and Mark B. N. Hansen. Durham: Duke University Press, 2009. 113–42.

Haraway, Donna. "A Cyborg Manifesto: Science, Technology, and Socialist-

Feminism in the Late Twentieth Century." In *Simians, Cyborgs, and Women: The Reinvention of Nature*. New York: Routledge, 1991. 149–81.

Harrigan, Pat, and Noah Wardrip-Fruin. *First Person: New Media as Story, Performance, and Game*. Cambridge: MIT Press, 2004.

Harrigan, Pat, and Noah Wardrip-Fruin. *Second Person: Role-Playing and Story in Games and Playable Media*. Cambridge: MIT Press, 2007.

Harrigan, Pat, and Noah Wardrip-Fruin. *Third Person: Authoring and Exploring Vast Narratives*. Cambridge: MIT Press, 2009.

Harvey, David. *The Condition of Postmodernity: An Enquiry into the Origins of Cultural Change*. Malden, MA: Blackwell, 1990.

Hawk, Byron, David M. Rieder, and Ollie Oviedo, eds. *Small Tech: The Culture of Digital Tools*. Minneapolis: University of Minnesota Press, 2008.

Hayles, N. Katherine. *Electronic Literature: New Horizons for the Literary*. Notre Dame, IN: Notre Dame University Press, 2008.

Hayles, N. Katherine. *How We Became Posthuman: Virtual Bodies in Cybernetics, Literature, and Informatics*. Chicago: University of Chicago Press, 1999.

Hayles, N. Katherine. *My Mother Was a Computer: Digital Subjects and Literary Texts*. Chicago: University of Chicago Press, 2005.

Hayles, N. Katherine. "Theory of a Different Order: A Conversation with Katherine Hayles and Niklas Luhmann." Interview with Niklas Luhmann; William Rasch; Eva Knodt; Cary Wolfe. *Cultural Critique* 31(Autumn 1995): 7–36.

Hayles, N. Katherine. *Writing Machines*. Cambridge: MIT Press, 2002.

Heims, Steve Joshua. *Constructing a Social Science for Postwar America: The Cybernetics Group, 1946–1953*. Cambridge: MIT Press, 1993.

Howe, Julia Ward. *The Hermaphrodite*. Ed. Gary Williams. Lincoln: University of Nebraska Press, 2004.

Ihde, Don. *Embodied Technics*. [Copenhagen]: Automatic Press, 2010.

Ihde, Don. *Ironic Technics*. [Copenhagen]: Automatic Press, 2008.

Ihde, Don. *Technology and the Lifeworld: From Garden to Earth*. Bloomington: Indiana University Press, 1990.

Irigaray, Luce. *This Sex Which Is Not One*. Trans. Catherine Porter with Carolyn Burke. Ithaca, NY: Cornell University Press, 1993.

Ishiguro, Kazuo. *Never Let Me Go*. NY: Vintage International, 2005.

Jackson, Shelley. *Patchwork Girl by Mary/Shelley and Herself*. Watertown, MA: Eastgate Systems, 1995. CD-ROM.

Jackson, Shelley. "Stitch Bitch: The Patchwork Girl." Transformations of the Book Conference, Massachusetts Institute of Technology, Cambridge, MA, October 24, 1998. Lecture. Online.

Jameson, Fredric. *Postmodernism, or, The Cultural Logic of Late Capitalism*. Durham, NC: Duke University Press, 1997.

Jenkins, Henry. "Game Design as Narrative Architecture." In *First Person: New Media as Story, Performance, and Game*, ed. Noah Wardrip-Fruin and Pat Harrigan. Cambridge: MIT Press, 2004. 118–29.

Johnson, Steven. *Interface Culture: How New Technology Transforms the Way We Create and Communicate*. San Francisco: Harper Collins, 1997.

Johnston, John. *Information Multiplicity: American Fiction in the Age of Media Saturation*. Baltimore: John Hopkins University Press, 1998.

Joyce, Michael. *Of Two Minds: Hypertext Pedagogy and Poetics*. Ann Arbor: University of Michigan Press, 1996.

Joyce, Michael. *Othermindedness: The Emergence of Network Culture*. Ann Arbor: University of Michigan Press, 2001.

Kaplan, Amy. "Manifest Domesticity." In *The Futures of American Studies*, ed. Donald Pease and Robyn Wiegman. Durham, NC: Duke University Press, 2002. 111–34.

Karkazis, Katrina. *Fixing Sex: Intersex, Medical Authority, and Lived Experience*. Durham, NC: Duke University Press, 2008.

Kelly, James Patrick, and John Kessel. *Rewired: The Post-Cyberpunk Anthology*. San Francisco: Tachyon Publicationss, 2007.

Kirschenbaum, Matthew G. *Mechanisms: New Media and the Forensic Imagination*. Cambridge: MIT Press, 2008.

Kitchin, Rob, and Martin Dodge. *Code/Space: Software and Everyday Life*. Cambridge: MIT Press, 2011.

Kittler, Friedrich A. *Discourse Networks: 1800/1900*. Trans. Michael Matteer with Chris Cullens. Stanford, CA: Stanford University Press, 1990.

Landow, George P. *Hypertext 2.0: The Convergence of Contemporary Critical Theory and Technology*. 2nd ed. Baltimore: Johns Hopkins University Press, 1997.

Landow, George P. "Twenty Minutes into the Future, or How Are We Moving Beyond the Book?" In *The Future of the Book*, ed. Geoffrey Nunberg (Berkeley: University of California Press, 1996). 209–37.

Lanham, Richard A. *The Electronic Word: Democracy, Technology, and the Arts*. Chicago: University of Chicago Press, 1994.

Lefebvre, Henri. *The Production of Space*. Trans. Donald Nicholson-Smith. Oxford: Blackwell, 1991.

Lemke, Thomas. "'The Birth of Biopolitics': Michel Foucault's Lecture at the Collège de France on Neo-liberal Governmentality." *Economy and Society* 30.2 (May 2001): 190–207.

Leroi-Gourhan, André. *Gesture and Speech*. Trans. Anna Bostock Berger. Cambridge: MIT Press, 1993.

Levin, Golan. "Art That Looks Back at You." TED Conference, California, 2009.

Lionnet, Françoise, and Shu-mei Shih, eds. "Introduction: Thinking Through the Minor, Transnationally." In *Minor Transnationalism*. Durham, NC: Duke University Press, 2005.

Lowe, Lisa. "Decolonization, Displacement, Disidentification: Asian American 'Novels' and the Question of History." In *Cultural Institutions of the Novel*, ed Deidre Lynch and William B. Warner. Durham, NC: Duke University Press, 1996. 96–128.

Lowe, Lisa. "The International within the National: American Studies and Asian

American Critique." In *The Futures of American Studies*, ed. Donald Pease and Robyn Wiegman. Durham, NC: Duke University Press, 2002. 76–92.

Luhmann, Niklas. "The Cognitive Program of Constructivism and the Reality That Remains Unknown." In *Theories of Distinction: Redescribing the Descriptions of Modernity*, ed. William Rasch. Stanford, CA: Stanford University Press, 2002. 128–52.

Luhmann, Niklas. *Social Systems*. Trans. John Bednarz Jr. with Dirk Baecker. Stanford, CA: Stanford University Press, 1995.

Mackenzie, Adrian. *Transductions: Bodies and Machines at Speed*. London: Continuum, 2002.

Macpherson, C. B. *The Political Theory of Possessive Individualism: Hobbes to Locke*. Don Mills, Ontario: Oxford University Press, 1962.

Manovich, Lev. *The Language of New Media*. 2nd ed. Cambridge: MIT Press, 2001.

Marks, Laura U. *Touch: Sensuous Theory and Multisensory Media*. Minneapolis: University of Minnesota Press, 2002.

Massey, Doreen. *For Space*. Thousand Oaks, CA: Sage, 2005.

Massey, Doreen. "Power-geometry and a Progressive Sense of Place." In *Mapping the Futures: Local Cultures, Global Change*, ed. Jon Bird, Barry Curtis, Tim Putnam, George Robertson, and Lisa Tickner. New York, Routledge, 1993. 59–69.

Massey, Doreen. *Space, Place, and Gender*. Cambridge: Polity Press, 1994.

Massumi, Brian. *Parables for the Virtual: Movement, Affect, Sensation*. Durham, NC: Duke University Press, 2002.

Maturana, Humberto, and Francisco Varela. *The Tree of Knowledge: The Biological Roots of Human Understanding*. Trans. Robert Paolucci. Rev. ed. Boston: Shambhala, 1998.

May, Jon, and Nigel Thrift, eds. *TimeSpace: Geographies of Temporality*. New York: Routledge Press, 2001.

Mbembe, Achille. "Necropolitics." Trans. Libby Meintjes. *Public Culture* 15.1 (2003): 11–40.

McHugh, Susan. "The Fictions and Futures of Farm Animals: Semi-living to 'Animalacra' Pig Tales." In *Animal Stories: Narrating across Species Lines*. Minneapolis: University of Minnesota Press, 2011. 163–209.

McLuhan, Marshall. *Understanding Media: The Extensions of Man*. New York: New American Library, Times Mirror, 1964.

Meikle, Graham. *Future Active: Media Activism and the Internet*. New York: Routledge Press, 2002.

Michaels, Walter Benn. *The Shape of the Signifier: 1967 to the End of History*. Princeton, NJ: Princeton University Press, 2004.

Miéville, China. *The City and the City*. New York: Ballantine Books, 2010.

Mignolo, Walter D. "The Many Faces of Cosmo-polis: Border Thinking and Critical Cosmopolitanism." *Public Culture* 12.3 (2000): 721–48. doi:10.1215/08992363-12-3-721.

Mitchell, David. *Cloud Atlas*. New York: Random House, 2004.

Moretti, Franco. "On Literary Evolution." In *Signs Taken for Wonders: Essays in the Sociology of Literary Forms*, trans. Susan Fischer, David Forgacs, and David Miller. New York: Verso Books, 1997. 262–78.

Morris, Adalaide, and Thomas Swiss, eds. *New Media Poetics: Contexts, Technotexts, and Theories*. Cambridge: MIT Press, 2006.

Murray, Janet H. *Hamlet on the Holodeck: The Future of Narrative in Cyberspace*. Cambridge: MIT Press, 1997.

Nakamura, Lisa. *Cybertypes: Race, Ethnicity, and Identity on the Internet*. New York: Routledge, 2002.

Nealon, Jeffrey T. *Post-Postmodernism or, The Cultural Logic of Just-in-Time Capitalism*. Stanford, CA: Stanford University Press, 2012.

Nelson, Theodor. *Literary Machines*. Sausalito, CA: Mindful Press, 1988.

Ong, Aihwa. "Latitudes of Citizenship: Membership, Meaning, and Multiculturalism." In *People out of Place: Globalization, Human Rights, and the Citizenship Gap*, ed. Alison Brysk and Gershon Shafir. New York: Routledge, 2004. 53–70.

Ozeki, Ruth L. *My Year of Meats*. New York: Penguin, 1998.

Page, Ruth, and Bronwen Thomas. *New Narratives: Stories and Storytelling in the Digital Age*. Lincoln: University of Nebraska Press, 2011.

Palumbo-Liu, David. "Rational and Irrational Choices: Form, Affect, and Ethics." In *Minor Transnationalism*, ed. Françoise Lionnet and Shu-mei Shih. Durham, NC: Duke University Press, 2005. 41–72.

Plant, Sadie. *Zeros + Ones: Digital Women + the New Technoculture*. New York: Doubleday, 1997.

Prigogine, Ilya, and Isabelle Stengers. *Order out of Chaos: Man's New Dialogue with Nature*. New York: Bantam Books, 1984.

Probyn, Elspeth. *Carnal Appetites: Food Sex Identities*. New York, Routledge, 2000.

Prosser, Jay. *Second Skins: The Body Narratives of Transsexuality*. New York: Columbia University Press, 1998.

Punday, Daniel. *Five Strands of Fictionality: The Institutional Construction of Contemporary American Fiction*. Columbus: Ohio State University Press, 2010.

Punday, Daniel. "Looking for Writing after Postmodernism." *Electronic Book Review* (ebr). 2012.06.28.

Punday, Daniel. *Writing at the Limit: The Novel in the New Media Ecology*. Lincoln: University of Nebraska Press, 2012.

Pynchon, Thomas. *Gravity's Rainbow*. New York: Penguin, 1995.

Raley, Rita. "Reveal Codes: Hypertext and Performance." *Postmodern Culture* 12.1 (2001). Project Muse. January 31, 2004.

Raley, Rita. *Tactical Media*. Minneapolis: University of Minnesota Press, 2009.

Rasch, William. *Niklas Luhmann's Modernity: The Paradoxes of Differentiation*. Stanford, CA: Stanford University Press, 2000.

Roof, Judith. *Come As You Are: Sexuality & Narrative*. New York: Columbia University Press, 1996.

Roof, Judith. "Is There Sex after Gender? Ungendering / *The Unnameable*." *Journal of the Midwest Modern Language Association* 35 (Spring 2002): 50–67.

Rueb, Teri. *Itinerant*. 2005. Accessed April 1, 2013. http://transition.turbulence.org/Works/itinerant.

Rueb, Teri. "Shifting Subjects in Locative Media." In *Small Tech: The Culture of Digital Tools*, ed. Byron Hawk, David M. Rieder, and Ollie Oviedo. Minneapolis: University of Minnesota Press, 2008. 129–33.

Ryan, Marie-Laure. "The Interactive Onion: Layers of User Participation in Digital Narrative Texts." In *New Narratives: Stories and Storytelling in the Digital Age*, ed. Rush Page and Bronwen Thomas. Lincoln: Nebraska University Press, 2011. 35–62.

Ryan, Marie-Laure. *Avatars of Story*. Minneapolis: University of Minnesota Press, 2006.

Ryan, Marie-Laure, ed. *Narrative across Media: The Languages of Storytelling*. Lincoln: University of Nebraska Press, 2004.

Schiff, James. "A Conversation with Jeffrey Eugenides." *Missouri Review* 29.3 (2006): 100–119. Accessed October 20, 2008, Project Muse, doi:10.1353/mis.2007.0007.

Shelley, Mary Wollstonecraft. *Frankenstein: The 1818 Text, Contexts, Nineteenth-Century Responses, Modern Criticism*, ed. Paul J. Hunter. 2nd ed. New York: W.W. Norton & Company, 2012.

Shōnagon, Sei. *The Pillow Book*. Trans. and ed. Ivan Morris. New York: Columbia University Press, 1991.

Silko, Leslie Marmon. *Almanac of the Dead*. New York: Penguin, 1991.

Silko, Leslie Marmon. "An Expression of Profound Gratitude to the Maya Zapatistas, January 1, 1994." In *Yellow Woman and A Beauty of the Spirit: Essays on Native American Life Today*. New York: Simon and Schuster, 1996. 152–54.

Simondon, Gilbert. *Du mode d'existence des objets techniques*. Paris: Aubier, 2001.

Sobchack, Vivian. *Carnal Thoughts: Embodiment and Moving Image Culture*. Berkeley: University of California Press, 2004.

Soja, Edward W. *Postmodern Geographies: The Reassertion of Space in Critical Social Theory*. London: Verso, 1989.

Spivak, Gayatri Chakravorty. "Can the Subaltern Speak?" In *Marxism and the Interpretation of Culture*, ed. Cary Nelson and Lawrence Grossberg. Urbana: University of Illinois Press, 1988. 271–314.

Stengers, Isabelle. *Cosmopolitics*. Trans. Robert Bononno. Vol. 1. Minneapolis: University of Minnesota Press, 2010.

Stiegler, Bernard. *Technics and Time, 1: The Fault of Epimetheus*. Trans. Richard Beardsworth and George Collins. Stanford, CA: Stanford University Press, 1998.

Stiegler, Bernard. *Technics and Time, 2: Disorientation*. Trans. Stephen Barker. Stanford, CA: Stanford University Press, 2009.

Strickland, Stephanie. "Dali Clocks: Time Dimensions of Hypermedia." *Electronic Book Review*, January 1, 2001. Accessed April 2, 2002.

Stryker, Susan. *Transgender History*. Berkeley, CA: Seal Press, 2008.

Sundén, Jenny. *Material Virtualities: Approaching Online Textual Embodiment*. New York: Peter Lang, 2003.

Sze, Julie. "Boundaries and Border Wars: DES, Technology, and Environmental Justice." *American Quarterly* 58.3 (September 2006): 791–814, 985.

Tabbi, Joseph. *Cognitive Fictions*. Minneapolis: University of Minnesota Press, 2002.

Teubner, Gunther. "Economics of Gift—Positivity of Justice: The Mutual Para-

..cques Derrida and Niklas Luhmann." *Theory, Culture, and Society* 18.1
⅃): 29–47.

⅃ker, Eugene. *Biomedia*. Minneapolis: University of Minnesota Press, 2004.

This Old House. Time, Inc. WXXI, Rochester. March 15, 2011. Television.

Thrift, Nigel. "Movement-Space: The Changing Domain of Thinking Resulting from the Development of New Kinds of Spatial Awareness." In *Non-representational Theory: Space, Theory, Affect*. New York: Routledge, 2008. 89–106.

Thrift, Nigel. "Remembering the Technological Unconscious by Foregrounding Knowledges of Position." In *Knowing Capitalism*. London: Sage, 2005. 212–26.

Tomasula, Steve. "Three Axioms for Projecting a Line (or why it will continue to be hard to write a title sans slashes or parentheses)." *Review of Contemporary Fiction* 16.1 (Spring 1996): 100. Proquest Research Library #02719290. 05.09.12.

Tsing, Anna Lowenhaupt. *Friction: An Ethnography of Global Connection*. Princeton, NJ: Princeton University Press, 2005.

Turkle, Sherry. *Life on the Screen: Identity in the Age of the Internet*. New York: Simon and Schuster, 1995.

Varela, Francisco J., Evan Thompson, and Eleanor Rosch. *The Embodied Mind: Cognitive Science and Human Experience*. Cambridge: MIT Press, 1996.

Village People. "Go West." Writers: Jacques Morali, Henri Belolo, Victor Willis. Casablanca, 1979.

VNS Matrix. *Media Art Net*. www.mediaartnet.org/artist/vns-matrix/biography. Accessed December 2011.

von Foerster, Heinz. *Observing Systems*. 2nd ed. Seaside, CA: Intersystems, 1985.

von Foerster, Heinz. "Cybernetics of Cybernetics." Urbana, University of Illinois at Urbana. 1979. Lecture.

Waldby, Catherine. "The Instruments of Life: Frankenstein and Cyberculture." In *Prefiguring Cyberculture: An Intellectual History*, ed. D. Tofts, A. Jonson, and A. Cavallaro. Cambridge: MIT Press, 2002. 28–37.

Wardrip-Fruin, Noah. *Expressive Processing: Digital Fiction, Computer Games, and Software Studies*. Cambridge: MIT Press, 2009.

Wellbery, David E.. "Foreword: Post-Hermeneutic Criticism." In Friedrich A. Kittler's *Discourse Networks: 1800/1900*, trans. Michael Metteer with Chris Cullens. Stanford, CA: Stanford University Press, 1990.

Wiener, Norbert. *The Human Use of Human Beings: Cybernetics and Society*. 1954. Cambridge, MA: Da Capo Press, 1988.

Williams, Gary. "Speaking with the Voices of Others: Julia Ward Howe's Laurence." Introduction to *The Hermaphrodite*, by Julia Ward Howe. Ed. Gary Williams. Lincoln: University of Nebraska Press, 2004.

Wolfe, Cary. *What Is Posthumanism?* Minneapolis: University of Minnesota Press, 2010.

Wolfe, Cary. *Critical Environments: Postmodern Theory and the Pragmatics of the "Outside."* Minneapolis: University of Minnesota Press, 1998.

Index

Wardrip-Fruin, Noah, 214, 222n2
Whobrey, William, 228n38
Wiener, Norbert, 12
Wolfe, Cary, *Critical Environments*, 13, 232n30; *What Is Posthumanism?*, 59
World War II, post–, 1, 2, 4, 7, 12, 64, 65, 147, 154, 222n9

"writing in reverse," 103, 128, 129

Zangwill, Israel, *The Melting Pot*, 245n29
Zapatista Army of National Liberation, 130, 240n102